Laurence Attwell's

LETTERS FROM THE FRONT

Laurence Attwell's

LETTERS FROM THE FRONT

edited by

W. A. Attwell

Pen & Sword
MILITARY

First published in Great Britain in 2005 by
Pen & Sword Military
an imprint of
Pen & Sword Books Ltd
47 Church Street
Barnsley
South Yorkshire
S70 2AS

ISBN 1 84415 233 2

A CIP catalogue record for this book is
available from the British Library

Typeset in Plantin by
Phoenix Typesetting, Auldgirth, Dumfriesshire

Printed and bound in England by
CPI UK

Pen & Sword Books Ltd incorporates the Imprints of Pen & Sword
Aviation, Pen & Sword Maritime, Pen & Sword Military, Wharncliffe
Local History, Pen & Sword Select, Pen & Sword Military Classics and
Leo Cooper.

For a complete list of Pen & Sword titles please contact
PEN & SWORD BOOKS LIMITED
47 Church Street, Barnsley, South Yorkshire, S70 2AS, England
E-mail: enquiries@pen-and-sword.co.uk
Website: www.pen-and-sword.co.uk

Contents

Foreword

Laurence Wesley Attwell was one of the lucky ones. He survived well over four years of horrific trench warfare with the British Expeditionary Forces in France on the Western Front during the First World War. In the whole of that time he had just two short periods of leave. The rest was spent enduring hardships, experiences and privations we find impossible to imagine in today's safe and cosy world.

In a quite extraordinary series of letters written to his family back home Laurence Attwell graphically recounts what life was like in those awful days for a soldier on active duty. These are no ordinary letters. Laurence had a wonderful way with words and no one could be anything but enthralled by his tales. Just dipping into the letters at random, young and old alike become immediately absorbed by the descriptions and images he portrays about his experiences during those four terrible years.

These captivating letters deserve a wider audience. I hope this book will allow many others to experience what life was really like for an infantryman in the trenches.

Laurence Attwell was my great uncle. He was known as "Laurie" by his friends and family. He was born in North London on 5 April 1888 and went to school at Harringay Board School in Hornsey. Leaving school at fourteen, he spent a year at Clark's Civil Service College in Holloway. At fifteen, Laurie's first job was as a Boy Clerk with the General Post Office in the city. He worked there for 1,496 days without a single day's absence from work, during which time his earnings increased annually by 1/- pw from 15/- to 19/-. He studied hard and took and passed a succession of exams which ultimately led to his obtaining jobs, first with the Accountant General's Department and later with the Inland Revenue.

Laurie was always of a literary turn of mind and keenly interested in church work, being connected with the Wesleyan (later Methodist) church in Winchmore Hill. Although he mentions it only briefly in his correspondence, it is clear he was gassed many times while in France and his health suffered in later life. He never married and died of lung cancer in 1957.

After the outbreak of war Laurie responded to Kitchener's "Your Country Needs You" call and at the age of twenty-six he joined the 1/15 Battalion (Civil Service Rifles). This was an infantry battalion attached to 140 Brigade, which in turn was part of 47 London Division. After training, he was assigned to the Military Police Unit of B (HQ) Company, 1/15 Battalion. He went to France in March 1915 where he and the battalion served with distinction on the Western Front for the remainder of the war.

Laurie maintained a regular correspondence during the period he was engaged in hostilities overseas, writing every few days to his family. His letters are mostly addressed to his mother, Emma Attwell, and his sister, Constance Isabel Attwell, to whom he was particularly close. Periodic references are made to his brother Arthur and his sister Flossie. There are around 150 surviving letters and, although it is clear a few were lost in transit or else were not kept, there remains a remarkable record of an ordinary soldier's wartime experiences.

Laurie's wonderfully descriptive letters caused a high level of interest back home when they were read by friends and members of his local church. It appears also that several organizations were interested in his literary talents, since he subsequently wrote various articles and pieces which, from comments in Laurie's letters, appear to have been published.

My father found the original letters among Constance's papers when she died in 1961. They are neatly written in pencil, mostly on small fragile sheets of notepaper.

I hope this record of days now long past will be of interest to all who read it and that it will form a small memorial to a kindly, generous man who uncomplainingly 'did his bit' in the Great War.

W. A. Attwell

NB.
To aid the reader I have inserted details of places and other clarifying information at appropriate points in Laurie's letters. These editorial inserts are shown italicized in square brackets, thus: [ ].

Sources and Acknowledgements

I have a strong interest in Family History and have for some years been engaged in researching the Attwell family. It was this that prompted me to seek more information on my Great Uncle Laurie. I was lucky enough to find that his Service records had survived the blitz and these were both fascinating and helpful in filling a few gaps. For instance, they revealed that he had been wounded, something that was not immediately apparent from his letters home, and hence explained a puzzling gap in the correspondence.

I also unearthed the 1/15 Battalion's War Diaries at the National Archives (Ref: WO 95/2732). These were written by the Adjutant and give a daily account of the battalion's activities and travels throughout the war. In particular, they provide detailed accounts of the major actions in which Laurie was involved. The War Diaries were invaluable in helping me to explain how Laurie's activities and travels contrasted with those of the Battalion and in providing other useful and interesting information. For instance, the censor would not allow details of casualties to be included in letters to England, but this information, obtained from the War Diaries, helps us to understand the severity of the fighting. The War Diaries' graphic descriptions of some of the battles provide an excellent background to Laurie's own experiences and these too I have used to make his story more complete. My thanks to the National Archives for allowing me to draw from this valuable resource.

The official record of the activities of 47 (London) Division (1914–18) edited by Alan Maude and published in 1922 by the Amalgamated Press Ltd is extremely interesting. It chronicles the movements and activities of 47 Division throughout the war and has been a useful source of reference.

W. A. Attwell

A Note on Laurie's Service Attachments

Since references are made throughout the book to 47 Division, 140 Brigade, 15 Battalion (and variations of all three!) and other related Brigades, Battalions, Companies and Units, it is helpful to understand the composition of each. Here is a brief explanation:

Laurie was in B (HQ) Company, a part of 1/15 Battalion, 140 Brigade, 47 (London) Division.

47 (London) Division

The 47 Division was a part of the Territorial Force sent to France in 1915. Although various changes were made during the war, the 47 Division broadly consisted of the following:

Artillery	– six Brigades
Trench Mortars	– two Batteries
Engineers	– three-four Companies
Pioneer Battalion	– 1/4 Battalion Royal Welch Fusiliers
Infantry	– **140 London Infantry Brigade**
	– 141 London Infantry Brigade
	– 142 London Infantry Brigade
Machine Gun Corps	– 47 Machine Gun Battalion
Royal Army Service Corps	
Royal Army Medical Corps	

140 London Infantry Brigade

During the period Laurie was with them, 140 Brigade consisted of six Battalions as follows:

1/6 (City of London) Battalion

1/7 (City of London) Battalion

1/8 (City of London) Battalion

1/15 (County of London) Battalion –
(Prince of Wales's Own, Civil Service Rifles)

1/17 (County of London) Battalion

1/21 County of London) Battalion

In civilian life Laurie had worked in the Accountant General's Department. It was natural, therefore, for him to join the Civil Service Rifles, a battalion made up entirely of Civil Servants.

1/15 Battalion

1/15 Battalion, London Regiment, was made up of volunteers from the Civil Service in London. It consisted of four Companies:

A Company

B (HQ) Company

C Company

D Company

Laurie was attached to B Company in the Military Police Unit. B Company in turn was made up of an unknown number of Platoons. Laurie was in No 1 Section, 5 Platoon, B Company. The extracts given from the War Diaries throughout this book are those belonging to 1/15 Battalion.

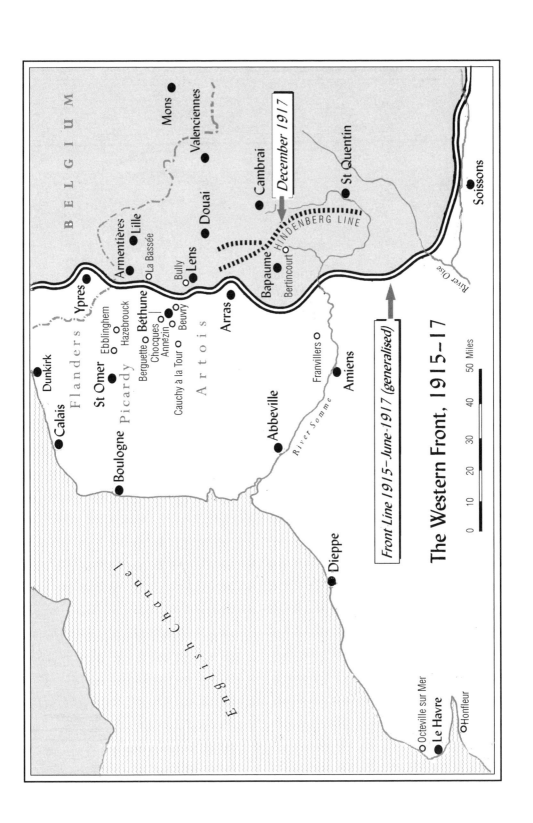

The Western Front, 1915–17

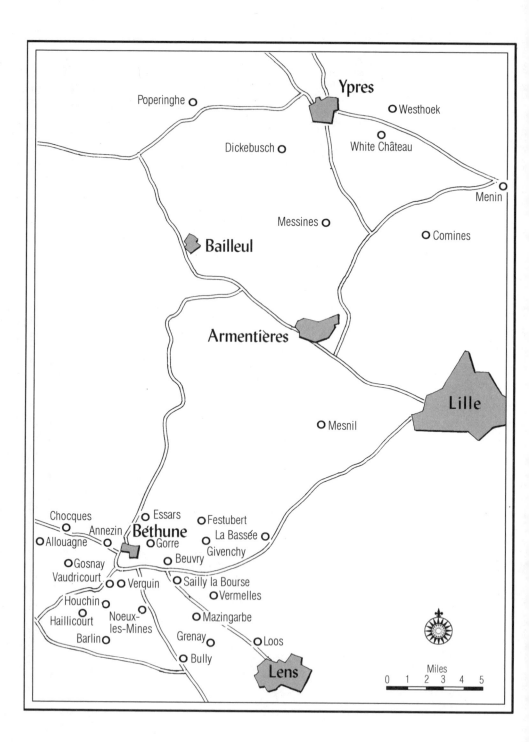

Poperinghe

Ypres

Westhoek

Dickebusch

White Château

Menin

Messines

Comines

Bailleul

Armentières

Lille

Mesnil

Chocques

Essars

Festubert

Annezin

Béthune

La Bassée

Allouagne

Gorre

Givenchy

Gosnay

Beuvry

Vaudricourt

Verquin

Sailly la Bourse

Houchin

Vermelles

Haillicourt

Noeux-
les-Mines

Mazingarbe

Barlin

Grenay

Loos

Bully

Lens

Miles

0 1 2 3 4 5

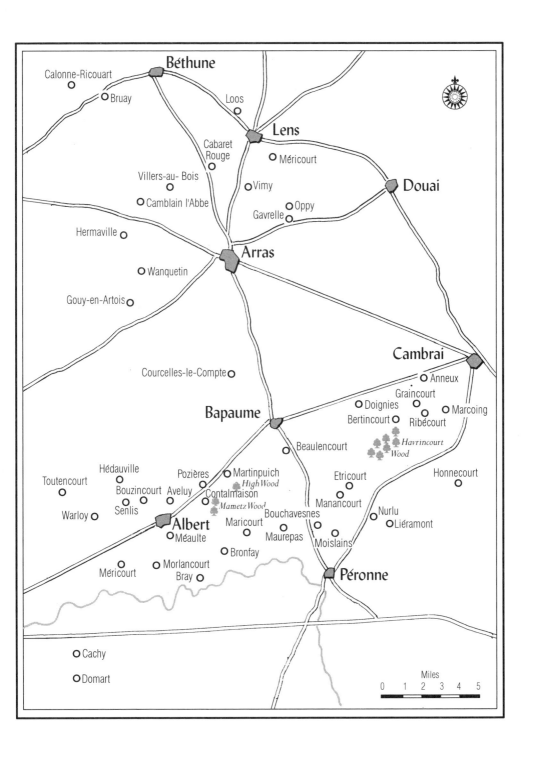

Chapter One

A Foretaste of What's to Come

When Germany invaded Belgium on 4 August 1914 Britain declared war on Germany. Before the month was out, Laurence Wesley Attwell had joined 15 Battalion, London Regiment (Civil Service Rifles) to do his duty for King and Country with the Territorial Forces.

At the end of October 47 London Division was selected as one of the Territorial Divisions to be taken to France. An appallingly wet period from November to March 1915, together with considerable delays in the acquisition of equipment and clothing, made life extremely uncomfortable for the recruits and did not help to prepare them well for the rigours of a real war. Nevertheless, along with the rest of the Infantry Brigades, Laurie completed several months of basic training, during which he underwent a spell of trench-digging near Braintree.

Then, on Sunday, 7 March 1915 orders were received for 15 Battalion London Regiment to leave their training centre at Watford and join the British Expeditionary Forces in France. Laurie's unit remained behind to clear up after them, but left Southampton some ten days later, and met up with them at the Rest Camp immediately on arrival in France.

WAR DIARY: SUNDAY, 7 MARCH 1915
Battalion under the Command of Colonel A.M.Renny.
Battalion strength: 30 Officers
                         1,046 Other ranks
Left Watford in two trains for Southampton. Embarked on four Steamers (*Balmoral, City of Chester, Jupiter and Munich*) between 7.30 and 8.30pm

War Diary: Monday 8 March 1915
Reached Havre early morning. Disembarked 9.00am. Marched to No.6 Rest Camp – went under canvas.

Thursday, 18 March 1915.

Dear Mother, Connie & Flossie,
Yesterday morning we rose at 4 in the morning, breakfasted at 4.30 and paraded at 5.30. We then did our last march in Watford down to the Station and entrained for . . . *[censored – but appears to be Southampton]*. When we arrived we all stayed in a large embarkation shed for some hours. Not until it was dark did we board our ship. It was a fairly large paddle-steamer, but we found ourselves very crowded down below.

I kept on deck for a long time – until the lights of Old England faded in the distance . . . *[censored]*. These forts had intensely powerful searchlights on and so had numerous warships. All these lights falling on the water and crossing each other made a peculiarly beautiful sight.

We arrived at our French port of landing – I suppose I must not tell you its name *[Havre]* – soon after 4 o'c this morning. While on board we had a ration of the Army biscuits and corned beef. The biscuits can only be broken with difficulty and the corned beef is very solid and satisfying. It is a very rough diet, but there was plenty of it.

On landing, we marched through the town up an extremely long and steep hill to our camp. There are hundreds of tents here. I share a tent with 14 others and you can guess it is something of a squeeze. We have had a pair of socks given to us and a woollen vest.

I expect that the main body will move away shortly, but that the base party will stay here for some time. I am still in good form. The weather is cold and rainy. The French people are interesting, especially the children, who clamour for biscuits and souvenirs and talk in broken English.
Goodbye, with love,
Laurie.

Saturday, 20 March 1915

Dear Mother
Yesterday afternoon the Battalion moved off and the Base party, including myself, had to clear up after they left. This done, we also

left the camp and marched a short distance to our present Base *[Harfleur]*. My address is now:

> 1/15 Batt. Co. of London Regiment,
> British Expeditionary Forces,
> 2nd London Division Base,
> via Havre.

and this is how you should address letters to me until you hear from me again.

The weather today is sunny and very bright but there is a cold nip in the air. We are 10 in a tent here and have two blankets each. Very little leave appears to be given to leave this camp. We have meals in large sheds and there are long washing sheds. The sanitary accommodation is better and it is altogether a more comfortable place. The other was on the summit of quite a large hill, while now we are in a large valley.

This morning we were inspected by the Officer Commanding at this Base and we are to be medically examined shortly. I will break off now for a little while and resume this letter later on today.

The medical inspection is now over and we have just had dinner. If we stay here much longer I shall be in a position to appreciate almost anything in the edible line that you could send me. The food here has been rougher than anything I have ever had before. Fortunately, there is a Canteen and I believe there will be a Y.M.C.A. building open here soon.

You might let me know if you received my letter safely and if it was mutilated at all by the censor. I am in good health and spirits. I hope you are well and not worrying about me. Are Connie and Flossie alright?

I have applied for a pass into the town. I am anxious to see as much of France as I can while I am out here.

Goodbye, my dear ones,

Laurie

So while a part of the Battalion moved off by train to Berguette and then marched on to Cauchy à la Tour in the Béthune area, Laurie was among a group who remained for the time being with the Base Party at Harfleur.

Dear Mother,

I got my pass all right and late in the afternoon walked through some typical French scenery to the town near our camp. It was very picturesque but there was a certain down-at-heels air about it. There were no signs of prosperity and the houses were somewhat tumble-down.

We went to a house which was open as a Soldiers Club and I had a bowl of soup and a bowl of cocoa (1d. each) and quite a collection of French pastries. There were some English papers to look at, so we had a very pleasant afternoon and evening.

On Sunday *[21 March]* we had to get up at 5.30 as we were on fatigue. Breakfast came at 6.50 and we marched off at 7 o'clock. We had to work rather hard levelling ground and making up beds. Just imagine me, after all this soldiering, making flower beds in a military camp.

The roads here are very rough and hard for walking. My money is beginning to get mixed up – French and English money are used indiscriminately. They are fitting up a Y.M.C.A. hut here now, so the camp will soon be more comfortable.

I have not heard from you yet. I will tell you when I have received your first letter. I should rather like another towel and a fresh pair of gloves.

My love to you all,

Laurie

Dear Mother,

You will perhaps be surprised to receive a letter from me on this paper, but the Y.M.C.A. building in our Camp is now in full swing. It is crowded out somewhat, but it is nevertheless a very great boon to us.

Today I am on what is called the "Fire Picket" and I have more time to myself than usual. The life in this camp seems to be an unending series of duties of one kind and another – fatigues, guards and pickets. On the other hand, we have so many things that the poor fellow in the firing line cannot get. The Y.M.C.A. have a small library and I have borrowed George Borrow's *Wild Wales*.

The money here is very mixed and you have to be careful, for you get English shillings (12d.) and French francs (10d.) looking at first sight very similar and the same risk of confusion between half-francs and sixpences. The weather has turned very rainy and the roads, which were very dusty, are now covered with sticky mud. It is quite an effort to keep upright.

Tent life is very curious. We have no room to spare and when we get down to sleep our feet are all crushed together round the tent-pole. We have plenty of fun and get on well together. I am not sure whether I told you about the Army biscuit. It is a large, thick biscuit, quite like a dog biscuit, and so hard that I make no effort to bite a piece off, but break it up small before eating it.

At present I have been able to keep up with the news, for we can purchase the Paris edition of the *Daily Mail*. It costs 1½d or 15 centimes and consists practically of the 4 middle pages of the London issue. My expenses at present have been quite moderate, so there will be no need to send me any money along.

I have been surprised that we can write so frequently, and if there should be any silence on my part you can put it down to the fact that we have at last been compelled to write less frequently. I hope you have received all the letters safely. So far nothing has turned up from you but I know that delays will occur. Kindly notice my address and use it until I tell you something different.

Some of the scenery here is fairly good but nothing compares with dear old England. Give my love to Arthur and Bert. I have not time nor sufficient energy left after the day's work to write to anyone save you, my dear one. I hope you are quite well. My best love to Connie and Floss. I am quite in good form. No room for worry yet.
Goodbye,
Laurie.

Friday, 26 March 1915

Dear Mother,
Yesterday was a hard day for me but a very interesting one. I was up at 5 o'clock and did not get off duty until quite late in the evening. We all travelled in the French tramcars to the big docks. The trams are single-deckers and passengers are allowed on both the driver's and conductor's platforms. Half the car is for smokers. Some of them are manned by women – notice the joke!

We went all through the town which was a great treat to me. Once at the docks, which are simply enormous and where there are a great many large vessels, I ceased to be a tourist and became a common dock labourer. I helped to load a train for the soldiers at the front. It was the longest train I have ever seen and a train like that goes up every day – Sunday and weekdays alike – just to one base. I was hauling bags of oats about, weighing 80lbs each – you never knows what you can do until you tries!

There are hosts of English labourers at the port – Army labourers – who are attached to the Army Service Corps. They are getting 3/- a day, or so I heard, for the same loading job for which we would get 1/-. My money is now very mixed. I have English, French and Belgian money. They have just paid us 5 francs of our soldier's pay. Today we were working like navvies at the bottom end of a cable railway – a light railway. The view at the top of the hill was very fine. We could see across the country for miles and the towns on the further side of the river.

I have done some washing of clothes! Dirty socks and hand-kerchiefs. I hope they will be alright. There is nothing else of interest, I fancy. I hope you three are well and happy. I think of you very often. Goodbye. All my love,
Laurie.

Easter Sunday, 4 April 1915 (Excerpts)

Dear Mother,
You will notice the special envelope to this letter. I believe we are allowed one of these each week. They give one practically a free hand in writing, for who is to give a definition of what are not private matters? Anyway, I take it that my own account of my doings and thoughts is quite a private matter.

Yesterday I was a platelayer, working on a light railway and seeing that the lines were level. We do get some queer jobs to be sure. In the afternoon it came on to rain and we had a soaking wet evening. There is a drying shed here and I put my overcoat in it for the night. Tent life at any time has its inconveniences, but when it pours with rain you must try to be a Mark Tapley *[servant of Martin Chuzzlewit]*. If you hit against the side of a tent in wet weather the rain drips through at that point, and of course in any case it comes in at the entrance flap. My position in the tent is, for the last week (since a poor old fellow went into hospital with sciatica) right athwart the door. I chose this spot, because, though it is draughty (you can always wrap yourself up against the draught) there is plenty of room to lie at full length. All the others have to sleep with their feet jammed up against the tent-pole in the centre. But of course last night the rain and mud was all round the entrance and I had to sleep in a sticky puddle. The rain oozed through the tent at various points and every hour or so there would be a report caused by a tent pole breaking. When a tent pole breaks a section of sopping wet canvas suddenly bulges inwards on top of you.

Did you receive the Company Roll which I sent off from Watford and has the regimental photo turned up? We draw our money in French notes now. I am enclosing one just as a curiosity. It is worth 4/2d. Please keep it for me as a relic of my stay on the Continent. We have just had an interesting time in our tent as we have had a Cameron Highlander in there, telling anecdotes about the front. He comes from Vancouver, has a fierce hatred of the Black Watch (strange feud) and was wounded in the scalp. The bullet made quite a furrow right along the top of his head. He possessed a keen sense of humour and kept us in constant laughter.

The mud here really beggars description, it is still sticky and slippery. It is as much as you can do to preserve your balance.

Well, a happy Easter to you all. I hope you will all have health and prosperity and may we soon see the end of this rotten business and be a united family once again.
Yours lovingly
Laurie.

Tuesday, 6 April 1915 (Excerpts)

Dear Mother,
I have very little that is fresh to tell you. This is our third rainy day and rain here is worse to bear than over in England. We go ankle deep in mud all over the camp, and if we are unlucky enough to hit a very soft spot, we go right up to the tops of our boots. Frequently fellows slip over in the mud, and a fine spectacle they present when they get up.

My birthday I spent down at the docks helping to unload a supply ship. The cargo at our crane was biscuits, cigarettes and tobacco. We were taking the stuff along on heavy wheelbarrows (or rather trucks), and we took three boxes of biscuits weighing 50lbs each at one go. In the afternoon we were shifting very heavy timber in the rain.

On our return we heard that a number of men had been commandeered to join the main battalion. There are 20 of them and they go off from here this afternoon. I am not a bit sorry to have missed this opportunity. For one thing, I have no doubt that we are more comfortable and secure here than the others are, and for another, I have strained the muscles of my foot a little. So you see chance, or whatever you like to call it, is keeping me a little longer in an absolutely safe position.

I believe we shall soon have a chance of fitting ourselves up with whatever we are deficient in. If so, I shall get a pair of pants, some new puttees and trousers, and a table-knife. My old table-knife suddenly snapped in half one cold morning when I was trying to spread some hard butter.

I hope all are well at home and that 82 Hatton Garden is flourishing. Enjoy yourselves as much as you can. You see, there is no need to worry about me.

My best love to you all,

Laurie

Thursday, 8 April 1915

Dear Mother,

We have been through some very wretched weather these last few days – chilly grey skies, filthy and treacherous ground to walk on, and steadily falling depressing rain. At night the tent is closed as carefully as possible, yet in the morning one is lying in a puddle of mud.

The evening time in a tent has a kind of romance and pleasure about it. The unaccustomed canvas walls, the flickering candle-light, the circle of faces, the cheerful joke and song, it is all very jolly. You can guess we are very tightly packed in. When the blankets are down, there is not an inch of floor-board showing.

Yesterday we went on a route march *[to the breastworks]*, which seemed to me to be halfway to a mountain climb. The French soldiers are very peculiar. They are by no means as smart in their bearing as the Terriers you are accustomed to see. Often their uniform is most grotesque – shabby-looking wide trousers and a great cloak with a hood to it covering the head. Others have vivid blue tunics and scarlet trousers.

The civilians are not wonderfully interesting, except the children. In many respects, of course, children are all the same all the world over, yet there are several points of difference between English and French youngsters. Usually they are somewhat sallow and, to my mind though I may be mistaken, less energetic than the English child. Most of them have rather nice oval faces with wistful eyes and the poorer ones are always pestering the soldiers for biscuits and bully beef or jam. Heaps of them wear black overalls and in the evening, cloaks with hoods. You don't see hoops or tops or marbles.

Today is ideal. France is at her best and I am very happy. There is a blue sky, white clouds, a genial sun and a view of hills and valleys and trees and fields. I am on Fire Picket duty – if there isn't a fire I shan't have much to do. We have been fitted out with various desirable things today. I have now an army vest, two pairs of pants, a new pair of puttees, a new table knife, an army towel, – everything that I wanted, in fact. My shirt-washing is quite a success.

Will you send out the safety-razor blades in the next parcel, please. There is no hurry. I have just had a long letter from Arthur. I send all my love to you my dearest ones. "Oh, to be in England, now that April's there!" Never mind, we shall come back some day.
Goodbye,
Laurie.

Meanwhile the advance party of the Battalion were digging trenches at Cauchy à la Tour, where they suffered their first casualties – two men wounded.

The state of the artillery at that time was parlous. They were so short of ammunition that during April, their daily allowance was three rounds per gun per day for the 15 pounders and one round only for the howitzers. Fortunately in due course things improved markedly.

The Germans had recently used gas with deadly effect at Ypres, so precautions against gas were hastily sought. Strange pads and masks were served out in quick succession. The first gas-pad was a home-made affair composed of a brown knitted "cap-comforter," folded into a pad to cover nose and mouth with four long white tapes. This the men were ordered to clamp on their faces after damping the pad with a solution of carbonate of soda, if they happened to have such a thing about them, but if not with another liquid which contained a certain amount of ammonia, and was available even in the trenches. Not surprisingly the combined supplies of carbonate of soda of every chemist within reach went only a very short way towards fulfilling the need.

Friday, 12 April 1915

Dear Mother,
I have described the day in the breastworks to you and our return to comparative civilisation. The return visit was however quite a short

one, for in the afternoon on the 10th we set out once more and marched to a village which had evidently suffered much from shells. I had before seen smashed-up buildings and shot-holes and so on, but I have never seen anything like this village. Not a complete house anywhere, all the windows gone, half the roofs, many houses a mere mass of wreckage, and of course, not a single inhabitant – a dead, smashed village.

We billeted in a farm not quite so dilapidated as the majority and in which the windows were blocked up with straw to prevent any light being visible at night time. We soon found out that our life here was not intended to be a rest cure, for we were put on carrying food and water etc. to the firing trenches. The journey to the trenches was carried out with great caution. Each man carried his rifle and ammunition, and proceeded along quietly in single file and spread out a bit. Several times en route invisible sentries challenged us and of course, guns were booming and flares going up the whole time. When we arrived at the trenches, we marched along behind them, quite safe on account of the high parapet of sandbags. All this is done at night, so we were not finished work until after 1 o'clock.

Our sleep was horribly brief, for soon after 2 o'clock we had to stand-to for three-quarters of an hour.

Yesterday, I was on my first guard in the danger zone, by which I do not mean that I was in danger. The night was made noisy, not only by the usual sounds of firing, but also by some croaking frogs. They keep their noise up all night long and for the greater part of the day as well, and at night-time it often sounds ridiculously like someone talking.

If you send me anything now, let it be in the shape of food, please. The Army biscuits are pretty hard, so we all welcome any addition to the Army diet. I hope all are well. Do not worry about me. I am quite alright. My very best love to you, Connie and Flossie.
Your affectionate son,
Laurie.

Meanwhile, with Laurie still relatively safely ensconced at Base Camp in Harfleur, up at the front, the advance party of the 15 Battalion saw its first action in the front line at Givenchy:

WAR DIARY: TUESDAY, 13 APRIL 1915
In the line at Givenchy.
Shelled – no casualties.

WAR DIARY: THURSDAY, 15 APRIL 1915
Out of the line – To Béthune.
Casualties: 1 killed
                    3 wounded

WAR DIARY: MONDAY, 19 APRIL 1915
In the line. Took over Section B.2.
Givenchy heavily shelled.

WAR DIARY: WEDNESDAY, 21 APRIL 1915
Billeted at Le Préol.

WAR DIARY: THURSDAY, 22 APRIL 1915
In the line. Took over Section B.1 again.

WAR DIARY: FRIDAY, 23 APRIL 1915
Heavy shelling of Givenchy. Back to Le Préol.

WAR DIARY: SATURDAY, 24 APRIL 1915
Le Préol to Labeuvrière (via Beuvry, Béthune, Chocques).

WAR DIARY: 25–30 APRIL 1915
Daily training at Labeuvrière.

Wednesday, 28 April 1915.

No. 1 Section, No. 5 Platoon,
"B" Company, 1/15th Battn. C. of London Regt.,
2nd London Division, B. E. F.

My Dear Mother,
I want you to notice that my address is changed as I have left the Base camp *[at Harfleur]* and joined up with the rest of the Battalion *[at Labeuvrière]*. I remember writing a very peaceful letter on Sunday, but my calm outlook was rudely disturbed that same night. We were told that a large draft was to leave the Base the following day.

After a medical parade we were busy packing up all our kit on Monday morning, and early in the afternoon we were on the road and bidding farewell to the little corner of France in which we have lived for so long. The day was sweltering hot, and the absence of any shade, combined with the great weight we were carrying, made the march

11

[back to Havre] extremely tiring. Several were quite overcome and I myself felt done up at the end of the journey.

We then got into the troop train – the longest train I have ever seen in my life – travelling eight in each little compartment. The railway journey was very interesting and quite comfortable, except at night, when our feet and legs seemed horribly in the way. We were in the train for something over 24 hours and seemed to make quite a tour through France. At any rate, I really feel that I have seen quite a bit of France now. I think it is better not to put down in a letter the names of any of the cities, etc., that we passed through, as I understand the censorship is pretty strict here. *[The route taken was: via Abbeville, Boulogne, Calais, Hazebrouk, St. Omer, Béthune and Chocques to Labeuvrière]*

On arriving here I was attached to my old company and section, so that I am once again with all my old friends and acquaintances. In fact I had a very hearty reception. At present No. 1 Section is billeted in a farmhouse, sleeping on straw in a barn. After being on tent-boards, straw seems deliciously soft. I understand that we are a good way off from the trenches, but we can hear the big guns. Last night there was a continuous cannonade, but this did not keep me awake for long. Today there is a pretty constant booming, just like distant thunder, and I saw an aeroplane very high up. The weather is sunny and warm and the countryside is pretty.

I have just seen the doctor about my foot. I have much more confidence in our doctor here than I had in the man at the Base, and so I lost no time over it. He says that it is a touch of neuritis and that my foot is a bit poisoned, so my idea of rheumatism seems all wrong. I am to have two days off duty and to bathe my foot pretty frequently. Except for this, I am in good health, so there is no need for you to worry over me.

Well, this is another move further away from you all, yet every day is bringing the end of the war nearer, so cheer up.

All my love to you and the girls. Your affectionate son,
Laurie.

Tuesday, 4 May 1915.

My dear Mother,
The weather since I last wrote to you has been extremely hot, but I am now writing just after a thunderstorm which has left things pleasantly cool.

Today, after drill and a practice advance through some pretty woods, we marched for some miles and finished up at a ——-(just guess)—- at a coal mine! We went in through the gates and had a shower bath. There was a large hall given up entirely to these shower baths, instead of course in peace time for the miners themselves. The shower was cool and refreshing, for I was very hot.

We are in a coal-mining area here. When I first came, I was greatly puzzled by two huge mounds on the horizon, with such regular sides that they looked like pyramids. I soon found out that they were the heaps of slag from the adjacent mines.

The result of being near mines is the provision of electric light in many of the tumble- down farmhouses. It seems a little incongruous, but then so does everything nowadays.

I have not yet received the thin underwear, nor have I heard from you for nearly a week, so there are some things hung up somewhere. On the whole we have had a very happy time here. The fellows I am with are the best set in the world and with their parcels of food we get some very good meals. We eat eggs for breakfast and French bread, which is curious stuff, not so close in texture as our loaves and almost sweet-tasting.

Yesterday I had a glorious feed in an estaminet *[small French cafés selling alcoholic liquor.]*, the French people certainly know how to serve up a good omelette. I had an omelette, fried potatoes, bread and butter, and of course coffee.

I expect my next letter will come from a different village. By the way, my envelopes are now quite exhausted, so please send on a supply. I hope they will not be the kind that stick together too easily in hot weather.

I guess whatever the garden is looking like now, it would be a pretty welcome sight to me. Let us hope that I shall be with you in time to smell the roses and the honeysuckle. Our trellis-work should be alright this summer.

Remember me to all the friends who ask after me.

All my love to you and to Connie and Flossie. Your affectionate son,
Laurie.

Chapter Two

Into Action at Last - Festubert, Givenchy and Maroc

Friday, 7 May 1915.

My dear Mother,

I have sent a Service Post Card. acknowledging the receipt of a batch of letters which have at last overtaken me on my travels and now I am the happy recipient of a parcel. Not the thin shirt one, however. I am afraid I must give that one up as lost in transit. The parcel was very welcome. You can well imagine that the shortbread and chocolate will not go begging and the socks came in the nick of time. When I asked for reading matter, I was thinking more of ordinary penny stuff, as I am afraid there will be little time for enjoying long tales. Still, my very best thanks for the kindness and generosity shown to me.

And now for my latest movements. On Wednesday at midday we left our quite comfortable barn and marched off in burning heat to a small village much nearer to the field of operations. We passed through *[Annezin and Béthune]* a town which I have no doubt is familiar enough to you, in name, that is. Indeed we are now in a very celebrated and historic region in France *[at Essars]*. The village was a poor place. Our barn was small, low-roofed, dirty and full of insects and smells. There was no water supply on the farm and no drainage system anywhere. Happily, we only spent one night in this wretched place.

Yesterday we advanced to our present station, where we are much more comfortable *[Gorre]*. We are billeted in a large barn over a bakery and it is possible to buy various little things in the village. Near to the church is a small place where a number of men are buried who have died in various actions in this district.

We are now within a short march of the firing line and in sight of the reserve trenches. There are a large number of guns concealed here and all day long firing is going on. When the big guns go off, there is a booming which seems to last for minutes and the barn gives a little tremble. Aeroplanes are common events in the sky and they are almost always shelled. The explosion is quite picturesque and the aeroplane always goes gaily on untouched. At night flares go up from the trenches looking like a bit of Brock's Benefit out of place. I have had some shell holes pointed out to me – great holes in the ground – quite close to our billet. Yesterday I saw a battalion of Indian Cavalry. Today, one of my little jobs was helping to sweep up the road and clean out the ditch at the side!! What a life!

The doctor is looking after me alright and I have been let off some marching jobs so as to give me as much rest as possible. I feel quite fit and cheerful in myself and there is absolutely no need for any worrying.

All my love to you, Connie and Flossie. How much longer to wait? Perhaps not long.

Yours lovingly,

Laurie.

On Friday, 7 May 1915 the Lusitania *was sunk. With Laurie starting to show signs of homesickness, this was the day the Battalion moved to Festubert (Tuning Fork) where it immediately became involved in action which was to last until they were relieved on 31 May.*

WAR DIARY: FRIDAY, 7 MAY 1915
Arrangements for attack on 8 May cancelled at 11pm.

WAR DIARY: SATURDAY, 8 MAY 1915
Arrangements for attack on 9 May.

WAR DIARY: SUNDAY, 9 MAY 1915
Occupied Intermediate line and breastworks at 3.00am – German lines heavily bombarded at 5.00am by all British batteries. Enemy replied a little.

Casualties: 1 wounded

WAR DIARY: MONDAY, 10 MAY 1915
15 Battalion relieved 6 Battalion in Sec. C.1. – B Company in support at "Welsh Chapel".

The bombardment on 9 May was the first big attack made by the First Army during May. Heavy fighting took place at and north of Festubert on the immediate left of the line held by the 15 Battalion, but the attack failed to break through.

Monday, 10 May 1915.

Dear Mother,

On Saturday we were served out with respirators and, in the evening, all preparations were made for a move on. We now carry some extra weight – a sand-bag and 100 rounds of extra ammunition – so you can see the thinner shirts are a boon to me.

We got up at 2 in the morning on Sunday, about my record for the "day of rest" and after a hurried breakfast, marched off towards the trenches. Quite a short march brought us to our position in some breastworks and at 4 in the morning we were all posted. We spent 30 hours in these very narrow breastworks, with just room enough to squeeze past the next man if necessary and not enough room to lie down at full length. There was a most terrific bombardment the whole time, but fortunately very little came over our heads. There were such a lot of different noises and there was not an absolutely quiet second the whole time we were there. Big guns and little guns, machine guns firing I know not how many times per second, howitzers, rifles doing their "fifteen rounds rapid", French, German and British guns all at it, hell-for-leather, as the saying goes, all the time. The shells made a curious swishing noise as they cut through the air. I kept on looking up as if I could see the shell. You could follow the noise along right up to the final explosion, but of course you could not see the shell.

The aeroplanes were very active and so were the anti-aircraft guns. When the night drew on, we had quite a firework display from the flares thrown up to a considerable height. The day had been brilliantly fine and at night there was a host of stars. Trying to sleep with heavy equipment on, in the midst of the racket and in such a narrow trench, proved a troublesome business. To add to the discomforts, it turned out bitterly cold. We all took a turn at watching and at 2 a.m. everybody stood to arms for an hour. After breakfast we marched back to our billets to stand by for a time. I thought of you all and of the contrast between your Sunday and mine.

My foot is much less troublesome now. How are you all getting on? Remember me to the Church friends. Well, every day brings us nearer together again, doesn't it? You may be sure I am looking forward to that homecoming with more than a little longing.

My best love to you three.

Laurie.

WAR DIARY: TUESDAY, 11 MAY 1915

Heavy bombardment by our artillery at 1.00am – No reply by enemy.

Casualties:-   1 killed
                1 wounded

WAR DIARY: WEDNESDAY, 12 MAY 1915

B Company in the line

Casualties:-   1 killed
                1 wounded

WAR DIARY: THURSDAY, 13 MAY 1915

Artillery bombardment

Casualties:-   2 wounded

WAR DIARY: FRIDAY, 14 MAY 1915

Fairly quiet day

Casualties:-   2 Lieutenant B. Scott wounded

Friday, 14 May 1915.

My dear Mother,

I have received your letter of the 9th and received it in a place which at one time I never expected to reach – the firing line.

It has been an unforgettable experience and certainly in many respects a very uncomfortable one. I have not shaved nor washed for three days, nor had my clothes or boots off. My sleep I get in brief snatches and my food when it is most convenient. I shall try to get a wash this afternoon, as I believe we may remain here another day.

I was again on guard on Thursday and came down with just a small party to the trenches at eleven at night. You can imagine us stumbling about in the darkness. Thursday night was very cold and rainy, and we slept where there was no shelter of any sort. Still, as I said before, you get little sleep at night in any weather, as you have to take your turn as sentry over your little bit of trench. The rain gave us a taste of the sticky mud business which was so terribly troublesome in the early stages of the war.

From the trench the German lines are easily seen (when you choose to pop your head over the parapet). The sentry is supposed to keep an eye on the enemy's lines and we usually get a periscope for the work. At 1.30 this morning we were all ordered to stand to arms and there was a terrific bombardment of the Germans by our artillery. It was cold, dark and wet, and the bombardment was absolutely terrifying, the noise was so immense and the shells burst with such a sense of such irresistible power. The whole sky was lit up by vivid flashes. The din when we do rapid fire at the Germans is also a thing which baffles all attempts of description.

We have rigged up a little shelter, in which we sit in our spare moments, but there are no dug-outs, this being not really a trench dug in the ground but a double parapet of sandbags raised above the ground level.

You will see from all this that I have reached the stage when such things as bread, cakes, butter, chocolate and so on are indeed luxuries. I should like a clean towel and a couple of handkerchiefs, and if you manage some eatables you will know that your parcel will help make trench life much happier. Of course I may not be here long, but in any case, I am not likely to be able to purchase them for myself.

You should see me cooking in my mess tin. I have done tea, cocoa, oxo, fried bacon and fried potatoes at various times and eat and drink the messes I make with wonderful appreciation.

I thought the anniversary hymns very good, particularly the first two. The first hymn has been a favourite of mine ever since I came across it in the Sunday School book one hot, happy, peaceful, Sunday afternoon.

At last I have fired some shots for my King and country. I wish they could be the last shots of the war. God bless you all, my dear ones. Let me know how everything goes on.

Yours ever,

Laurie.

The second big attack on Festubert came on 15 May. The front occupied by 47 London Division was heavily shelled and in the three days 15–18 May they suffered 320 casualties in killed and wounded.

War Diary: Saturday, 15 May 1915

B Company relieved

WAR DIARY: SUNDAY, 16 MAY 1915

Heavy fighting all day. Canadians on our left charged and took some trenches. 15 Battalion ordered to hold its ground. Enemy shelled trenches severely.

Casualties:-   1 killed

                    9 wounded (one subsequently died)

WAR DIARY: MONDAY, 17 MAY 1915

Rain – Operations seriously interfered with. Enemy still shelling our trenches.

Casualties:-   2 killed

                    4 wounded

Monday, 17 May 1915.

My dear Connie,

I found your letter of the 13th most interesting and was certainly pleased to hear that a few eatables are on the way. It is not by any means that we are starving, or the Army rations really insufficient, but these extras add a touch of comfort to what would otherwise be a rough meal indeed. You need not be anxious either to buy the very best stuff, anything pretty good in quality is bound to be well appreciated. I believe I asked for a towel and a pair of handkerchiefs in my last letter. Anyway, I should be glad to get besides these a duster and a bit of flannel for washing. The new holdall is a great success.

Your graphic account of the treatment of Germans in London was so good that I read it out to some of the fellows here. Most of them were rather pleased, but I am not so sure about it myself. I cannot yet even reconcile myself to the idea that a German atrocity justifies a British outrage. Even when the actual perpetrators are caught, it seems to me that a clean swift death is the only honourable course to adopt. Shooting is, perhaps, far too easy a death for some of them. So it may be we will leave the execution of exact justice to One who is higher than ourselves.

Now, as to my doings. Late on Saturday night we were back from the firing line [at Festubert] for a 'rest' – so called. We sleep and eat in a farm which is only half there, so to speak, and right in front of our batteries of artillery, which deafen us day and night with their continual firing. We have had a few return shells, but they are intended for the batteries and consequently our risk is very slight. We have been told that the news is good for our section of the line, for

19

which I am profoundly thankful. Several German trenches near us have fallen into British hands and a large batch of German prisoners came by here only yesterday.

Sunday was spent in taking up ammunition, food and water to the firing line, a fatiguing operation, and just as risky, in some ways, as being behind a good strong parapet of sandbags. I believe we are to go into the trenches again this evening for a short time.

I am getting along quite alright. So glad to hear all are well. I hope that happy state will continue. I was thinking yesterday evening of you in the family pew, just while I was carrying the stone water-jars to the troops. In a way, that is a service too, isn't it?

My fondest love to you all. I write as often as I can, but perhaps the time will come when I cannot write very frequently. If it does, try to be patient and not to worry.

Yours affectionately,

Laurie.

War Diary: Tuesday, 18 May 1915

Festubert – Shelling

Casualties:-   1 killed
                6 wounded
                Captain W.F.K.Newson wounded

War Diary: Wednesday, 19 May 1915

Advance on our left contained – more prisoners taken. Transport lines shelled. Two Horses killed.

Casualties:-   2 wounded

War Diary: Thursday, 20 May 1915

Battalion relieved at night – Moved to billets at Tuning Fork. Heavily shelled.

Casualties:-   6 wounded

War Diary: Friday, 21 May 1915

Resting in Billets

At this point Laurie left the main body of the Battalion and went back to Gorre, well out of the firing line. His next few letters show he was sent back to undertake special guard duties by the canal at Pont d'Essars in his capacity with the military police attached to B (H.Q.) Company. This wonderful period of rest and relaxation lasted until 2 June.

My dear Connie,

We are now out of the firing line and back in the reserves *[at Gorre]* revelling in the rest which we are able to get. This last turn in the trenches proved very fatiguing indeed. For days on end one seemed to get no sleep at all and of course the tension was rather acute the whole time. I was surprised to find my health kept so good. I believe I am now in better form than before I saw the firing line and certainly my feet are easier. Perhaps the necessity for vigilance and wariness bucked me up.

The weather was usually wet and the slime and mud were terrible. I got just a taste of what those heroic men must have endured in the trenches all through the winter, and can only wonder how they pulled through so well.

On Wednesday I had an interesting job. With just a few others, I was sent forward to an advance trench, which jutted out from the main line and was about 150 yards from the Germans. We had to make the enemy believe that the trench was occupied by a whole company instead of only a handful. We did this by continually walking up and down and firing over the parapet at intervals (irregular intervals of course). If the enemy had attacked, we should have retired to the main trench which was covered by several machine guns. In short it was a trap set for the Germans. At various times a good quantity of shrapnel and other shells was sent over for our edification, but fortunately it did us no great harm.

The dull rainy weather helped the Germans, for, in fine weather, our aeroplanes are constantly on the watch and search out the positions of the German batteries. So far as I can judge, we have a great superiority in artillery here. You cannot conceive the grandeur and the awfulness too of an artillery duel. The flashes are very bright, and when the explosion takes place a dense cloud of smoke gradually unrolls. The shell usually falls harmlessly into the fields, sending clods of mud high in the air. The shells pass overhead with a sort of scream. Some, the very long-distance ones, hustle along, talking to themselves quietly all the way. Others buzz like a motor driven madly. You get the impression of concentrated energy and irresistible force. Once or twice all the din stopped and, for just half a minute, there was absolute quiet over the battle line, save for the singing of birds. Then a stray shot, and then the din all over again.

Your parcel was absolutely grand. Even the box and the shavings came in useful, for without them I doubt whether we could have lit our bit of fire in the rain. The fellows with whom I shared greatly enjoyed the stuff, especially the pineapple. You get grimy and thirsty, and pineapple is like a gift from Heaven. The beef was very nice and the parcel was a great success. I don't want you people to go spending too much money, but an occasional parcel would be vastly appreciated.

By the way, you would scarcely recognise me now, for I am growing a military moustache. It has a tendency to be ginger, alas.

We shall soon have another Bank Holiday along. I hope it will be the last on which the dark shadow of war rests.
All my love,
Laurie.

Monday, 24 May 1915.

My dear ones,
I cannot but think of you all this Bank Holiday and wish I could be with you in our little Eden at No. 52. You can be quite sure I shall never shake off the recollections which are associated with our peaceful and happy years in Palmers Green. They are the happiest in my life, so you may guess with what longing I wait to return.

As I write, your letter of the 21st is before me. How sorry I am. The thought of you all worrying is very bitter to me, and see how useless it has been, for I am writing to you in health and security.

On Saturday our village was struck by a few shells, one of which smashed our chimney and wounded one man in the leg. We spent the rest of the day in lazy positions as far from danger as we could get. In the night we had one of the most terrible thunderstorms I have ever seen or heard. Do you remember the evening when everyone sat up late at Coleraine Road watching the lightning? This was even worse than that. It was a constant vivid, blinding, flashing of lightning and one continuous roar of thunder whilst the rain simply pelted down in torrents. The flashes were too bright for the eyes to bear and the thunder was like a tremendous battery of guns. I compared it to Heaven's artillery and found man's artillery greatly outmatched.

Early yesterday morning I was one of a small party to leave the village and march to a fine large prosperous town *[Béthune]*. Here, although still the military element predominated, there were all the un-accustomed attractions of an active civilian population. It was Sunday and they were all in their best attire, little kiddies dressed up in most curious fashions, very French indeed. I saw some young exquisites also,

22

with wonderful boots, ties and soft hats. There were numerous fine shops and a pleasant bustle pervaded the streets. After a short stay in this town, we moved to an absolutely arcadian spot by the side of a lazy canal *[at Pont d'Essars]*. Here, at a bridge, where the roads cross both railway and canal, our party are stationed on guard. It is a charming place and, unless the enemy advance unexpectedly, not likely to be so unquiet as my other billets have been. Now, you see, you are worrying about my dangers in the trenches and here I am, a long way from the trenches and quite a long way from any fighting at all. The guard may last for a fortnight. It is like a country holiday to us. We do not have to dodge shells or go without washing. We are in clover.

I am glad to hear another parcel is on the way. You really don't know how grateful I am to you all. Will you please express my sincerest sympathy to Miss Edith in her loss. My love to you all. Yours affectionately,
Laurie.

Wednesday, 26 May 1915.

Dear Mother,
I am still doing guards day in and day out by the side of this lazy canal and find the occupation quite to my liking. It means of course that my liberty of action is very restricted, for we must not leave the vicinity of the guard-room for long, but if you were here you would join me in saying "what a pleasant prison".

The canal bridge is the centre of interest for the whole neighbourhood and there is usually something to watch. By now I have seen selections from most of the famous regiments at some place or other. We get all kinds of people past our post – French interpreters, A.S.C. men, signallers, Red Cross people, French civilians, and despatch riders. In the district are several British and French batteries and all their horses are brought down to the canal for water. In the afternoon numbers of the soldiers swim about and others catch sprats and other little fish by letting down nets made of wire gauze. There is a little barge traffic as well, for which the canal bridge swings round on a pivot. Quite close, the French observation balloon hangs in the air. It is not the ordinary spherical type but shaped like a Zeppelin with a cancer on its side.

The weather is very hot, as hot as the English June or July, and we are always glad to get out of the sun when our turn on guard is done.

I have received a final parcel of food from Clovelly Road and some toffee from Plaistow. It is a curious life here, quite cut off as it were from the world, but it will take a lot of it to upset me. As there are no shops, the eatables are as welcome as if I were in the trenches, and I have more time to appreciate them.

I hope all of you are well. The news of the war seems fairly good lately. Let us hope that it means the beginning of the end.
Your affectionately, etc.
Laurie

Saturday, 29 May 1915.

My dear Mother,
I am still on the road guard I described to you and am by no means disposed to grumble at it. On Thursday I got a pass and went with a friend up the canal path to the large French town not far from here. It was most interesting to walk through the streets. The place was quite flourishing, except in one quarter which had been slightly shelled, and where most of the houses were closely shuttered. There were some really good shops, some of them cafes and pastry-cooks, crowded with French officers in glorious uniforms. Some of the colour schemes of these uniforms were really splendid, though more reminiscent of an Alhambra ballet than of the grimness of this present war. Some of the civilians too were worth more than a passing glance, many of the fashions being quite Parisian. Of course, before leaving, we had our tea, a meal in which omelettes figures largely.

The sunsets are particularly fine here and the country, though flat, very picturesque. The weather though, is not quite as pleasant, a very cold wind having sprung up during the past few days.

We are now nearly into June, the month in which the war is to end, according to forecasts by Generals French and Joffre. May it be so, that's all. I should like to be back in time for our roses and to see how the arches look.
My best love to you all,
Yours,
Laurie.

While Laurie was enjoying his time relaxing in Pont d'Essars, things back at the front were entirely different for the remainder of the Battalion. The Battle of Festubert was in full flow, and 15 Battalion was actively engaging the enemy and starting to suffer some noticeable casualties.

War Diary: Monday, 24 May 1915

Fatigue party carrying trench mortar up to advanced trench at 2.00am heavily shelled.

Casualties:-   3 killed
                5 wounded

War Diary: Tuesday, 25 May 1915

Trenches heavily shelled. Started a Communication trench. Night very bright and exposed to heavy shell fire and machine guns, but were able to dig enough to give cover to men crawling.

Casualties:-   Officers: 1 killed, 1 wounded
                Men: 7 killed, 10 wounded

War Diary: Sunday, 30 May 1915

Since 26 May 25,000 sandbags have been filled and used for breast-works. Men greatly hampered by the amount of water which has reached 2ft 6ins level.

Casualties:-   2 killed
                4 wounded

War Diary: Monday, 31 May 1915

Battalion relieved.

With this they were finally relieved on 31 May 1915 and moved out of the immediate war zone. Meanwhile, Laurie's period of relaxation was shortly to come to an end.

Monday, 31 May 1915.

Dear old girl,

You are as true as ever to your old partner. If you were not my sister, I should think of you as my fairy godmother. This all means of course that your letter and parcel of the 27th have reached me safely. They found me still by the side of that placid canal, which by this time I know so well, having studied it at every separate hour of the twenty-four. The French soldiers here are wonderfully adept at catching small fish, about four or five inches long, which they fry for their breakfasts.

I believe our term of office as road patrol is soon to cease and I will let you know quickly of any movements on my part. The other day I went back to our headquarters to get our letters, and a Frenchwoman at a cottage where we had coffee and an omelette told us that 41 shells had fallen near the village during that day.

Yesterday I could not but think of you all. Sundays are woefully different days here. I have had no chance of a service of any kind since I left the Base, and I have never even seen a Chaplain, save at a great distance. Once the Wesleyans paraded and I hoped, but the Chaplain was detained elsewhere and we were dismissed. Still, I believe, if I could come home next Sunday, I should fall into the old life as easily as though I had only broken with it for a week. It would take a great deal to change some things in me, I am sure. If I were in civilians once again, and walking down that dear old garden you are looking after so well for me, you would rub your eyes and say "There has been no war, it was all a dream".

Another month gone, you dear foolish ones, and here I am, safe and sound. Why, when I first told you on the 1st of last September that I had joined, you as good as gave me up for lost. Yet here I am, still kept for you all, and I believe I shall be.
Etc., Yours,
Laurie.

Thursday, 3 June 1915. (Excerpts)

Dear Mother,
On going through my pockets I find 9 unanswered letters. This is to answer no fewer than 3 of them – Flossie's of the 23rd, and yours of the 23rd and 30th. Auntie Louey has both written and sent a very fine parcel. Cliff has evidently been in the same district as myself – that should give you an idea.

Last Tuesday evening I was on guard at the bridge over the canal while battalion after battalion trooped past. It was the occasion of a general shuffle round in the trenches. The men coming out were covered in mud and dirt; they had not washed for a week, they had beards to correspond, and they were incredibly weary. It was really pitiful to see all these strong men almost tottering along – dead-beat. For a week they had, many of them, only cold water to drink and not much of that, it being too risky to light fires in the trenches.

Yesterday I came off that pleasant task of mine and marched through one or two towns *[Béthune, Beuvry and Vermelles]*, a matter of about 6 miles, laden like a pack mule in the burning heat to my present quarters *[at Sailly la Bourse]*. Here I am now, once again with the main body of the Battalion, and billeted in a fairly clean barn.

The woman at the house in which we lived by the canal was offered a banana and did not know how to eat it, saying that she had never seen one before! How is that for civilised France? My best love, etc. Laurie.

Sunday, 6 June 1915.

My dear Connie,

Sunday afternoon and hot, so hot. It certainly is the hottest day we have had so far. The effect on the troops is soporific. They sprawl about and move as little as possible. Only by a great effort of will do I sit up and write to you! Don't think I grudge you the effort. Indeed it is a pleasure.

I scarcely know what to say about the news from England. Even yet half the people seem to be asleep – and so thoroughly selfish. Isn't it obvious that Germany can only be overthrown by the exertion of every ounce of energy that Britain possesses? And isn't it also obvious that so far we are not exerting every ounce of our strength? Germany is at the top of her effort, granted, and she is being held. But we have to do more than hold, we have to crush. It is the duty of every man, whether he be a tram driver or a worker on some Government order, or whatever he be, to say always to himself "How can I best serve the country of which I am a citizen?". Arms and ammunition, food and clothing – the prompt and efficient supply of these is as important as the supply of men. We are up against an enormous, soulless, pitilessly efficient machine and we must meet it in an organised way.

I have seen any amount of German helmets with their flamboyant eagles and flaunting motto – "Mitt Gott fur Koenig und Vaterland". Then I think of their methods of warfare. Strange that the soldiers of God should use the weapons of Hell. Isn't Owen S. Watkins hot on the subject?

This is a very pleasant corner of France we are now in *[Sailly la Bourse]*. Not far off are some scars on the landscape – giant heaps of slag just outside the mines. There are other scars too – nasty zigzag trenches cut ruthlessly across the fertile fields. The wayside flowers are very beautiful and round here there are scarlet poppies in amongst the grass.

You mention masks in your letter. It is feared that the Germans will drop bombs containing terrible chlorine gas. The dastards! We have got proper respirators, soaked in chemicals, and we even have

a respirator drill. The officer shouts out "Gas!" and we all get our respirators on in about ten seconds with an undercurrent of laughter. If you could see us, you would understand the laughter. We are muffled up over our eyes, peering through a black veil and with a pad over nose and mouth. Yet it is rather pitiful too. It cannot be an honest, clean foe that has to be met so muffled up against disease, etc.
Yours affectionately,
Laurie.

Thursday, 10 June 1915. (Excerpts)

Dear Mother,
This town is a very curious place *[Les Brebis]*. It makes me think of Leiston. Just as the whole population of Leiston depended on one ironworks, so the whole population of this town depends on the mines. The employees all live in model cottages, about 700 all of one design and set in rows like a French Port Sunlight. Beyond all these and on the outskirts of the town are some fine large houses, presumably the residence of the managers and bigwigs generally. The town is undamaged by bombardments and the civil population is undisturbed.

A very different state of affairs reigns just a mile away. Here there is a village, no not a village, merely the tortured remains of a village, which shows only too plainly the power of the modern projectile. The houses are just like the photos of Italian earthquakes, and of course there is not an inhabitant left. For the last two nights I have been out with working parties and it has been very interesting though depressing. We started out with our rifles, a supply of ammunition and a spade or pick. Naturally we are not supposed to make much noise or to show lights, so we stumble along in the darkness.

After calmly wandering about in the open fields, with French trenches on one hand and German trenches on the other (and not knowing clearly which were which), we set to work digging a communication trench. It was hard work, for the heat was stifling.

Yesterday evening we went further afield and came through a desolate town – street after street of big houses, all empty and battered about – the most melancholy place I think I have seen so far. How terribly the French must feel to see their land so spoiled, and think of the ruin implied in just that one deserted town. Quite suddenly we came to the trenches, and then began that strange Indian file march along the trench, full of zigzags and unexpected turnings and about eight or nine feet deep. At one point we went right underground and groped in inky blackness for about 30 yards.

Will you please send me out a new toothbrush and a change of socks before very long, etc. I hope there will be no more worrying of London by these rascally Zeppelins. All my love,
Laurie.

Sunday, 13 June 1915. (Excerpts)

Dear Connie,
This is the reply to Mother's letter of the 5th and yours which accompanied the parcel of the 9th. I am grateful, indeed I am. I told you about Auntie Louey's parcel. No sooner had the last traces of that disappeared than I received a lovely gift from Plaistow. It consisted of 2 tins of pineapple, a large tin of peaches, Skipper sardines and a little tin of cream.

Now for our parcel. It is splendid, as it was bound to be. There is only one item which is unnecessary – or rather, two – and you weren't to know about these. I have plenty of boracic ointment, as my feet are not giving me any trouble now, and I use that tea very slowly, so that I now have about 2 months supply.

Now, as to my doings. I am now in reserve trenches or really they are a collection of wooden huts which I will describe later. We left the French mining town *[Les Brebis]* on Thursday evening in a fierce thunderstorm. It was horribly dark, so dark that you lost sight of the man only a foot in front of you and you could not see your own boot. Occasionally a flash of lightening or a flare from the lines lit up the road and the dripping file of men trudging slowly along. We did several miles like this and at last came to a place that had once been a village *[Grenay]*. We put up near a mine. I don't know whether you have ever seen a mine close at hand, but you can guess that there are plenty of large buildings and machinery, trucks and railway lines. All this was smashed in an indescribable way. Great holes in a tall brick chimney, huge girders twisted and with jagged rents in them, roofs without an unbroken slate, thousands of panes of shattered glass, pipes twisted into fantastic shapes, trucks over-turned and piles of fallen bricks everywhere. I wandered through some of the deserted buildings and peered down the cavernous gloom of the shaft. I couldn't see the bottom of course and was content with quite a short peep into such a depth. Well, a mine requires wooden props. There are thousands upon thousands of these pit props stacked up near the mine-head and these have been laid so as to form a chain of long huts. In these we shelter, screened fairly away from the enemy. We get some shells over us daily, but they are not aimed at our huts but at the village. The German artillery probably believes us to be sheltering in the ruined houses, as in so many other parts of the line.

Yesterday we went up to the front line with barbed wire and rations. Oh, these dark wanderings through narrow twisting communication trenches. They are weird, that is the only word for them.

This is the continuation of the letter which I brought to such an abrupt conclusion. I was describing the walks in the evenings up to the firing line and showing how uncanny they were. First of all, you must not make a noise or show a light. Then you go along in Indian file over the most varied country, over loose stones, across ditches, through anything, in darkness.

When you come to the communication trenches you wander along a trench about five feet deep with a parapet of earth thrown up two feet above on each side. It twists and turns when you least expect it and is so narrow that you rub your elbows on the sides. Occasionally bullets whistle overhead and seem to follow you along, showing that some German has suspected your presence. You then duck so as not to show half an inch above the top of the trench.

On Friday I was out on an "observation post". We were out in the open, flat on our stomachs on the edge of a great heap of slag, simply listening and watching all the country below us for signs of the enemy. There are lovely wild flowers here – roses, pinks and poppies and after that dreadful thunderstorm the weather has greatly improved.

The salary is quite right. 2/2d is deducted annually as an insurance against consumption. If I had consumption I could go to one of the Service Sanatoria and get various benefits. It is not an ordinary life insurance. Next month's salary should be something good, as I get an increment and it is a quarter month as well!

All my love to you all,

Yours ever,

Laurie.

War Diary: Wednesday, 16 June 1915
Subjected to a great deal of heavy artillery fire most of which was directed at dummy trenches built half a mile behind our line.

Saturday, 19 June 1915. (Excerpts)

My dear Connie,
You surprise me when you tell me that my letters are receiving so much praise. "Like a book!" What sort of book? I wonder? I am glad however that you like them. One thing I do claim and that is that I only speak of things I know by personal experience. What news there is in my letters is reliable, and any exaggeration is not intentional, in fact, I try to avoid mere sensationalism.

What things we hear! I have just heard of an aeroplane attack by the French on Karlsruhe. Oh Ho, how about a certain worthy firm? Perhaps Stuttgart is none too safe either. I am not fond, however, of hearing of these air raids save on actual forts, etc. You at home are beginning to feel something of German frightfulness now. I do hope London may be spared a repetition of that night of incendiary bombs. Anyway, I know that every Attwell will keep a steady courage and a trust in Providence, just as I out here strive to do.

Now for my latest movements. As I foretold in my last letter, we moved from our log huts on Thursday evening and proceeded on our walking tour through France, in single file, of course, and close up against the walls. Unfortunately the beauties of French scenery are not very obvious in the darkness, so I cannot describe our march *[through Mazingarbe to Le Philosophe]*. At last we arrived, a bit weary at a small and ugly village situated on a very important military road, the use of which is prohibited to civilians.

We put up in a school – deserted and somewhat in need of repair. There are a few panes of glass left, but this is more than many of the houses can boast. Some of them show terrific holes in the walls or roofs where shells have penetrated. Since our arrival however there has been very little bombardment. It is curious to be here and see the blackboards and little school forms and desks, but no little pupils.

Yesterday we were busy constructing a dugout in the garden (what vandals we have to be!) so that if the shells came too close we might have a haven of refuge. It was no light work. The dugout has to be six feet deep with steps down and roofed over with stout logs, several layers of filled sandbags and earth over all. Its capacity was 24 men "standing room only" and it was highly uncomfortable. Well, do you expect armchairs on active service?

Today we are packed up (in a hurry) and waiting for orders, but perhaps nothing will come of it. Etc.
Laurie

WAR DIARY: TUESDAY, 22 JUNE 1915
One shell burst in the front trench wounding five men.

Wednesday, 23 June 1915. (Excerpts)

My Dear Connie,

We are now suffering from a positive plague of flies, both in the school-room and now in these trenches. I am not over-fond of these big bloated bluebottles here, for they may have come straight off some poor human body half decomposed. Yesterday a party went out to bury some of the poor fellows – French soldiers dead for some weeks or even months. There are the first symptoms of another trouble too and I should like you to send me some reliable insecticides as a precautionary measure. I told you I might ask for it if I felt it might be useful.

From the above you will have gathered that we have again moved on. We left the village [Le Philosophe] on Monday evening, the same day that several shells played havoc with some of the houses. You should have seen the branches of trees tossed all across the roadway. One lucky shot hit a waggon containing shells, which blew up at short intervals.

The trenches we now occupy were once, I have been told, in the hands of the Germans, and were only captured by very hard fighting. This is the first time I have been in a German trench. For the rest of Monday and most of Tuesday we were (myself, two other privates and a corporal) on duty in a sap. This is a narrow trench running right out from the firing line towards the German main trench. Our duty was merely that of observation. Of course we had to be pretty careful not to show ourselves above the parapet, which was rather low. Last night I was one of a digging party, so what with digging all night without a pause and being on guard in the daytime I am beginning to need sleep very badly.

I came here with a scalded hand, the result of some spilt tea just off the boil, but it has healed wonderfully well and will soon be as right as before.

Will you please make a purchase for me of a cheap watch? Anything, however large, will do, so long that it is a watch in good working order and not too easily broken. Connie's little wristwatch was smashed at last under the weight of a very heavy box I was staggering along with. Etc.

Laurie.

WAR DIARY: FRIDAY, 25 JUNE 1915
Quiet day. A good deal of rain which made the trenches almost impassable. Water was in some places over two feet deep.

Saturday, 26 June 1915. (Excerpts)

Dear Mother,

Many thanks for your letter of the 20th. What surprising news about Arthur! Another feather in the cap of the "Coleraines". *[Laurie's family then lived in Coleraine Road, Hornsey.]*

I am still in these same trenches and perhaps you would like to have some description of them, as they are different from any others I have been in. They would delight the heart of a schoolboy, for they are sheer chalk. Every piece you pick up will serve to mark with. The glare of the sun on the white trenches is almost intolerable. There is not much chance of concealing such a dazzling place from aeroplanes, for you must remember the trenches zigzag through beautifully green fields. Many of those fields are thick with flowers – red poppies and blue cornflowers. Such a sight I have never seen before. The scarlet, blue and green are simply gorgeous. The flowers are as thick as those bluebells in the Welsh woods which Connie will remember.

The dugouts <u>are</u> dug out and no mistake. They are simply holes in the side of the trench and we crawl into them like bears going into a den. Once in, you fill the place up completely, and sitting up almost invariably means banging your head on the roof. At night, if you get the chance of a sleep, you crawl in and hope to goodness the whole place won't collapse on top of your prostrate form.

We have had a curious job on while here. Apparently those in power think we are too far away from the Germans, and so we have gradually dug an advance trench in the night time, not far from their own trench. Today we are acting as sentinels in this advance trench, which is naturally still in a rather rough condition. We are cautioned to keep very quiet and hidden, so that the Germans may not know too much about our advance towards them.

The heat has been very fierce and the flies nearly as fierce as the heat. There are literally thousands of great bloated bluebottles covering everything.

The water supply has been scanty, so you can think of us, absolutely dirty, unshaven and unwashed, covered with chalk from head to foot, hot and dry, eking out our water-bottle supply so as to last out the day. The finishing touch came yesterday, when a period of drought ended in a great thunderstorm. At the end we were wallowing in chalky mud and puddles six inches deep, yards long and covering the whole width of the trench. There was no escape. You had to splash right through everything. After this we had to go right into the advance trench and dig all night and then sleep on the ground.

Today the sun is very fierce again and there are great billowy clouds in an azure sky. We hope to be leaving these trenches soon, where we shall go next is unknown. Etc.

Yours affectionately,

Laurie.

WAR DIARY: MONDAY, 28 JUNE 1915

Battalion HQ were subjected to heavy bombardment in which four civilians were killed and five wounded (whom we had taken in for safety). We also had eleven wounded. Curious coincidence that each of the Battalion HQ in Le Philosophie had been bombarded in the same way. Evidently some spies about who had given our position away.

On 26 June Laurie and the Battalion left the trenches and returned to Le Philosophe, moving on to Noeux-les-Mines on 28 June where they rested for a couple of days before returning to Mazingarbe on 1 July.

Friday, 2 July 1915.

My dear Connie,

I have received your letter containing the little tin, for which many thanks, and the parcel containing my old watch. I had quite forgotten that old gunmetal ticker. Many thanks for it.

I am very glad to hear that your injuries are clearing up and that the business has not suffered greatly from your enforced absence. Your note of indignation about our lot out here rather amuses me. The greater the hardships and discomforts we endure out here, the higher we shall hold our heads when we return and the more we shall feel that we have repaid in some measure the debt we owe to our motherland.

Now to the latest items in my itinerary through France, items which may possibly keep alive that very active indignation of yours. Indeed, this time I myself must have a little growl. When I last wrote, we were settling down in a large French town and visions of rest floated before our eyes. But alas, the Civil Service Rifles are not as other regiments. For instance, we invariably move into rather dirty billets – floors littered with old scraps of cheese, filthy newspaper, and so on – and as invariably we clean up thoroughly and leave <u>our</u> billet scrupulously clean. Again, to march on drill with full pack on is considered a punishment in most regiments, yet we always wear full equipment on every possible occasion. A walk (or rather a march) which would form a nice exercise in ordinary equipment becomes hard labour with the addition of a pack.

On Wednesday we rose at 5 and started our day's rest with a route march of 9½ miles, finishing in a sharp shower of rain. Thursday we packed up suddenly and marched off again.

Let me however give you a description of the town we have just left *[Noeux-les-Mines]*. Although an industrial mining town, it was quite a rural sort of place. Every available piece of ground bore some crop. This, indeed, is characteristic of France. Do I praise them for it? Well, if I may be allowed to criticise our fine allies, la belle France seem to me to almost overdo thrift. There is, after all, a better thing than saving and that is wise spending. Although fairly close to the 'front', the town had been untouched by shells and we had the delight of seeing normal civilian population and the quaint little kiddies who are now enjoying such a long holiday from school. Many of them are surprisingly sallow-complexioned, weedy little children, very different from our English romps, but others have very fetching mischievous faces. They do not seem to have such organised games and cliques as we have in our streets in London. I saw in this town, more than ever before, those quaint little carts drawn by dogs. The newspapers are sold by little boys, who announce their coming by blowing on a trumpet and then crying their wares. I think if little Arthur or Bert saw one of these little urchins with his trumpet, they would have an ambition to be a French newsboy when they were a few years older.

A very interesting sight in this town was the body of Indian troops billeted there. They were, I believe, the Bengal Lancers. Anyway, they were striking characters, with long black hair, glittering eyes and flashing white teeth. Some looked very dignified and proud, others like half-tamed savages. The French soldiers were very interested in them.

An hour or so of marching yesterday evening brought us to our present abiding place – still another schoolroom! I shall soon be an expert on French schools. This one has still the desks and I had a curious boyish feeling when I sat eating my dinner and thinking of the days when my knees would have fitted in perfectly. Oh, to be a boy again! Nothing of the sort. Oh, to be with you again, that is all!
My love to you all, yours affectionately,
Laurie.

Between 5 and 20 July, although in and out of the front line, the Battalion enjoyed a fairly quiet time, suffering only the occasional casualty.

Tuesday, 6 July 1915. (Excerpts)

Dear Mother,

On Friday the authorities were apparently possessed with the idea that we were in danger of being shelled, for we were put to work feverishly digging dugouts. On top of this rather heavy work, most of us were put on an all-night job. We marched out armed with picks and spades towards that part of the line which I have before described, where we lived in log huts. A second line of trenches was being dug right along the roadside. My particular form of exercise was to carry filled sand-bags incessantly a distance of about 250 yards. At a quarter past one in the morning we stopped work and marched back, reaching our schoolroom at 2.30 a.m.

After a few hours rest we set out once again and were working on the dugouts with intervals for meals until Saturday evening. Sunday actually brought us a little respite. We were to have gone again to the trench-digging in the evening, but were let off as we had done so much work on Friday and Saturday. On Monday evening however we were off again.

We were working on a communication trench, cutting our way through solid chalk. At 12.30 the heap of chalk which we had excavated shone white under a bright moon and we had to cover it with a thin layer of soil to prevent detection by aeroplane or field observation. Some of the shopkeepers have still clung to their old homes here, so this village is not the desolation that we occasionally live in, where one never sees a civilian or a little child.

I had a long letter from Arthur the other day. How I can sympathise with him. It must have been a great strain and a very cruel disappointment. I am amazed that he can keep going so long and at such responsible work. We can certainly feel pride in the eldest male of the "Coleraines".

Etc.

Laurie.

Dear Mother,

Many thanks for your last letter. You really must try not to fret so much over the inconveniences which may come my way. I try in my letters to give you a faithful account of my doings, and I do hope I have not given you the impression that ours is a life of perpetual misery.

My last letter took us as far as last Tuesday. In the evening, under a very threatening sky we left our schoolroom home and marched across country in the direction of the ruined mine and log-huts. We did not go into the log-huts this time however but turned off into a portion of the firing trenches not a great way off. So once more I am in the front line, this time for a fairly long spell I imagine.

The trenches were originally dug and occupied by the French, so I have now been in English, French and German trenches. Our stretch runs along a whole line of back gardens. The houses are, of course, riddled with holes and ransacked of everything. The gardens are waist-high in weeds, a rank profusion of flowers, but there are still some fine poppies and some beautiful rose bushes. In one or two places there are those lovely large white lilies. Cherry trees come right up to the edge of the trench, and even the back of the trench, technically known as the parados, is covered with little wild plants.

One of my chums here is full of information about trees, birds and flowers. Like myself, he is a nature lover. He told me the name of a tiny little flower, such a red gem set in the chalk. It was the scarlet pimpernel.

The German trenches are visible for miles in this level country. They are a fair way off, and, on the whole, this has been a very quiet trench so far.

Wednesday was showery. In the evening three of us were on a listening post and had a little trench to ourselves. One was a bomber and the other two were bayonet men. The bomber throws hand grenades or little bombs at the enemy, and the bayonet men then advance and finish off the job. That is the idea of the teams in cold-blood language. Our business that night, however, was quite innocent – merely to listen and observe, and nothing untoward happened.

Will you tell Connie that the watch has now recovered from the effects of the journey and keeps satisfactory time. The letters from the boys are very quaint, but I rather value them. They show that I made more than a passing impression on them. They were really nice little fellows and I got quite fond of them. *[This probably refers to his nephews, Arthur and Bert Attwell]*.

Yours affectionately,
Laurie.

Tuesday, 20 July 1915.

My dear Mother,

Now to make an effort to bring my story up to date. The night of the 14th was notable for a very heavy bombardment on our right, where persistent attacks and counter-attacks are being made. The blackness of the night was lit up in that quarter by countless flares and star-lights. These last are like gigantic rockets and finish up in a ball of white light, very powerful, which floats in the air for quite a long time. There were also white signal lights, red lights and green lights – quite a firework display, you see. The most frightful sight was the lurid flame and red glow caused by the exploding shells. Rifle fire was of course continuous. Yet I tell you the shooting stars which flashed gloriously across the sky, and which possibly you saw as well as I, seemed to me far grander and more awe-inspiring than any of the warlights invented by man.

The 15th was dull and uneventful, but on the 16th a curious little incident occurred. An elderly German wandered, by some curious blunder, into an advanced part of our trench, a mistake which cost the poor fellow his life. The weather was showery and quite cold.

We have recently been served out with sunshields, which fasten on the back of the cap and hang down over the neck. They are now very useful, for, after a spell of dull weather, we are now panting in proper Continental summer heat. The nights, however, are still quite cool and this great range of temperature in the same 24 hours is a little trying.

The 18th, being Sunday, was the occasion of a fierce engagement on our right. Most of the attacking seems to begin on the day which should by rights be given to quietness and peace. The 19th was quite uneventful and frightfully hot and today is ditto. There is still no sign of our being relieved from these trenches, but I cannot think that we shall stay here very much longer.

I am just going to give a little table of the places we have visited in France, though you will require a good map to be able to locate them all:

March	17/18	From Southampton to Havre.
"	19	Harfleur, at the Base Camp.
April	15	Octeville-sur-Mer.
"	19	Montevilliers.
"	22	Harfleur.
"	26/27	By troop-train from Havre, through Abbeville, Boulogne, Calais, Hazebrouk, St. Omer, Béthune and Chocques to Labeuvrière, not far from La Bassée region.
May	5	Essars.
"	6	Gorre. Firing line only a short march up the road.
"	9	First day in the firing line itself.
"	10	Gorre and afterwards Festubert, which was the centre of very fierce attacking, the Germans being gradually driven back. The C.S.R.'s *[Civil Service Rifles]* did their share in this advance.
May	10/12	In and out of firing line at Festubert.
"	20	Gorre.
"	23	Béthune and afterwards Pont d'Essars.
June	2	Béthune, Beuvry, Vermelles and Sailly la Bourse.
"	7	Les Brebis.
"	10	Bully, Grenay (this is the place with the ruined mine and the log huts).
"	17	Through Mazingarbe to Le Philosophe.
"	21	Trenches again.
"	26	Le Philosophe.
"	28	Noeux-les-Mines.

This is as far as I will take the list. Ever since May 9th we have been in and out of the trenches, for varying periods, then coming out to a place a little to the rear of the firing line. We have been under shell fire ever since May 9th, even when out of the firing line itself.

Perhaps this long list conveys little to you, but it will be useful to keep and at any rate it shows we have trotted about.

I am keeping very fit, considering how little sleep I get and the general discomforts of the place. The flies are a great pest, especially at meal times.

All my love to you three. Your affectionate son,
Laurie.

My dear Connie,

I have received your parcel and letter of the 18th and am very pleased with the contents. The clean underlinen is very welcome and will replace some very dirty rags which have been doing duty as shirt and pants recently. Etc.

I have seen the booklet on the C.S.R.'s *[Civil Service Rifles]* and must plead guilty to the photo you mention. I hope that Fred (Tanner) and Frank will come safely through the Dardanelles campaign, for in my mind they are off to the most risky battlefield of all this world war.

The battalion has been feeling quite perky for the past few days, for one evening a number of Seaforth Highlanders, members of Kitchener's army, were put alongside us in the trenches, and we were told to instruct them in the methods of trench warfare. They were very largely miners, of small stature, and spoke appallingly broad Scotch. Their eagerness was wonderful and they had heaps of energy and go. I only hope all Kitchener's men are as sturdy and as likely to become thorns in the side of the enemy as these Highlanders showed them-selves to be. It seemed very strange to me to be regarded as an authority on military matters, rather comic in fact. Curious enough, the bombardment on the 21st and 22nd was much more severe than usual. These men, miners remember, complimented us on the under-ground dugouts we had made, with pit-props holding the roof up securely.

On the evening of the 22nd, in a pitiless rainstorm, we moved out of the trenches. At last we were relieved. For sixteen days we had dug and watched, and here at last we had a respite. We moved back to a schoolroom *[in Mazingarbe]* about 3 miles off, a place we have been billeted in before. On the way, to add the final touch to my discom-fort, my ankle seemed to give way and I flopped full length on a very wet, cindery road, with my waterproof sheet entangled over my head and my rifle about a yard off. Fortunately, nothing happened to my ankle, so I finished the journey alright, though wet through and covered with cinder grit.

My love to you all,
Laurie.

War Diary: Saturday, 24 July 1915
Accident at bomb school at Noeux-les-Mines.

Casualties: –   Officers –   1 – Wounded
             Sergeant   1 – Killed
             Other ranks –   3 – Killed
                               3 – Wounded

Monday, 26 July 1915. (Excerpts)

My dear one,

Many thanks for your letter of the 21st. In future you can shorten my address to:-

> Pte. 2607 L. W. Attwell
> 5 Platoon, B. Coy.
> 1/15, Batt. Co. of Ldn. Reg.
> B. E. F.

The weather had turned very pleasant now, the sun being tempered by a brisk breeze. Friday, our first day out of the trenches, was showery, and we spent it very idly, though I think there was good excuse for our merely wishing to lie still and quiet. On Saturday we had a thorough kit inspection and, in the evening, marched out on a reserve trench-digging exploit. Sunday, fortunately, was a day of complete rest. The only parade was a voluntary church parade. There was no Chaplain available, so our Captain read the prayers and lesson, and did it very efficiently, like everything else he puts his hand to. We had "For all the Saints" in memory of some comrades who have only recently been killed. The incident is rather a horrid one. We have a bombing school, and the instructor was handling what he thought was a harmless bomb, when it exploded with ghastly effect. There were naturally men clustered round the instructor. Several were killed outright and scarcely anyone present escaped without serious injury.

Soon after the service we had a treat in the shape of the Adjutant's gramophone loaned to B Company for the evening. This made the troops exceedingly merry and we had quite a concert long after lights were out, corporals and sergeants joining in with great gusto. We sang a lot of queer soldiers' songs with weird choruses and had some fine solos as well. Our Platoon is rich in men who have good voices and a knowledge of music, so it was really a great treat.

Do I seem to be always cracking up the old Civil Service Rifles? Well, I don't care. There are very few Battalions with such high level of intelligence amongst the privates as ours. A very big military bug came through our trenches a short while ago, and we were pointed out to him by our Brigadier as "my brainiest Battalion"! There are not many Battalions in which the privates are equal in social standing and everything else to their officers. Yet the discipline is good. Our crime record is always a short one and we always become popular amongst the French people who have to billet us.

Today we have practised making barbed-wire entanglements, those terrible obstacles to advancing troops. There is nothing more for me to say on military matters. I am keeping pretty well and expect to be very lively after a few more quiet days.

How unnatural it is that we two should be separated for so long. But in thought and feeling surely we are nearer to each other than ever before in our lives.

> "There is a strong wall about to protect me:
> "It is built of the words you have said to me:
> "Before me goes a shield to guard me from harm:
> "It is the shadow of your arms between me and danger."

My love to you and to my sisters. Let us hope for a near meeting.
Yours affectionately,
Laurie.

Friday, 6 August 1915. (Excerpts).

My dear Mother,
I have quite a batch of letters to acknowledge this time. Yours of the 30th July, Flossie's of the 2nd and lastly Connie's of the 3rd August, all three being very charming and welcome letters. I have also received the parcel sent off on the 3rd.

It may relieve you to learn that I am no longer in the region of the trenches *[Vermelles]*, but I am at least out of range of shells, for the first time since the beginning of May *[the Battalion was by then resting at Labeuvrière]*.

I wrote to you last on Bank Holiday. The chief incident of that day was a sudden bombardment at teatime, which caused many of the chaps to finish their meal in the cellars of the houses we were living in. In the afternoon of the 3rd we were relieved; I shall not tell you yet by whom, and marched back through the communication trench to a place we have stayed in before *[Le Philosophe]*. At 9.30 in the evening we started off once more in the pouring rain, turning our backs on the firing line and settling down for an all-night march *[via Noyelles, Vermelles, Sailly La Bourse, Vaudricourt and Gosnay]*. It was quite a romantic experience, this long march through the darkest hours, though of course tiring. Soon after 1 o'clock we had hot tea served to us in the roadway from our travelling cookers and this freshened us up considerably. Then, very gradually, the dawn came. Still the march went on until about 3.30 in the morning and we left the rather dismal mining district behind us and saw before us the lovely green fields, golden corn, silver oats and a big hill up which we had to trudge. The hill surmounted, we came fairly soon to our destination *[Labeuvrière]*.

I will conclude now, as the Corporal is waiting for the letters.
Love to you all,
Laurie.

Sunday, 8 August 1915. (Excerpts)

My dear Connie,

Thursday was a glorious day. France was at her best. The horizon was bounded by the woods, wonderfully thick and luxuriant, and in one place, right on the skyline, was a crucifix. Everywhere the eye rested it found beauty.

On Friday we had a very thorough inspection by our Commanding Officer. As you may know by now, it is quite alright to be a foul-mouthed, thieving ruffian in the Army, but to have a speck of dirt on your tunic is only one degree short of treason. The British Army is already a fine institution. If it were only controlled by the dictates of common-sense it would be irresistible. However, "Ours not to reason why"! During the day, by the way, I formed part of the escort for a prisoner, a man put under arrest for breaking military regulations.

Yesterday we went for a 9-mile route march and on our return set to polish up our equipment in readiness for yet another inspection. Is the Army for use or ornament? Perhaps you will send me a little fine emery paper.

So much for grumbling. Now for a real treat. Today, being Sunday, we had a Church Parade. The Church of England service was not up to much, I hear, as there were too many present to hear the Chaplain's voice and the music was poor. The benighted Nonconformists, however, had a separate service conducted by the Wesleyan Chaplain, the first I have seen in France. We had the service in a schoolroom, sat down in comfort, sang old Methodist hymns in rare style, and

43

listened with great enjoyment to a fine, thoughtful address. It was a treat!

Here is a further list of places. I am not sure if I have told you of them before:

June	17	Le Philosophe
"	21	Bully-Grenay (Trenches)
"	26	Le Philosophe
"	28	Noeux-les-Mines
July	1	Mazingarbe
"	6	Vermelles (Trenches)
"	22	Mazingarbe
"	30	Vermelles

My love to you all. Let us hope for an early meeting.
Laurie.

Friday, 13 August 1915. (Excerpts)

My dear Connie,

Our life this week, even though we are out of the firing line and back in Brigade Reserve, has not been an uncrumpled bed of roses. The Civil Service turns out a great many tape-bound officials every year, but for devotion to precedent and hide-bound minds the military system is supreme. Half the discomforts which came to us are occasioned by some authority who must try, in the thick of the world's most gigantic war, to govern the men under his control as if they were still on a peaceful English barrack-square.

On Monday we drilled and drilled and drilled again, the object being not so much to do us good as to polish up the knowledge of certain junior officers and N.C.O.s. Wednesday was a bright and glad-some day. Chalk it up! It was a pleasant march out *[to Auchel]* in the early morning and, on the way we passed within a few yards of one of the Army aeroplane centres. I had not seen these machines so near before and was glad of the opportunity. A few bombs dropped there would have done great damage.

The shower bath was in a mine. We used the showers erected for the miners. The country was glorious, very fertile just here, and the girls in bright coloured skirts and blouses helping in the harvest fields made a very pretty picture.

Yesterday was given up to polishing and cleaning every particle of our equipment to the point of lunacy. All this in preparation for a terrific inspection by our Brigadier, which had been threatened for some days. The inspection came off this morning, in pouring rain part of the time, and on the whole we seem to have pleased the military "powers that be". We were up and about at 5.30 in the morning and tonight I am on guard, so you can see that our "rest" is hardly complete.

Etc. Yours affectionately,

Laurie.

War Diary: Thursday, 26 August 1915
15th Battn. moved up to trenches at Bully-Grenay.

War Diary: Friday, 27 August 1915
8 out of 10 killed (by aerial torpedo) in a Royal Engineers Working Party.

War Diary: Saturday, 28 – Monday, 30 August 1915
Aerial torpedoes cause a lot of trouble.

War Diary: Tuesday, 31 August 1915
Commenced bombardment.

Sunday, 29 August 1915.

My dear Connie,

It is bad news to hear that London is so troubled by these pestilential Zeppelins. I can sympathise with the nervous when they hear the explosions caused by the bombs, for many men out here, even after months of experience, can hardly control themselves during a bombardment. I know one fellow very well, a school-teacher who belonged to "B" Company, who was so upset by the sights and sounds at Festubert that his nerves broke completely. Poor fellow, he is now in an asylum in England. Most of us, however, became almost accustomed to the racket and the whirring fragments.

Poor old Dennis! I am sorry to hear of his wound. Most certainly I will write to him and to Auntie Louey too. She can well feel proud of her boys.

In my last letter I warned you of our coming move to the firing line. We left our comfortable billets on Thursday at 2 o'clock and started a weary, weary march which culminated in the trenches [at Bully-Grenay] at 10 in the evening. The sun at this start was frightfully hot and, as our loads were heavy, we were soon wet with perspiration.

After having some tea in a field, we moved on once more at a rapid rate. The march became an agony. I have never seen so many men fall out from our Battalion before. A stretcher-bearer I know said there were thirty cases of exhaustion. You will not be surprised then when I say I was never more tired in my life. Being on sentry duty that night fell to my lot and was no joke, I can assure you.

We are in trenches again by the ruined mine, but there have been big alterations and I am afraid the place is not quite so quiet and safe as it was. A new trench has been dug in front of the original one and much nearer to the German lines and this is to be occupied in a day or two.

On Friday night I was one of a small party told off to repair part of a trench which had been blown in. Of course in daylight such work is impossible, but at night we calmly wandered about the fields and on top of the trench parapet. Last night I was, with three others, on a listening post. We were about 300 yards in front of the main trench and stood in a narrow place, technically called a sap. During the night, which was rainy, a working party on our left was shelled.

All my love to you three, your affectionate brother,

Laurie.

Chapter Three

The Battle of Loos

High level overview of the Battle

The basic plan was simple. The French and British Armies would attack the German lines from two directions, while strong reserves of cavalry and infantry would exploit the breakthrough as soon as the German line had been breached.

There were several major problems, however. Many of the British infantry reserves had never fought before, were not sufficiently trained to go straight into the line and were thus very much an unknown quantity; and the artillery was short of guns and ammunition. Perhaps even more disturbing was a profound disagreement between the British and French commanders on battle strategy.

The attack was preceded by a four-day artillery bombardment aimed at cutting the enemy wire and destroying his batteries. 533 guns fired over a quarter of a million shells. The attack itself commenced at 6.30am on 25 September 1915. The British, for the first time using poison gas, released 5,100 cylinders of chlorine in the direction of the German lines. The wind made it behave erratically, at some points blowing it back across the British trenches and ultimately causing 2,632 British gas casualties, of whom seven later died.

The French made initial progress at Artois, but were later driven back. The British, attacking at Loos, failed to capitalize on strong early gains and vigorous German counter-attacks forced them back by the end of the first day. The chance to capitalize on these initial gains was thus lost when our reserve divisions were held back far too long. They were belatedly deployed on the afternoon of the 26th, with disastrous consequences.

The assaulting infantry were arranged (eight men to each yard of front) over a depth of 3,000–4,000 yards in successive lines 50 yards apart. They advanced in ten columns of extended lines, coming forward as if on parade.

The German machine guns opened fire at 1,500 yards and, although men fell in their hundreds, the remainder continued to advance. One German regimental history described the assault thus: "Never had machine guns had so straightforward a task, nor done it so effectively. With barrels burning hot and swimming with oil, they traversed to and fro along the enemy's ranks unceasingly. One machine gun alone fired 12,500 rounds that afternoon." Some British infantrymen actually reached the German wire, but, "confronted by this impenetrable obstacle, the survivors turned and began to retire."

The battle continued for another two weeks. Then, when a second British attack suffered heavy losses on 13 October, the offensive was terminated. The Battle of Loos had cost the British Expeditionary Force 50,000 casualties, the French 48,000 and the Germans around 24,000.

Thursday, 9 September 1915. (Excerpts)

My dear Mother,
So there is to be another Attwell launched into this stormy world *[His niece, Olive Attwell]*, Daisy will find three youngsters a pretty handful, I expect.

We are now billeted in empty houses. The town was uninjured when we last came into it, but now considerable damage has been done by shell-fire. Houses which before were occupied are now ghastly ruined.

Last night we again went on a digging expedition in front of the firing line. For some reason or other we were under shell-fire and the night was rendered rather uncomfortable as we had to keep on flopping down when flares went up or bullets whistled by or shells went over. For all this excitement the casualties only numbered four. Anyway, we expect to move back again after tonight so we are not worrying much.
All my love to you three, your loving son,
Laurie.

Tuesday, 14 September 1915. (Excerpts)

My dear Connie,
On the 9th we went for a night digging affair and had a less exciting time than on the previous evening. After the digging the motors came to our rescue; several miles march first, of course, and carried us off

48

in the small hours of the morning to our present village *[Houchin]*, a place we have never visited before.

Our billet here was formerly a hospital for sick and diseased horses and possesses one of the largest cesspools I have ever seen, even in France! The place has the supreme merit of being 8 to 10 miles from the trenches.

We have been supplied with new smoke helmets – each man carrying two. Respirators are abandoned now. One of the helmets is of improved pattern, which means also that we look even more ghastly than in the older type. The ammunition we are using now is all American stuff, rather an interesting fact.

Two old acquaintances have rejoined the battalion from Base. One of them is a chess enthusiast, so I can have as many games as I want. I have acquired an entirely undeserved reputation as the Platoon poet and at the evening sing-songs I generally get called upon for an item. I make up topical skits and sing them to well-known tunes and they always go down well. I think the fellows out here are far more easy to amuse and please than an audience of young men at home would be.

We are expecting to leave here soon, probably to do some more digging. Northern France will soon be a labyrinth of trenches. All my love, etc.
Laurie.

Saturday, 18 September 1915. (Excerpts)

My dear Mother,
I am very sorry to hear that you are all having such disturbed evenings lately. I can quite understand lonely women being terrified at these Zeppelins and the uncertainty as to where the next bomb will fall. The sole idea of these air-raids is to create panic and confusion, and it is the duty of the people at home to remain calm and resolute.
Laurie.

WAR DIARY: SATURDAY, 18 SEPTEMBER 1915
"Battalion employed in carrying gas cylinders into the new gas trench and placing them in position. It required a good deal of organisation but the men did well and it was successfully carried out without incident."

Tuesday, 21 September 1915. (Excerpts)

My dear old Connie,

On Saturday evening our Battalion was put on special fatigue and absolute secrecy was enjoined. I am therefore unable to tell you what we did *[See War Diary entry above]*, but undoubtedly it was one of the most important jobs we have had to do so far. The Sunday evening following we were on the business of fortifying a large cellar by means of large sandbags. The cellar is to be used as Brigade Headquarters and will be the home of regimental bigwigs. We were congratulated on a good evening's work. The early hours of the next morning saw us back in a most unsavoury barn. Here we slept till midday and then rested and cleaned ourselves and our equipment. There is no knowing when we shall go back again, but we are such a roaming Brigade recently that I fully expect another move before long.

Here is a list of places touched during August:

August	1/3	Vermelles (firing line)
"	3/25	Labeuvrière
"	11, 18 & 24	Auchel
"	23	Allouagne
"	26/31	Bully-Grenay (firing line)

God bless you all. Yours lovingly,
Laurie

WAR DIARY:, THURSDAY, 23 SEPTEMBER 1915
15 Battalion into new trench. Takes over front. Artillery very active the whole time.

WAR DIARY:, FRIDAY, 24 SEPTEMBER 1915
"More rain and the trenches awful – a bad look out for tomorrow's attack. During the night we were relieved by the 6 and 7 Battalion and retired to a new trench near Maroc church."

WAR DIARY: SATURDAY, 25 SEPTEMBER 1915
"The Battalion was in Brigade reserve and moved up to our now old front line as soon as the 6 and 7 Battalions had carried out their successful attack.

"We supplied a party of twenty-five men to carry over bombs. They had a bad time crossing and only four men neither killed nor wounded. Immediately they left our front trench they came under heavy fire from the right.

"A most striking event of the attack was the absolute silence of the German guns as our first four lines went over. There was also not enough wire cut. The Germans had machine guns concentrated on all places where it was cut and our men lost heavily at these points. The gas seemed to do no actual damage and not a single dead German killed by gas was found opposite us though without doubt it frightened many. The prisoners who were brought in certainly did not appear to be in any way affected and except for a very few respirators, the only thing they had was a wad of cotton wool."

WAR DIARY: SUNDAY, 26 SEPTEMBER 1915
"Stood to arms all day awaiting counter-attack. Nothing happened."

WAR DIARY: MONDAY, 27 SEPTEMBER 1915
"The Battalion now holds the ground from Double Crassier to our old front line at the Quarries, which is the actual pivot of the whole advance. The trench is very shallow and less than 3ft in a lot of places. We were lucky not to have that particular part of the trench shelled."

WAR DIARY: TUESDAY, 28 SEPTEMBER 1915
"Another wet day. They shelled N Maroc with gas shells. Upset a lot of the men. We were inexperienced and tried to stay in a cellar when one had knocked the house down on top of us. Our smoke helmets were useless and we were eventually driven into the street and then the fresh air revived us. – Cocaine placed into our eyes proved a great relief.

"During the night we relieved the 6 Battalion London Regt. In the captured German second and front lines. Relief very slow."

Tuesday, 28 September 1915.

My dear Mother,
I am afraid that this long silence of mine must have set you all worrying, but you know me well enough, I am sure, to believe me when I tell you that no letters have been collected from us for several days now. Besides there has been absolutely no chance to write and explain matters. Well, anyway, I am fit and well at the time of writing, so you can all ease your minds a bit.

Now I suppose you want to know about my latest experiences. I have been passing through the worst time I have had so far, so it is a great cause for thankfulness that I am still fit and well.

On the 21st we moved to a town near the firing line *[Les Brebis]* and deepened a trench in the evening. A heavy cannonade was going on all the time. Tuesday we were again up in the trenches, this time as carriers of huge baulks of timber. It is surprising how I now shoulder a load and walk off with it, which before I should never have attempted. While carrying, I came across a large dog – an Airedale Terrier, I believe. They are now being introduced as watch dogs in the trenches.

Thursday, the 23rd, saw us packing up and in the evening we marched off to the firing line *[at Bully]*. The elements were unkind and we marched through a terrific thunderstorm which so drenched us that in a few minutes I could feel the rain right through to my skin.

Friday was notable chiefly for a most terrific cannonade. The noise was one long appalling Boom — crash! Boom — crash! Hour after hour.

Saturday, 2nd October 1915

My letter has been postponed for another three days unfortunately, and three such days as I have never experienced before and never want again. Now I will go on with my interrupted account.

On Saturday *[25th]* a fierce attack was made on the Germans, who held a position which their prisoners stated was thought to be impregnable. Our Brigade played a splendid part, capturing three lines of trenches, and our Battalion suffered some casualties in giving assistance to the others.

An entire Platoon, which carried out a fresh stock of bombs to the men who were attacking the trenches, was very nearly annihilated, only six or seven men returning without a wound. We kept the supply of ammunition in the front lines up to the full amount during the day. At night, I was one of a small party told off to carry a trench mortar battery over to a captured German trench. A trench mortar is a heavy apparatus, which flings large-sized bombs – two-thirds as big as a foot-ball – and very heavy. We had heavy loads and consequently could only crawl along slowly. It was an unforgettable experience to cross that modern battlefield at night, and the night after a heavy attack. Away on the left a town was ablaze, lighting up the sky and sending up huge flames. The barbed wire was a mass of tangled broken wires, with here and there, alas, a body. Near the captured trench was a scene of great confusion.

Again I am interrupted. I will write again soon, all is well.
Best love,
Laurie.

WAR DIARY: WEDNESDAY, 29 SEPTEMBER 1915
"Burying dead"

WAR DIARY: THURSDAY, 30 SEPTEMBER 1915
Relieved by the French.

"When we left there were still a large number of dead to bury and rifles, etc. to be salvaged.

"Moved to Loos Road redoubt, then Mazingarbe."

Sunday, 3 October 1915

My dear Connie,
Yesterday's letter was rudely interrupted. Perhaps I shall be more successful today.

I was describing the scene just outside the German trench on the night following the attack and its capture. For a space of thirty yards in front of the chalky parapet were many evidences of the hard, hand-to-hand struggles. All manner of pieces of equipment lay on the ground. Here and there were unexploded bombs, some just fallen out of the stiff fingers of some unfortunate bomber. There were also rifles and "coshers" lying about. A cosher is a short wooden club tipped with iron and armed with a spike. They were intended for use by bombers at short distances – when face to face, in fact. Barbarous? Yes, of course, all the whole business is one long sickening barbarity. There is nothing good, nothing noble, in war. They say it calls into play courage and heroism. What of that? Is an evil thing good because it must be faced by virtue?

On Sunday we moved to a position which we were told must be held at all costs and to the last man. Such an event was highly improbable in view of the fact that the French and English alike were gaining ground from the Germans, and, as a matter of fact, our stay here was quite pleasant. We moved out again on Tuesday evening and marched through a long maze of trenches to the captured German line. We went right along this, and I found it a most interesting journey. Of course the trench was much damaged and contained a vast litter of things. Fortunately, nearly everything ghastly had been cleared away by this time. I found some correspondence tucked away at one point and enclose two postcards as souvenirs. I daresay you will be able to decipher them.

All through this fearful time we have been fighting cold and damp. Our boots have been full of water for days on end and we have been caked with mud. I can now appreciate the suffering of our men during last winter. The nights were terrible and even in our sleep (we had no shelter) we were chilled to the very marrow.

In the evening I was one of a party sent off for water. We went out of the trench and along a road which before was a kind of "no-man's-land". Now it is in our control. Thursday, the 30th, was slightly better, and in the evening we left the trench. I was not sorry to go, for when on sentry duty one stared at the beaten Germans and thought of those huddled-up forms among the barbed wire.

The night was spent in the most smashed-up trench I have ever seen. We were acting as a mobile reserve unit. In other words, we were ready to go anywhere. In the afternoon of Friday we turned our back on the trenches altogether and marched away *[from Mazingarbe, through Houchin and Vaudricourt to Verquin]*, past refugees, with all their belongings crammed onto a cart, past endless batteries, and past long ranks of blue-overcoated French soldiers with those casques on, which protect their heads from wounds.

We were still marching when evening came, but very weary now, and when we finally reached our destination, the Battalion was a mere horde of cripples. I have rarely seen them so worn out. Heaven only knows how I finished, but "all's well that ends well!"

Is it not wonderful that I am still preserved? Remember me to the friends who ask after me. All my love, my dearest ones. Yours ever, Laurie.

WAR DIARY: FRIDAY, 8 OCTOBER 1915
Inspected by General Sir H. Rawlinson. Moved back to Mazingarbe.

The aftermath of battle

Private George Coppard took part in the Battle of Loos. He later recalled in his book, With a Machine Gun to Cambrai, *how he returned to the battlefield some two months later to witness the appalling residues of the battle. He describes how for several hundred yards adjacent to the original German trenches masses of British soldiers still lay where they had fallen two months earlier. Shells from the enemy artillery had since tossed them around into grotesque shapes. The macabre scene was amazingly colourful with bloodied wounds on naked limbs and bodies clothed in multicoloured Scottish kilts, glengarries and bonnets. He describes how the heat had darkened the skin of the corpses and the awful smell of death hung everywhere, making a ghastly and repulsive spectacle. Hundreds of rifles lay around, some impaled in the ground by their bayonets as if transfixed as their owners had fallen forward.*

Chapter Four

Winter in the Loos Salient

On 8 October the anticipated German counter-attack was launched, but repulsed right along the line with considerable enemy casualties. The next few days brought fierce attacks and counter-attacks from both sides with each suffering severe casualties.

Throughout October and up until mid-November 47 Division held an exposed portion of the line well down the forward slope of the ground, enfiladed by enemy guns on both sides. The Germans harassed the exposed British trenches continuously.

The incessant rain turned the trenches into an appalling state. There was no dugout accommodation, and what recesses that existed were constantly falling in with a grave risk of premature burial of any soldiers unlucky enough to be within. There was little protective barbed wire in front of the British trenches; they were full of tangled derelict telephone cables to trip the unwary and, with up to two feet of mud in them, these trenches were the only means of daylight access to the forward positions.

WAR DIARY: WEDNESDAY, 13 OCTOBER 1915
Back into the trenches.

WAR DIARY: SATURDAY, 16 OCTOBER 1915
Heavily shelled in the afternoon and a good deal of damage was done to our front line.

Saturday 16 October 1915.

My dear Connie,
I have woken up from a snatched sleep and take the quiet opportunity to let you know that I am still alright. I have received Flossie's letter

and was particularly delighted to find the chocolate and sweets. The circumstances of our lives in this trench are such that just a few sweets were an absolute godsend. The Mackintosh's "Mint de Luxe" are grand. Now for the tale of my doings:

The 11th was memorable for the finest air fight I have ever witnessed. A German Taube aircraft ventured too far over the British lines and was surrounded by quite a number of our machines. They gradually closed in on the German, which darted about as if to find a way out, but at length it was forced to descend in our territory.

Tuesday, the 12th, was the beginning of personal adventures again. I was put on Brigade guard – a much more important thing, of course, than an ordinary Company or Battalion guard. While on guard over the Brigade Headquarters, the whole staff moved to a village nearer the firing line. Naturally the guard must go too. So we marched behind some of the transport waggons. This meant that we alternately halted and then almost ran out of time. Arriving at our Headquarters, half the guard (three men, one being myself) was dismissed. We were told to join up with the Battalion once more – the Battalion having marched off the same evening to the trenches. For that night we were to find our way to the little deserted village where our travelling cookers were halted. I was the only one who knew the right turning, so I led. It seemed a very strange night walk, all on our own. At last we arrived at the village and found the cookers. We then reported to the sergeant and had a good sleep in a deserted house.

In the morning, after a good breakfast, we started out to find the Battalion in the trenches. Our directions were very vague. We proceeded up the most desolate-looking street on God's earth, past empty ammunition boxes and bits of equipment, dead horses and broken-up transport limbers and carts. The whole road was pitted with shell-holes and most of the trees were smashed in half and the trunks were all over the place. On each side of the road was a level, hedgeless, treeless plain, through which twisted and turned the maze of chalk trenches.

We followed our directions to the letter, but came only to a very badly damaged trench with a few French soldiers in it, so the three of us turned about and marched back to the cooking again. The latter part of the journey was under a bit of shell-fire, and I think we were all very glad to get back safely. We stayed with the cookers until after dinner, when they suddenly received orders to pack everything and move back. Nobody knew where the Battalion was, so we had to go with the cooks. The carts went along the road, but we took to the communication trench. They had moved guns right up to the edge and in places you could see the muzzle of the gun peeping over the parados (the rear wall of the trench). These batteries were firing as we passed underneath and the noise was terrible. You can perhaps imagine what it was like to be only two or three feet in front of a battery when it fires. A cloud of chalk, dirt and powder covered us each time, and our eardrums ached horribly.

We then joined up with the rest of the guard at Brigade Headquarters and in the evening moved off to join up with the Battalion. We had to proceed right across a recent battlefield – you know what that means – and at last came upon our fellows in a German trench. No sooner had we reached the top of the trench than the order came for everyone to climb out and lie down. After a cautious wait, we all advanced in the dusk, over barbed wire and round shell holes to the next German line. This was quite empty and we had but little firing at us as we crossed over. We settled down in this trench as best we could but in two hours we had to advance again. This time we went through a road which was somewhat sheltered, and through communication trenches which were a tangle of telephone wires.

We are still in this same trench, but I will describe the remainder of the days in my next letter.

This is a list of the places we went to in September:

Sept.	1/3	Bully-Grenay (trenches)
"	3	Les Brebis and Haillicourt
"	4/7	Haillicourt
"	7	Bruay and Les Brebis
"	8/9	Les Brebis
"	9/14	Houchin
"	14	Barlin and Houchin
"	16	Béthune
"	17/19	Les Brebis
"	19/23	Haillicourt
"	23/30	Trenches at Bully and Vermelles – the great attack during this spell
"	30	Vermelles

I am still keeping up and quite uninjured. My best love to you all, Laurie.

WAR DIARY: SUNDAY, 17 OCTOBER 1915

Relieved and moved back to the old German front line where we were during 18 and 19 September.

Dear Connie,

I am now about to try and answer your letter of the 13th and Mother's of the 15th. The parcel was a tremendous boon. The marrow and ginger jam was eaten with gusto and relish. Don't forget to thank the Church Sewing Meeting from me for the socks (which I am now wearing) and mittens. The shirt I have put on today and is quite alright.

In my last letter I got as far as the 13th, but I missed out perhaps the most interesting feature of that day. During the morning I gained a comprehensive view of a big attack along many miles of the front – a unique thing in this war. Generally one is boxed up and can see but little of the surrounding country.

The continuous roll of the big guns lasted for nearly three hours and it was one vast turmoil of noise from start to finish. From the line issued dense masses of smoke – smoke of all hues, white of shrapnel shell, black and sulphur-coloured of high explosive shell, and also the great pall of smoke screen behind which our troops advance.

That night saw us in the front line of all, and what a line! Over yonder the Germans, and here we stood in a mere shallow ditch, hardly worthy of the name of trench. During the 14th we worked like madmen, deepening the trench and building up firing positions. This we did under snipers' fire and not without casualties.

The 15th was a repetition of the 14th, though I shall always remember my thirst, for our water ration was only a water bottle-full in two days, during which we were on thirsty work. A wounded man was rescued after two whole days in the open, and was carried off in the evening with good hope for his recovery. He had chewed grass to get a little food and moisture.

On Saturday *[16th]* I was on a rather curious job, being one of four men sent out to warn a working party should any Germans advance upon them. The men were out putting up barbed wire entanglements and we were concealed in twos in long grass between them and the German trenches. It was a cold night and we had to be there for five and a half hours. We could hear the Germans talking, singing, digging, etc., and even a gramophone going somewhere. My companion was little more than a boy and did not relish his job. He was continually seeing "a man over there". I was not so easily frightened, for I realised that anyone approaching through that thick grass would make quite a considerable swishing sound.

On Sunday we moved out of the front line to the support trench. This is also a captured German trench and is still in dilapidation, owing to the shelling it received before the attack. It was so bitterly cold that night that sleep proved absolutely impossible. The cold snap came suddenly and we all suffered badly from it. Two men from the platoon had to go off to hospital. We are now more or less hardened to it and can sleep better.

Yesterday started brightly but ended sadly enough. In the evening we were out on a fatigue which I must keep secret at present. At night I was on sentry duty from one till two and when I went out to take up my post I was just in time to see a very dear friend being lifted on to a stretcher. I feel very grief-stricken at it all. Oh, stop the war, stop the war! He was bleeding from the head badly and was scarcely conscious. It was pitiful to see so strong a young man – he excelled in strength – suddenly become so feeble. Things became all black and bitter for me for a time. Never let me hear a word about the glory of war.

Still, we have to bear these losses. I have an unfinished game of chess in my pocket which we were enjoying hugely. He is only wounded, thank God, and <u>may</u> recover.

I am suffering from a cold in the head and have perpetually cold feet, but otherwise I am in great form. How many fitter and stronger men have I seen go under!

I trust you are all well. Is Mother's rheumatism troubling her? Please thank Arthur from me for his share in the last parcel. I have now been just over seven months in France. Who thought our parting was for so long?

My fondest love to the three dearest ones in the world.
Laurie.

WAR DIARY: WEDNESDAY, 20 OCTOBER 1915
Back in the front line.

Sunday, 24 October 1915.

My dear Connie,
Thank you for the eatables. They are just right. I think I might mention here that these parcels of yours and those which a special chum of mine always shares with me are, I am convinced, responsible for my continued good health. But for the additional food and the dainties they contain I feel sure that the severity of the weather, added

to the hard work we have had to do recently, would have broken me down. I admit that my appetite has been positively enormous, eclipsing even the traditional Attwell capacity, but the circumstances of my life are the excuse.

Now let me tell you of the last few days. On the 19th we were on a digging expedition. It was noticeable how the bullets kept flying quite near and yet nobody was hurt. The next evening, Wednesday, we did some salvage work, collecting equipment, rifles, bayonets, ammunition, and so on. The whole field of battle is littered with stuff and we were out to save some of it. This time one poor fellow was hit by a bullet.

On Thursday we changed trenches, moving up to the firing line again. It was raining slightly and was hopelessly miserable. We carry blankets now – more weight – and these do keep the life in us, but you have no idea how cold you can feel sleeping out in the open, utterly unsheltered. For days I have had the sky as my ceiling and the hard ground as my floor. I can appreciate the verse now,

> "Though like the wanderer, the sun gone down,
> Darkness be over me, my rest a stone, etc."

Friday afternoon was conspicuous by reason of a bad bombardment of our trench. They seemed to have the distance judged to a nicety and knocked the place about terribly. We certainly spent a bad half hour. The gun was believed to be on an armoured train, and it started on one end of the trench and then went right up, sending a shell at every twenty yards. We all filed away in the opposite direction but suddenly the blessed thing started at the beginning again and nearly caught a crowd of us. Personally I think we would have been better to crouch still, every man in his usual place. Yesterday we came back in the evening to a reserve trench where we are at present. I am more fortunate here, having a small place to sleep in which shelters me fairly well.

My fondest love, etc. Your affectionate brother,
Laurie.

WAR DIARY: WEDNESDAY, 27 OCTOBER 1915
"Returned to Mazingarbe, and we supplied a Company for the King's inspection."

My dear Mother,

Many thanks for your letter of the 22nd and for the sweater, etc. I shall not want the sleeping helmet yet, and we are now served out with a warm shirt and pair of pants each, so I am much better protected against the cold. I have run out of trouser buttons and safety pins.

We have had an extremely bad time of it recently. You shall judge. Heaven knows, I try not to complain without cause. On Sunday evening, the 24th, we were all called out for digging. It was cold, dark and raining hard. We had a long march over slippery mud and along so-called roads full of hidden shell-holes nearly up to a village recently become famous. Here we worked in the rain until everyone was so wet that falling into a river would have made little difference. On the tramp back to the trench, now flooded, our men were more dispirited than I have ever seen them before.

The rain continued during the whole of the next day, giving no opportunity for getting either warm or dry. Tuesday was better and we had some wintry sunshine which we used to the uttermost. On the evening of Wednesday *[27th]* we left the trench and marched back to a village just behind the lines. The going was so sticky and difficult that I found it impossible to keep up with the others. I obtained permission to have a rest and, as soon as we came off the field paths on to the roadway I halted and watched the others fade away into the gloom. Then I sank down in a ruined house and had a rest. You can picture me afterwards making my way along the road, inches deep in black ooze, feeling tired and rather dejected, and reflecting on the futility of war.

By dint of asking a sentry at occasional cross-roads I followed up the Battalion to their present billet – a not overclean barn. In the morning, I paraded before the doctor and obtained two days' rest. I cannot think at present that this will be sufficient, as the chill I have caught has given me a constantly aching back. However I am confident things will work out alright. I am only a bit unwell and there is no need at all for you to worry. Just to convince you that I have not given up lightly, let me give you some figures. No. 5 Platoon started on this war 50 strong, and we have had reinforcements from time to time. Yet today the Platoon only numbers about 20, and some of these are sick like myself.

I must confess that times come as I think about this war and I am a broken-hearted man. What about these American massacres? I read that the entire population of one town (10,000) was drowned in a single afternoon. How hopeless and devil-ridden the world seems. I have gazed at times across to the German lines and fired at enemies. But at other times I have stood at night on a desolated battlefield and looked down at the still forms of Germans. Somehow I cannot call them enemies then. I can only say "poor fellow!" Have I any right to think myself a better man than he? Why do we kill each other?

Yet do not think of me as always miserable. I see things in a clearer light than ever before. I have tried to do my best out here and, sooner or later, this war will come to an end. <u>Then</u> it is for everyone to live for one object – the rendering impossible of such another conflict forever. It is well expressed in the national hymn:

> "And may the nations see
> That men should brothers be,
> And from one family,
> The world o'er."

I will let you know how things go on, but do not worry. Etc. Laurie.

WAR DIARY: MONDAY, 1 NOVEMBER 1915
Heavy German shelling.
Casualties: 2 Killed
                3 Wounded

WAR DIARY: TUESDAY, 2 NOVEMBER 1915
Intermittent shelling.
Casualties: 2 Killed
                3 Wounded

WAR DIARY: WEDNESDAY, 3 NOVEMBER 1915
Took over A.2 Sector.
Water in trenches 12 – 15" deep.
Casualties: 4 Wounded

WAR DIARY: THURSDAY, 4 NOVEMBER 1915
Casualties: 4 Wounded

Thursday, 4 November 1915.

Dear Mother,

This is just a short message to let you all know that I am still going along alright. You will be very glad to hear that I am now feeling better in health than the last time I wrote, and I hope to be quite well again in a few days. I am in the firing line and it will be impossible for me to write a proper letter here. I have had your letter of the 31st.

My fondest love, etc.

Laurie.

WAR DIARY: FRIDAY, 5 NOVEMBER 1915

Moved back to old German front line around Loos Road redoubt.

Casualties: 8 Wounded

WAR DIARY: SATURDAY, 6 NOVEMBER 1915

"The Lord Mayor of London inspected the Battalion as it stood by Platoons in the trenches. He was no doubt impressed by the appearance of the men who had been five days in front line trenches in very wet weather and no supply of water for washing or shaving purposes."

Sunday, 7 November 1915.

Dear Connie,

At last my chance arrives of writing to you and acquainting you with the strange tricks which fate has recently played on me.

Two companies of our Battalion were sent out of the trenches a day earlier than the others *[on 27th]* in order to attend the Royal Inspection, but "B" Coy. was not one of them.

I missed a most important piece of news from my last letter. When we came from the trenches on the 27th we had spent 15 days in them and were in a condition of filth quite impossible for you to realise. Most of us had at least a 10-days' beard and 10 days' dirt on our faces. Even the officers were verminous! I need say no more. Well, the very next morning we were marched out for a bath, Hurrah! I have told you of our washing in a coal mine. This time we had a bath in a brewery! We stripped in one place and then went on to an enclosure where there stood a dozen large wooden tubs, filled with warm water. In another minute all you could see was a dozen heads and pairs of shoulders sticking out of the tops of the tubs. We had a most glorious bath. An R.A.M.C. man poured in more hot water when we wanted it and at the end we received a new shirt and pair of pants each. What a relief it was once more to be clean!

As you know, I paraded sick for a chill. I was given a complete rest until Sunday evening, the 31st, when we again set off for the firing line. I still felt queer, the march was longer than usual and most tiring, and the trench we were bound for had a bad, bad reputation. Half the journey through, I asked for permission to fall out, being on the verge of collapsing, but this was not granted. The fellows were highly indignant, including our Platoon Sergeant. Indeed, I cannot speak too highly of the Sergeant. While I was in the trenches he was most kind. He tried his hardest to keep me in some warmth and comfort, and was careful not to give me too much to do. How I finished that long march I cannot understand, even now. I was as weak as a child and the muscles of my back ached incessantly. Yet in the trenches I gradually recovered my usual health, and now as I write to you I feel as well as ever.

Life in the firing line was rendered exciting by bombardments. We had one the very first evening and at frequent intervals afterwards during our stay. On Monday the 1st we had rain and the trench fell in in several places. The rain continued throughout Tuesday. Altogether we had quite 30 hours continuous rain. Ah! pity us! I tell you, you would have wept to see how utterly wretched and miserable we were. Our trench was inches deep in mud and icy cold water, we had no dug-outs or shelters, we were soaked to the skin, a keen wind chilled us to the bone, we were continuously being shelled, and our trench was literally falling to pieces on top of us! And all the time, rain, rain, rain!

One of the shells struck a large tree just in front of the trench. The tree was smashed into two jagged pieces, one of which nearly crushed some of the men. This incident was repeated the day after, and we undoubtedly had some very narrow escapes from injury during our stay. The weather was improving on Wednesday, Thursday and Friday, which were quite dry. On Friday evening *[5th]* we left the firing line and proceeded to a reserve trench. Here fate interposed curiously.

One of the draft men had gone off to hospital and it appears he has enteric. Well, nine of us were regarded with suspicion by the doctor, as we have been living in close contact with a man who turns out to be an enteric patient. So we were ordered to leave the trenches and report to the 6th London Field Ambulance. We piled all our stuff on a limber, which had come up with the daily food for the men in the trenches, and I got in the limber as well. I shall never forget the ride through the night over bumpy, shell-holed roads from the trenches to the hospital.

Well, to cut a long story short, we are now isolated, and live in a tent all on our own. As we feel perfectly well, we are a happy party and don't mind isolation from the Battalion at all.

This move does not cut you off from me, but it does cut me off from you. I am afraid that the parcel will be lost entirely, so don't send me any more parcels till I give the word. Letters will probably be hung up until I join the Battalion. What a happy turn of events! This is a piece of good fortune after a most trying time. Remember me to the different friends. March to November, and still alright!
My fondest love to you all, my heart is with you.
Laurie.

WAR DIARY: SUNDAY, 7 NOVEMBER 1915
A quiet day.
Casualties: 1 Killed
               3 Wounded

WAR DIARY: TUESDAY, 9 NOVEMBER 1915
Intermittent shelling.
Casualties: 3 Killed
               9 Wounded

WAR DIARY: WEDNESDAY, 10 NOVEMBER 1915
Considerable shelling during the day. Very wet, windy and cold.
The damage to trenches caused by weather and bombardment is so bad that it is almost impossible to keep pace with the work of repairs. In places the trenches are quite impassable by day.
Casualties: 3 Killed
               13 Wounded

Wednesday, 10 November 1915. (Excerpts)

My dear Connie,
You can imagine my delight when your letter and the parcel reached me safely. This was due to the kindness of the Quartermaster Sergeant and his assistant. They pick out our post from the rest and bring it up to us specially, so I shall probably get any letters just the same as before.

The parcel is an extra good one this time. I have been in luck lately, for a splendid parcel came along from Plaistow, with a letter from Erica. It contained sardines and sausages and all manner of luxuries. There were also some little throat pellets called "Meloids", manufactured by Boots, and very efficacious.

In my last letter I promised to describe the hospital to you. It was 3 o'clock in the morning when we first set foot inside its portals. We entered a huge bare hall, originally part of a brewery, divided by a partition into the hospital itself and a sort of waiting room. The place, which was very lofty, was warmed by a large number of coke braziers, exactly resembling the fires you have seen roadwatchers crouch over. At first the coke fumes were very noticeable, but we soon became accustomed to them. Beyond the partition, we caught glimpses of the hospital floor, crowded with stretchers used as beds.

Having explained our errand, we were treated with great kindness. We had a stretcher to lie on and were served with some French bread and butter and a hot bowl of tea. How well we slept! Early the next morning, we got up and had breakfast. The cases now began to arrive and, as we were not urgently requiring treatment, we sat in a corner and could watch the working of a Field Hospital.

Everything was done in a quick methodical way and the thing worked like a well-oiled machine. A good many had to be carried in, others could walk. One of our own Corporals turned up with his left arm in a sling and a bullet hole clean through his wrist. There were several cases of "chilled feet". These were rather pitiful. The cold and damp in the trenches causes the feet to swell and become very tender. Many of the sufferers could not get their boots on again because of their swollen feet and had been for a day or more with just stockings on, plus all the rags etc. they could get to wind round and round. A lot of the poor fellows had to be carried.

During the day a large number of people who had received preliminary treatment were packed off in ambulances to the large permanent hospitals. The officer in charge was most business-like. He would call out "Now three more sitting cases" and so on, and car after car drew up and was filled in a few minutes.

At length we were examined and our temperatures taken. Two of our party of nine were apparently feverish and they were promptly packed off to hospital by the next car. The rest of us were taken round to a tent and told we were to live there. We have three blankets apiece and a brazier just outside the tent, so we can keep quite warm and comfortable.

On Sunday evening we went to a voluntary service in the hospital, sitting apart, of course. It was a curious sight to see all those men down on stretchers listening to the chaplain and joining in the singing, I also had a warm bath, the first for a long time, on Sunday.

Every morning we have our temperatures taken. Personally the rest and comfort are doing me a world of good. On Monday we did a bit of work round at the Divisional Baths, which is the high-sounding name applied to those tubs I have described to you before. Being a brewery, there are plenty of barrels about and we had the job of stacking these up in a corner. Imagine me rolling wine and beer casks about. We had since done several jobs round at the Baths, including shovelling coke into sacks and then carrying the sacks up a large number of stairs. Yesterday turned out to be very wet and windy. Our tent threatened to blow away bodily, but fortunately most of the ropes held. We contrasted our lot with that of the poor fellows in the trenches (our Battalion is in the firing line again) and felt ourselves very fortunate.

Before I close, I have a favour to ask. One of my friends is a married man, and he would like to send his wife a birthday gift. I have mentioned the Regent Toilet Co. *[later Parfumerie Delafine Limited]* to him and he would like his wife to have a tasty little parcel of your stuff. Can you please make up a dainty parcel, containing some shampoo, powders, fancy soap, a bottle of scent (not a large one, but let the scent be good) and some tooth powder. He has given me 7 francs, the equivalent of just over 5/-, so you can deduct the cost from my next month's pay. Please do your best for my chum and let me know what you have sent, but there is no need to lose on the transaction. I know I can rely on you to please the lady in question. Her address is given on the enclosed slip.

Etc. All my love to you. Your affectionate brother,
Laurie.

WAR DIARY: THURSDAY, 11 NOVEMBER 1915
A quieter day. Moved to support line.

Casualties: 2 Killed
             6 Wounded

Over the next few days 15 Battalion marched to Mazingarbe, then to Noeux les Mines. They finally entrained for the Lillers area, where for the period from 16–30 November they rested in Corps Reserve. The daily routine involved parading each day from 10.00am until 1.00pm for platoon, company and battalion drills, bayonet fighting and rifle exercises.

An entry in Laurie's official Army Casualty Form shows he rejoined 15 Battalion on Monday, 15 November 1915.

Friday, 26 November 1915.

My dear Mother,

The parcel of the 22nd has reached me safely. In view of my cold, the handkerchiefs were most timely. The eatables shall have very short shrift, for this cold weather sharpens the appetite. I can see that the Continental winter under war conditions is going to be no joke. Last night we had a heavy hailstorm and another cut short our drill this morning. The hail descended on us very slantingly, cutting on to one side of our faces. Such details as shaving in the early morning, when the pump handle has to be thawed before it will move, make us think longingly of civilisazation and peace.

There is little to tell you, and no news is certainly good news in this case, as it means first of all that we are still in this large town, and likely to stay here for some long time. On Sunday, the 21st, we had the unusual organised hypocrisy of church parade. The service was dead-and-alive and most uninteresting. How different to the little chapel at Winchmore Hill, where I used to sit every Sunday morning and get so warmed up that I would vow impossible things.

On Sunday evening we were on "inlying picket". This meant that we must keep in our billets during the next 24 hours, being available to quell riots, put out fires, assist the military police, form a guard of honour, or do any other unusual job which might crop up. We had Sir John French through the town yesterday in his motor. On Tuesday a treat came my way. A few privates from each platoon were allowed to attend a swagger Brigade concert, and I was one of the fortunates. The concert was held in the little French theatre and was splendid. The second part of the programme was taken up by a group of officers who called themselves "The Follies" and dressed up in the usual pierrots costume. They gave numerous selections – solos and concerted pieces, songs humorous and sentimental, and recitations. I almost fancied myself back in gay old Shaftesbury Avenue.

Wednesday evening was very different, for I was on guard. Of course, we are doing a lot of drill while at rest. In fact, the young subalterns seem to delight in putting us through elementary drill of the kind we practised at Somerset House in September 1914. I am not a very disciplined person even yet, and it riles me to be ordered about by young men for whom I have no trace of respect. Sometimes my blood boils with suppressed rage at the infinite gulf fixed between the officer and the private. Some of our officers are not fit to black the boots of the men they order about like dogs. This war will be won in spite of the officers, I believe, not because of them. The army tries hard to crush the soul out of every private, but, you know, nothing on earth <u>can</u> crush the soul out of a man. What sacrifice have the officers made that the men have not made? What dangers are there which the men do not share? What discomforts which the men do not bear the heavier weight of? Then why are men to be treated as though they were criminals or conscripts, being made from commoner clay? The Army will make quite a democrat of me before long. Still, these are just grumbles to ease my mind. This is a delightful town, and the rest here is doing me a lot of good. Etc.

Your affectionate son,

Laurie.

The winter saw a radical improvement in artillery methods. 18-pounders replaced the ancient 15-pounders, many of which had become unserviceable through not being able to cope with the rate of fire-power thrust on them, and we obtained a good supply of new high explosive shells. The flatness of the battlefield caused us to change our artillery defences, replacing rows of sandbags and foliage with tunnelled dugouts and covered gun-pits.

Two pieces of new equipment made trial appearances during the winter. The gumboot was introduced and was an immediate hit with soldiers who had to endure long hours standing in wet trenches, and the steel helmet soon to become a standard issue.

The fighting since the battle of Loos had taken its toll and many men were sick. All Battalions were well below strength and replacements were insufficient and irregular.

By mid-December 15 Battalion held a portion of Essex Trench, considered to be a key tactical position. The day after they took over the trench, the enemy raided it. They were repulsed twice, but a few days later the Boche succeeded in bombing 15 Battalion out of some 20 yards of Essex Trench. 15 and 18 Battalions launched two counter-attacks but failed to regain the captured ground, losing fifty men in the process.

War Diary: Thursday, 20 December 1915

Essex Trench attacked at dawn. We had to withdraw about 18 yards. At night we attacked to recover the lost ground but owing to bright moonlight the movement was seen too soon to affect a surprise. Our men however pushed on well and three entered the German trenches but they could not be properly supported and after nearly three hours fighting we took up and consolidated the morning position.

Casualties: 2nd Lieutenant A.M.Thompson Killed
Lieutenant G.C Grunsdale Wounded
9 Killed
57 Wounded
3 Missing

On 30 December an area close to Essex Trench known as Hairpin was blown up. Some days earlier infantry had reported sounds of mining under the Hairpin and, although these had initially been disregarded, the garrison on the top had fortunately been reduced. Immediately following the explosion the Germans began an extremely heavy bombardment, causing many casualties in the garrison and badly damaging the trenches.

The Battalion continued to take part in the actions throughout the remainder of the winter in the vicinity of Loos.

Chapter Five

1916 and Vimy Ridge

On 27 January 1916 Laurie received a shell wound to his left heel. On 31 January he was sent to Etretat for treatment, being discharged on 26 February and reporting back to the Base Camp in Havre where he spent two months recuperating. He eventually rejoined 15 Battalion in the field on 18 April 1916. No letters survive during the time he was away from active duties.

Only two weeks after rejoining his Battalion Laurie was thrown into the thick of the Battle for Vimy Ridge. He subsequently wrote a graphic account, reproduced below, of his dramatic involvement in the action.

15 Battalion's involvement in the Battle for Vimy Ridge

The offensive started in the area of Villers-au-Bois on 26 April 1916 when the first German mine went up, creating a massive crater in the British front line. This was the prelude to several other massive explosions over the forthcoming days, causing substantial damage and many casualties. By the start of May the Germans were suspected of having tunnelled at least eleven galleries towards the British front line which was in imminent danger. British miners worked frantically, burrowing forward from the old French trenches. On 4 May they fired four mines and opened a massive bombardment in support of an advance to occupy the craters. The British infantry fought really well and by dawn had secured a notable success. By 15 May, however, the Germans counter-mined and re-occupied their old lines.

140 Brigade (to which 15 Battalion belonged) took over this troubled sector four days later. It was not a welcome inheritance. The line was in a bad state of disrepair; there was no wire to protect the front or supporting lines; the front line consisted simply of a series of disconnected and isolated posts and there were no shelters of any kind. The Boche relentlessly harassed the unprotected British lines with trench mortars, and inflicted many casualties.

On 20 May the Germans began a heavy bombardment of the trenches at 5.00am which lasted until 7.45pm and was far heavier than anything the British had experienced before. As the bombardment ceased, the enemy infantry attacked across the whole front occupied by 140 Brigade. They attacked in considerable strength and drove two Battalions out of the front trench, across two supporting lines and into a line halfway down the slope.

Many survivors were taken prisoner. Communications were very badly affected and there was a great deal of confusion when the first lull came in the fighting around 10.00pm which hampered any attempts at a counter-attack. At 2.00am on 22 May 15 Battalion attempted to retrieve some of the lost ground, but without success. The Battalion commander, Captain H. B. Farquhar, was reported wounded and missing in this action.

Fierce fighting continued until 25 May at which time the Battalion, and indeed the whole of 47 Division, were relieved and placed in reserve. The Division's artillery fired 32,000 rounds between noon on 21 May and 4.00pm on 24 May. During the same period 47 Division suffered the loss of 63 officers and 2,044 other ranks killed, wounded or missing. There were also many instances of great gallantry for which numerous medals were awarded, including seven Military Crosses going to members of 21 Battalion (probably a record for one Battalion in a single operation).

WAR DIARY: SATURDAY, 20 MAY 1916
Moved to Camblain L'Abbé where Battalion was well billeted in huts.

WAR DIARY: SUNDAY, 21 MAY 1916
Shortly after 3.00pm heavy bombardment was heard.

4.15pm – Ordered to move to Villers-au-Bois

7.50pm – Ordered to occupy position south of Cabaret Road

8.20pm – B and C Companies, two Lewis guns and two sections of Grenadiers moved forward first.

10.15pm – Captain Farquhar with B Company reported to Brigade Headquarters at Cabaret Rouge. 200 extra rounds of ammunition per rifleman and extra bombs were issued. This Company was sent forward with Major Newson to report to the officer commanding the 8 Battalion London Regt on left. During the move, the area was heavily shelled with lachrymatory shells. Owing to these the progress made was very slow.

WAR DIARY: MONDAY, 22 MAY 1916

1.00am – B Company reported to Hdqrs 8 Battn and were informed that our resistance and support lines had been lost. A counter-attack was being organised in which one Company of 18 Battalion, 25 Bombers and details of 8 Battalion and B Company 15 Battalion were to take part and that the whole would move forward at 2.00am it having been arranged that the 6 and 7 Battalions would co-operate on the right.

2.10am – B Company moved forward attacking in two lines two Platoons in each line.

2.15am – Lieutenant Colonel Warrenden cmdg 15 Battalion, one Company – D – and details arrived at the same time, and very heavy musketry and machine gun fire was opened by the enemy supported by strong artillery barrage fire.

2.27am – Captain Hobbs commanding company of 18 Battalion London Regt reported and asked for reinforcements – two Platoons of C Company under 2nd Lieutenant F. Osborne were sent forward and though unable to get in touch with the company of the 18 Battalion, were able to get into and secure Granby Street as a defensive flank.

2.45am – Two platoons of D Company under Captain Roberts were sent forward on the left to support B Company, but only got in touch with some small scattered parties; he was however able to get into the support line trench and made good his position here.

4.00am – The line was generally quiet.

4.30am – Colonel Maxwell cmdg 8 Battalion wounded left handing over to O.C. 15 Battalion London Regiment. During the afternoon there was an intense bombardment lasting an hour from 4.50pm to 5.50pm and this was followed by another between 9.00 and 11.00pm when the 24 Battalion London Regiment was coming to relieve us.

Casualties: –   2 Officers   Captain H. B. Farquhar and Lieutenant B. Scott wounded and missing

Other ranks   9 – Killed
                     73 – Wounded
                     8 – Missing

WAR DIARY: TUESDAY, 23 MAY 1916

Relief complete and moved back to Camblain l'Abbé where battalion arrived between 4.00 and 5.00am.

WAR DIARY: THURSDAY, 25 MAY 1916

Marched at 8.00am to Calonne Ricuoart where Battalion arrived 12.45pm.

WAR DIARY: FRIDAY, 26 MAY 1916

Leave re-opened, and commanding officer started Battalion training and cleaning up.

WAR DIARY: SATURDAY, 27 MAY 1916

Battalion had baths and clean clothes issued.
Casualties: – 1 died of wounds

WAR DIARY: WEDNESDAY, 31 MAY 1916

Brigade inspected by Brigadier General commanding. He expressed his entire satisfaction with the appearance and steadiness of the Battalion.

Letter written by Laurie shortly after the Vimy Ridge assault.

On Sunday afternoon on the 21st May, just as we were about to have our tea, we received thc alarm. We packed up hurriedly and marched from our hut at Camblain l'Abbé to Villers-au-Bois, at a pace which put us all in a sweat. We were not long at Villers and as the evening drew on we went down the Cabaret Rouge Road. As we neared the trenches, the noise of terrible bombardment reached us. The whole of the line seemed full of flashes and smoke. Presently, as we went along the communication trench a very pungent smoke reached our eyes and nostrils. It was gas from "tear shells". In a few minutes our eyes were running with copious tears and before long they began to smart unbearably and we groped along half-blinded with the pain. A halt was called and, as the bombardment had slackened, we marched to a dug-out on the top of the hill, Cabaret Rouge. Here we stayed for half an hour and then, leaving our packs behind, made our way carrying 5 bandoliers each to the foot of the notorious Vimy Ridge in the Souchez district.

Before we had gone far, at the foot of the Ridge the Germans began to shell the whole of the valley. We crouched against the side of the hill for over an hour, whilst thousands of shells shrieked and hissed into the valley. It was miraculous that there were few casualties from this awful bombardment which exceeded anything I had ever before experienced.

At length when things had somewhat quietened down, we received the order to load our rifles and to fix our bayonets and we then knew that we were to make a night attack. At 2 o'clock on Monday morning we climbed to the top of the Vimy Ridge. No sooner were we at the top than pandemonium was let loose upon us. Lights went up from the German lines, machine guns and rifles poured their murderous hail at us, bombs came hurtling over, shrapnel burst overhead. It was one continuous agony of sound. We kept on quite steadily and crossed our front trench and then, passing through our barbed wire defences, found ourselves in ground which was torn up by shells to so great an extent that it resembled a ploughed field with great holes in it. Men were falling all round and the bullets sang past like hail. Simmons was hit and Shaw. I spoke to Simmons – shot in the leg – and he told me he was alright and that I had better go on. I went from shell-hole to shell-hole escaping death I know not how.

Presently I found myself almost alone. Men were groaning or lying grimly silent, others were creeping back to the British line. The order to retire had been given, our bayonet charge being stopped by the German barbed wire. I was then with Bishop, but otherwise alone. We turned back, but Bishop was hit in the leg and soon after hit badly somewhere else. I had to leave him in a deep shell-hole.

Just beyond was Lawson, wounded in both arms. I gave him water. The light – it was now 3 o'clock – was getting brighter and dawn had come. Still the bullets came and, as I looked round cautiously, I saw half a dozen Germans firing not more than twenty yards away. I knew I must get back to the trench quickly or remain outside the whole day. Very cautiously I crept backward, facing those Germans all the time, and reached a deep hole before I was seen. I was fired at but they missed! An officer told me to run for it, calling from the trench which was only thirty yards away. I hesitated and then ran, reaching the trench safely. For two hours I was in the front trench with a mixed lot of men of several battalions and then the scattered remnants of "B" Company were collected as far as possible and we went back to the foot of the Ridge again where we were shelled nearly the whole day.

Late on Monday evening, after another most terrible shelling, we were relieved by another Battalion and marched back to Camblain, reaching it early Tuesday morning. "B" Company were about 40 strong, having set out with nearly 100. Praise God for His protection through all this danger.

When I returned from the charge on Monday morning I found decisive proof of the narrowness of my escape from injury. A bullet had entered my right breast pocket, bending the ring on my clasp knife, then tearing through a letter, my pay book and my pocket chessboard. It must then have come out of that pocket and across my chest (without even touching my skin) and entered the left-hand breast pocket. Here it tore nearly through my pocket-book diary and out of my tunic. All told, my tunic had six holes through it! Another half-inch would have meant a wound, possibly a serious one through the lungs. Accustomed as the fellows are to narrow escapes, everyone was amazed at this good fortune and my knife, pockets, etc, had to be examined by dozens of fellows. Truly an escape for which to praise God!

The remnants of the pocket chess set, etc. together with the letter written but never posted to his sister, all having the tops shot off, have been preserved and are held by the Editor (See illustrations). In the unposted letter, seemingly dated 21 May, Laurie writes:-

"The Battalion is jubilant over some new honours. We have two French Military Medals and a recommendation for a VC."

Wednesday, 7 June 1916.

Dear Arthur, *[Laurie's brother]*
You have set me a somewhat difficult task when you ask me for an account of my feelings when I went over the top. There are so many currents of thought and such a confusion of sensation. Still, I will try.

We had received an alarm just as we were about to have our tea, and made a forced march (on a hot day) to the trenches. As soon as we arrived in the trench area we were assailed by "tear shells". Before long we were groping about half-blinded, our eyes red and stinging, and shedding copious tears. Arriving at the place where our attack was to be made, we came under the fiercest bombardment I have ever seen. The contour of the country was our salvation. The men all crowded into a series of dugouts, where they spent an uneasy hour listening to the explosions, every successive one seeming to come nearer. I acted as a sort of sentry outside one of these dugouts, which were at the foot of a hill and not in a trench in the ordinary way. I could therefore see the bombardment perfectly.

The explosion of a shell is nearly all forward, so although I was out in the open (flat down of course), all the shells passed beyond me, and I only got an occasional pelting with dirt, stones etc. The flashes were blinding and there was not a second's intermission for over an hour. The noise half-stunned one and the ground rocked till the very spot on which one lay seemed insecure. Our faces became grimed with dirt and powder. I was wearing a shrapnel helmet, which I kept tilting over my face whenever a fiercer flash than usual lit up the ground in front.

The scene had a sort of savage magnificence. I don't know of anything else on earth which gives so terrific an impression of irresistible, unthinking power than the passage and explosion of a high explosive shell. Sometimes I hunched myself up until I was as small as a rabbit, and once I put my collar up, till I remembered that that wouldn't help much. This was the prelude. The bombardment ceased, the signal was given, and in dead silence we climbed the hill, leaped over a trench and commenced our advance on the Germans. Before we had got properly clear of our own barbed wire we were spotted. In a moment it seemed to me as though I was out in the worst thunderstorm I had ever known. Bullets sung by viciously and signal lights were sent up by the Germans, flares lit up the whole scene, bombs and rifle grenades came amongst us in dozens and shrapnel screamed overhead. I kept on thinking "what an unspeakable noise!" There seemed so much din that the ears could not hear it all. One of the worst noises was the spitting of machine guns.

As I went on, I kept on saying "not hit yet, not hit yet" in an inane way. I got quite light-hearted about it. When friends went down, I felt disgustingly cool. Just a little twinge of regret, and then I would help them to a comfortable position, give them a drink and go on again. My ammunition (nearly 400 rounds) and equipment seemed terribly in the way. The German wire stopped me. I raged about and at last barged through, tearing my tunic nearly in half. I became unusually wily, taking advantage of every shell hole and running in between the flashes. All along I thought, "I am not strong enough for bayonet fighting, what shall I do?" And then the order to retire had been given and I found myself almost alone. I did that return journey on my stomach, and before the light was really bright had reached a deep shell hole not far from our front line. I had been observed and shot at, but the aim was wild.

I could see a group of Germans firing and running about on the parapet of their trench. I so hated the idea of a wound in the back that I crawled backwards, and kept my eyes on this group. An officer saw me and shouted "run for it!" after a little hesitation, I made a dash for the trench and got back safely.

On the whole I felt remarkably well considering all I had been through. I am quite fit now, except that I have just been inoculated against typhoid, and naturally this has pulled me down a bit.

My fondest love to you all, Yours ever,

Laurie.

Saturday, 24 June 1916. (Excerpts)

Dear Connie,

I have received your interesting letter of the 19th and also a parcel and a letter from Flossie. I had no idea my escape would become known to so many people. The evening following our return from the trenches I was a billet guard. With the attack fresh in my mind, I scribbled down an account by the light of a candle. It gives news of places, but, as it is now more than a month old, there can be little danger in sending it to you as an enclosure *[unfortunately missing]*. There is no wonder that I thought the German bombardment particularly vehement, for in the newspaper reports we read that the fire of a hundred batteries (400 guns) was concentrated upon our small section of the front.

If I could come on leave now, you would think me a perfect scare-crow. My tunic is torn up the back nearly from top to bottom, and my shirt is always on view. My trousers are covered with soot and my cap is like nothing on earth. Add to this frayed puttees and old boots and you have your quite sedate brother in uniform on active service.

I wrote you last on Monday. That evening I was a billet guard. The following evening I went with a carrying party, taking heavy bombs to a store in the trenches. Wednesday evening I had free and slept like a child. This was my first sleep in the evening for nine days, so you can imagine how much I enjoyed it. Of course, where we are now we cannot go far in daylight without coming under observation from the Germans, so we do all our work at night.

Thursday we carried huge barrels of drinking water to the front line, but Friday provided the climax. In the morning I was put to work in the baths. We have a large marquee divided into two compartments. One is the dressing room and the other has twelve small sprays. The water is pumped into a tank and then heated to a temperature of about 40°f. The men put dirty pants and vests in a big crate and then get clean garments in exchange. I had to walk round and superintend generally. Of course, I had a bath myself in the afternoon. While I was pumping, a heavy storm came on, and for nearly an hour the rain poured in torrents, accompanied by a violent wind. The same evening we went carrying sandbags to the front line. Once in the trenches our troubles began. We were always ankle deep in water; more often than not it was over the tops of our boots, while in the really bad patches the water came well over the knees. I have never walked through quite so much before. Now you see how your socks came just in the nick of time. I slept very well after it and feel no ill effects.

I am having quite a jolly time with my companions and have got a man who is keen on chess to play with. There are some fine fellows in the Battalion. Talk about England being degenerate! Come out here and live with young England. It is a constant surprise to me that, possessing little physical strength, etc., I should be one of the popular men of the company.

Mosquitoes have plagued us and dozens of fellows are going about with huge lumps caused by the stings. I have been stung once or twice, but nothing happens, unless, of course, the mosquito is poisoned and dies!

My fondest love to you all,

Yours affectionately,

Laurie.

1-3. Photographs of Laurie taken in 1915 when he was 27.

4. Laurie's sister Connie.

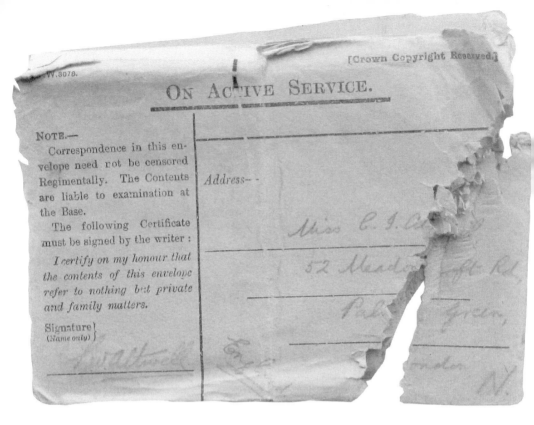

[Crown Copyright Reserved]

W.3078.

ON ACTIVE SERVICE.

NOTE.—
Correspondence in this envelope need not be censored Regimentally. The Contents are liable to examination at the Base.

The following Certificate must be signed by the writer :

I certify on my honour that the contents of this envelope refer to nothing but private and family matters.

Signature }
(*Name only*) }

Address— —

Miss C. I. ...

52 Meadow ... Rd.

Purl ... Green,

... don

N.

5. An unposted letter damaged by the German bullet that tore six holes in his tunic but never touched his skin. (see p.77)

6-7. The chess set that was in the same pocket.

When I returned from the charge on Monday morning, I found decisive proof of the narrowness of my escape from injury. A bullet had entered my right-hand breast pocket, bending the ring on my clasp-knife, then tearing through a letter, my pay-book & my pocket-chess board. It must then have come out of that pocket & crossed my chest (without touching my skin even), & entered the left-hand breast pocket. Here it tore nearly through my pocket-book diary & out of my tunic. All told, my tunic had six holes through it. Another half-inch would have meant a wound, possibly a serious one through the lungs. Accustomed as the fellows are to narrow escapes, everyone was amazed at this good fortune, & my knife, pockets &c. had to be examined by dozens of fellows. Truly an escape for which to praise God.

8. Laurie's letter describing his escape. (see p.77)

9. H.Q Company, 1/15 Battalion London Regiment, 7 July 1918. Laurie is on the extreme right. (see p.188)

10. Laurie after the war.

Chapter Six

The Battle of the Somme, 1916

From this point there is an unfortunate gap in Laurie's correspondence, which is not resumed until February 1917, some seven months later. However, the Battalion's War Diaries give a good account of his activities during this period.

The Battalion moved south at the beginning of August marching for five days to Drucat near Abbeville, then subsequently on to Franvillers for three weeks of training in preparation for a major attack. This was an entirely new theatre of war for Laurie amongst a completely different landscape. Everywhere the slopes were covered with transport of all kinds, whole divisions of cavalry awaited an opportunity to engage the enemy, and all manner of artillery spent their time lobbing shells at distant targets.

The middle of September saw Laurie thrust into the midst of another major offensive – the Battle for High Wood.

High Wood had been attacked by 7 Division two months earlier, but since then it had proved an impenetrable obstacle. The 47 Division now took over the allied trench. This ran roughly through the middle of the wood, leaving more than half of it still in German hands. High Wood itself consisted only of large numbers of dismembered and jagged tree stumps protruding from a mass of churned-up soil. A description written at the time read:

"Imagine Hampstead Heath made of cocoa-powder, and the natural surface folds further complicated by countless shell-holes, each deep enough to hold a man, and everywhere meandering crevices where men live below the surface of the ground, and you will get some idea of the terrain of the attack."

Aside from High Wood, the surrounding countryside was a featureless wilderness. The absence of landmarks inevitably played a large part in the confusion of the forthcoming action caused by poor map-reading.

The attack on High Wood was conceived by the High Command on a grand scale. The German positions at High Wood were now preventing the allies from moving forward, and it was hoped we could break through their lines and achieve a decisive victory after the inconclusive fighting of the previous two months. Accordingly, the 47 Division was one of many brought in to make a major assault on High Wood.

Laurie's Battalion made the initial attack. They were supported by four tanks making their first appearance on the battlefield. Unfortunately, the broken tree stumps and deeply pitted terrain was too much for them and they were very soon bogged down. The 15 Battalion's assault was thus deprived not only of the tanks' support, but also that of the remainder of the allied artillery who would not fire close to the new tanks for fear of damaging these new weapons. The 15 Battalion, left on their own, had to fight desperately for every yard of ground. Their attack was countered with bombs, and heavy rifle-fire from the opposing trenches. But most damaging of all were the German machine guns positioned in concrete emplacements. Their withering fire unmercifully mowed Laurie's colleagues down as they advanced across the open ground, and in the face of massive casualties, the 15 Battalion's attack was repulsed.

WAR DIARY: FRIDAY, 15 SEPTEMBER 1916

Battalion took part in general attack on High Wood by the Fourth Army.

5.50am –	'A' Company on right immediately successful and pushed through to Support line. 'B', 'C' and 'D' Companies were cut up by machine gun fire and were unsuccessful.
11.00am	Enemy front line bombarded by Stokes Mortars. As a result of this and progress of Divisions on right and left, enemy surrendered and by 12 noon we were in possession of whole of High Wood. Rest of day spent consolidating new position.
6.00pm	21 London Regt attacked from High Wood. Practically annihilated by Artillery and machine gun fire.

Casualties:
> Officers:Killed:
>
>> Captain Roberts, Captain Gaze, Captain Davies, 2 Lieutenant Hoole
>
> Wounded:
>
>> 2 Lieutenant Fallon, 2 Lieutenant Townsend, 2 Lieutenant Thomas, 2 Lieutenant Richardson, 2 Lieutenant Ray, 2 Lieutenant Roberts, 2 Lieutenant Houslop, 2 Lieutenant Barnes, 2 Lieutenant Burtt
>
> Missing:
>
>> 2 Lieutenant Fletcher
>
> Other ranks:
>
>> About 250 killed, wounded and missing

The fighting throughout 15 September was extremely fierce. High Wood was eventually captured but not without considerable losses. One attack by 24 Battalion during the afternoon resulted in only 62 remaining alive and unwounded out of the 567 officers and men who started out.

47 Division was then ordered to capture a ridge running north-east from High Wood consisting of a lozenge-shaped group of trenches known as Cough Drop and a communication trench called Drop Alley which ran towards the Flers Line.

WAR DIARY: SATURDAY, 16 SEPTEMBER 1916

Morning quiet, Consolidation proceeded.

> 9.00am
>
>> 23 Battalion, London Regt attacked from High Wood. Practically annihilated by shell & machine-gun fire.
>>
>> Day quiet, except for intermittent shelling of High Wood by heavy howitzers.
>
> 9.00pm
>
>> 15 Battalion moved up to take over position held by 6 Battalion, London Regt. On arrival found that 6 Battalion were not occupying their expected position but were in Cough Drop. 15 Battalion accordingly occupied western half of Cough Drop and threw back defensive flank. Night quiet. Consolidation of Cough Drop proceeded.

WAR DIARY: SUNDAY, 17 SEPTEMBER 1916
Cough Drop heavily shelled. Consolidation proceeded. 2 Lieutenant
E.L.Townsend died of wounds.

WAR DIARY: MONDAY, 18 SEPTEMBER 1916

5.30am	6, 8 & 15 Battalions London Regt attacked Flers Line. At same time 15 Battalion occupied Drop Alley and established a block at its junction with Flers Line. Attack successful but owing to loss of direction, troops in Flers Line and Drop Alley did not quite join up. Several unsuccessful attempts made during day to link up.
12 noon	6, 8 & 15 Battalions London Regt relieved in Flers Line by 8 Otago Battalion New Zealand Division & moved back to Drop Alley.
6.00pm	Combined bombing attack by New Zealanders and 15 Battalion up Drop Alley failed. Night fairly quiet.

WAR DIARY: TUESDAY, 19 SEPTEMBER 1916

6.00am	Enemy bombed down Drop Alley but was easily driven back.
7.00pm	Enemy again bombed down Drop Alley, and owing to state of exhaustion of troops it was not possible again to dislodge him.
Casualties:	2 Lieutenant B.K.Ware killed

WAR DIARY: WEDNESDAY, 20 SEPTEMBER 1916

3.00am	Relieved by 1 Battalion Black Watch and moved back to Bottom Wood near Mametz Wood. Total casualties 15–20:

Killed, Wounded or Missing:
Officers = 15
Other Ranks = 365

[Thus, the Battalion lost in these few days well over one third of it's strength.]
Left Bottom Wood and moved to Albert

WAR DIARY: 21 – 29 SEPTEMBER 1916
Left Albert and moved to Henencourt Wood for training and refitting.

An account of the battle for High Wood written in the official record of the activities of 47 London Division (1914–18) edited by Alan Maude and published in 1922 by the Amalgamated Press Ltd is followed by the following passage:

"Such a bald account as the foregoing attempts no more than to give a general idea of the progress of the operations, to suggest to those who took part in them the significance of events which, at the time, they almost certainly did not appreciate. It cannot in any way represent the strenuousness, the wonderful heroism, the appalling discomfort and weariness of those days. Battalions went in fit and strong, full of confidence to take their part in the great British offensive. They came out a few days later, a handful of men, muddy and tired out. Four days' fighting cost the Division just over 4,500 officers and men in casualties, and it is notable that those battalions lost most heavily which had been in the open, under the German machine-gun fire and artillery barrage. Every battalion went into battle magnificently – wave after wave, just as at the last rehearsal when every detail was perfected. The lines of dead later bore mute testimony to the quality of our men and their training. That the momentum of the attack was spent in High Wood is no wonder, and the difficulty of making good the delay afterwards can but emphasise the value to the enemy of the position we had won. There are several divisional memorial crosses in High Wood. The 47th Division gained no higher honour than that its cross should stand among them, and that it should bear the latest date."

The battle for High Wood was a harder fight than any before endured by the 15th Battalion. Laurie was lucky indeed to survive, but by early October he was back in the thick of the fighting which had now advanced to Eaucourt L'Abbaye.

The objective of 15 Battalion was a new German trench dug across our front over the high ground north of Eaucourt L'Abbaye. The attack started at 1.45pm on 7 October and immediately the whole attacking line came under heavy fire apparently from automatic rifles. The advance was up sloping ground across which the enemy had a clear view. They responded in full force with artillery and machine guns and brought to bear a withering cross-fire from well sited gun positions. Not a man turned back. Some got right up below the German lines but were not seen again. Men dug themselves in where they could, but it was not possible to hold a permanent position.

WAR DIARY: SATURDAY, 7 OCTOBER 1916
Unsuccessful attack by 140 Brigade. Battalion badly cut up. The remnants of the Battalion under Captain G.G.Bates dig themselves in in an advanced position on the right of the Brigade front astride the Eaucourt L'Abbaye – Le Barque road

Casualties:
Officers: Killed 1   Other ranks: Killed 22
           Wounded 4   Wounded 257
           Missing 1   Missing 65 approx.

WAR DIARY: MONDAY, 9 OCTOBER 1916
Moved back from front line to the horse lines at Mametz Wood

Casualties 8–9 October: Other ranks: Wounded 9

On 9 October the 47 Division was relieved and Laurie had finished his part in the summer fighting of 1916. Although repeatedly attacked by the allies, the Germans held on to the high ground at Eaucourt L'Abbaye that the allies had fought so hard to capture, until their general retirement at the end of February 1917. This underlines the strength of the positions held by the enemy.

While engaged on the Somme 47 Division had lost 296 officers and 7,475 other ranks killed, wounded or missing. They had played a valuable part in the summer's advance during which two German defence positions of prime importance had been taken, and the line was moved forward by three miles.

Many aspects of the operations of the Somme in 1916 were radically different from those Laurie encountered in 1915. One of the things which affected him as an infantryman was the additional role he had to play in supporting the artillery. Guns were positioned much further forward in positions which provided little or no cover. They were in almost constant use in putting up hastily prepared barrages or in prolonged shelling of enemy positions. Ensuring the guns were supplied with sufficient ammunition had by summer 1916 become a major problem. Whereas in 1915 at Loos, it was a simple matter to transport supplies by road right up to the front line, in September 1916 it took nearly two weeks to get a mule track through over High Wood.

As the weather deteriorated, roads and tracks were entirely lost, and long queues of vehicles plunged up to their axles in mud and fought their way around shell-holes and across impossible terrain, often under shell-fire. So it fell to the infantry-carrying parties to bring in supplies of ammunition and food each night to the front-line batteries. Pack-animals and limbered wagons were not then effectively used for supplying the forward areas, so a heavy burden fell on the infantry.

Field Ambulances too often worked under the most appalling conditions. Since it was not possible for wheeled transport to get through to the front-line positions, the wounded had to be carried back to the dressing station which lay some considerable distance to the rear. The awful conditions meant the bearers could easily take between five and six hours of almost unimaginable hardship, falling into pot-holes and sliding for miles in ankle deep mud, often at night, across an almost featureless landscape with non-existent sign-posting.

On 14 October Laurie, no doubt relieved to be leaving, marched into Albert from his billet to entrain for Ypres in the north.

Letter written to the Wesleyan Methodist Church and published in their Special Roll of Honour edition of *Our Magazine*

March 1916

A Pair of Gloves

The saddest thing I have seen in France is a pair of gloves. A parcel came to our trenches with our rations, addressed to a bomber, a personal friend of mine, who had been killed the previous day. It is the practice for such parcels to be split up amongst the addressee's friends. This parcel contained many little things which we find useful in the trenches, and amongst them a pair of gloves. These were given to a fellow who had lost his, but half-an-hour later he called us together again and said: "I say, you chaps, listen to this. I can't use these gloves." He then read out, not in a very steady voice, a short message written on a slip of paper, which he had found tucked inside one of the gloves. It was just to say that they were sent to dear Harry with his mother's love, and nobody save her had ever touched them. Just before packing them up she had put them on, so Harry could imagine when he wore them that he was touching his mother's hands. He was our friend, but it was not grief for him, lying there so quiet and peaceful, that made us separate without another word, not daring to look in each other's eyes. It was the thought of that mother, yes, and other mothers, watching and waiting. Some of the men out here have served their country nobly, but what of the sacrifice of love and the burden resting on many who must perforce sit at home? If I could have the bestowal of one of those coveted emblems – the Victoria Cross – I should, and so would every right-thinking man, pin it on the breast of a woman, the mother who sent out the very light of her life to play his part in this great struggle for King and Empire.

Private Laurence W. Attwell

Chapter Seven

Ypres, 1916 – 1917

47 Division arrived in Ypres on 16 October 1916. For Laurie November and early December was mainly spent in training with his battalion while they enjoyed a well-earned spell out of the line. But things were not to be quiet for long.

The battlefield at Ypres sloped gently up to a low ridge possession of which was considered vital by both sides. A small hill known as Hill 60 was held by the enemy and overlooked allied positions. As a consequence, despite considerable care being taken, enemy snipers were continually claiming casualties.

There was a great deal of mining activity which had been going on in the area for the previous twelve months. As a result we had a large mine positioned underneath Hill 60 in readiness for the coming Battle of Messines. To the north of the hill the ground was extremely swampy and no-man's-land was quite impassable for both sides.

Laurie was back in the front line on 19 December. Four days later, after a very short bombardment, 15 Battalion sent a raiding party across to the enemy lines. They entered the enemy's front line and, after violent resistance, killed all the twelve German occupants. The raiders lost two missing believed killed and eleven wounded in the assault.

During late January it snowed and a hard frost continued through into February with temperatures falling below zero. Virtually all work became impossible in these conditions, but water still seeped into the trenches. However, as soon as it did it froze, with the effect that ground level in the trenches began to rise. It seemed possible after several days that defenders in both sets of opposing trenches would eventually rise upwards on the frozen water until they were in full view of one another!

There was now a massive demand for ammunition and supplies. The Divisional Commander had ordered all troops in the forward lines to receive either a hot meal or a hot drink every four hours. As a result convoys from the Divisional Ammunition Column, the Supply Column, Field Ambulances and many others clogged the shell-holed roads as they trekked backwards and forwards each night. Laurie, in his role with the Police, had a major problem controlling the never-ending streams of traffic in the winter darkness and freezing conditions.

Throughout this period 15 Battalion was in and out of the front line at Hill 60, Ypres.

Saturday, 10 February 1917.

Dear Connie,

There is quite a budget of letters for me to answer this time. Flossie has sent two letters, dated the 30th Jan and the 6th Feb, Mother wrote on the 1st and you on the 2nd. Besides these, the parcel of the 31st must be acknowledged.

The parcel was a really good one. The pork was delicious and the sweets did my throat good. I was delighted to see the Bryant & May cookers. Please tell Flossie that I could do with a pair of mittens.

We have heard that the USA will, after the war is over, close a port to Germany for every American merchantman that Germany sinks. I should imagine that there will be a big trade boom between France and England after the war.

The past few days in the line have been extremely quiet. On Monday a shrapnel shell landed in the middle of a working party and did great havoc. My dear, you should be very thankful that I am in Headquarters Company. Although there are times of risk, taking things all round, we are far more able to secure our own safety than the men in the Companies. As you know, I speak now from a good long experience of both.

On Wednesday evening *[7th]* we moved into the . . . *[censored – but the Battalion then moved back from the front line into a support position.]* You will remember my description of the place with its tiled servants quarters down below. It has been badly shelled since we last saw it and is now quite a ruin. We do the usual gas guard, ration fatigues, cleaning up and so on, and are quite happy. Of course, we shall soon be back in the front line again.

Yesterday evening there was a tremendous artillery duel going on for hours. I and a friend were out on a short walk to a little canteen and we had an excellent view. The trouble is, I cannot possibly describe the brilliance of the flashes on the frosty night, nor the reverberating crashes of the guns. There is a certain beauty about it but no pleasure.

Fondest love to you all.
Your ever affectionate brother,
Laurie

Thursday, 15 February 1917.

Dear Mother
This is just a short note to reassure you that I am jogging along alright. We moved up to the line on Monday evening. I was about the last to go, being on the job of guarding some stuff and seeing it safely packed on one of our transport waggons. The police have a small dugout to themselves. It is a marvel how six men (two of them big specimens of humanity) can possibly live and sleep in so confined a space. The miracle is accomplished however and we are quite comfortable. My bed is largely composed of signal rockets, with pads of sand-bags to ease my all too prominent bones at the hard corners.

The intense cold is now over, but we still have sharp frosts nightly and the ground is ice -bound. You will be relieved to learn that I am at last recovering my voice. It has been a shocking cold. Miss Marshall was kind enough to send me some "Licorice & Menthol Pellets" which have been of great service.

The post is not working with its usual regularity recently. Both letters and parcels are taking longer in delivery.

We got hot porridge for breakfast, prepared by our cooks. Not bad for the trenches is it?
My best fondest love to you all,
Your affectionate son,
Laurie.

Friday, 23 February 1917. (Excerpts)

Dear Connie,
I am sorry that recent shifting about on the part of our Battn. has put a stop to letter writing. However, we have settled down now and I am spending my first really free evening in a Church Army hut with this sheet in front of me.

Now to resume my account of our movements. On the 16th we left the trenches for the château I have before told you of. The night was so dark that one had to grope with one hand outstretched or else risk walking into every tree or even a sudden drop into a shell-hole or a seven-foot-deep trench. There was any amount of frozen water in the trenches too, so it was slippery as well as dark. On ration-carrying stint, I measured my length on the ice with a heavy box of bully beef planted firmly on my stomach.

We remained in the château until the evening of the 19th, when we left for camp *[Ottawa Camp]*. I and one other policeman were put in charge of a quantity of stores, (blankets, dixies, Officers' valises, etc). We had to see the stuff safely loaded upon our limbers before leaving. At length all was packed and the driver of the last limber, a friend of mine, offered us a lift home. This practice is strictly "verboten". However, we preferred a ride even on a bone-shaking limber to a heavy march in the fog of eight long miles.

Aha! It was a joy ride!. The driver, more than a little intoxicated, wanted to get back to camp quickly. The bursting of a shrapnel shell in the road made us somewhat sympathetic with his eagerness. So the horses moved some! Gee, I should say so! Road controls shouted at us, foot soldiers sprang into ditches to get out of our way, the driver's shrapnel helmet fell onto one of the horses' back. The frightened animals ran away with us. We went round corners on two wheels. We missed deep ditches by inches. Your foolish brother was so exhilarated by the speed that he nearly lost his voice again in shouting to the horses to get a move on. We arrived at the camp with our necks unbroken, but bruised all over.

On the 22nd we left the Camp. The whole Battn. is on working party. I am with a party of 20 other Headquarters men. Our dinner was some boiled eggs and brown bread and butter. We live in tents and have three blankets apiece.

I am enclosing a photo of one of my very best friends – a Lance Corporal who lives in Eaton Park Road. I think you will agree that he looks a jolly comrade. So he is!

Well, I will write again before long. I am further away from the line than I have been for months. Hope you and Flossie are in the best of health and spirits.
Yours, etc.
Laurie.

Postcard dated Thursday, 1 March 1917.

My dear Connie,
I have just received a parcel from you dated the 14th February. A fortnight to get here! Poor old cake! Still it was very good. I hope you have

received my letter and postcard. I am in the best of health and having quite a good time. You would be astonished to see the huge logs we tackle on the railway sidings each day. Trust Mother is well and that you and Flossie are in good health. Will write a letter soon.
Best love,
Laurie.

P.S. Have had a scarf and vest from the Sunday School.

Sunday, 4 March 1917. (Excerpts)

My Dear Mother,
There seems surprisingly little to relate this week. We are living for a brief space in a kind of backwater to the war, as it were. No news is certainly good news in this instance. Separated, as the Battalion is, into numerous working parties, our postal arrangements are necessarily spasmodic. I have had Flossie's letter of the 18th Feb. and the parcels of the 14th and 23rd, for all of which many thanks.

We are still doing the heavy carrying work at the Railway Station. You speak of church services. My dear, while, in England, people were sitting in their comfortable pews listening to the various services, your humble and obedient was helping to unload 15 trucksful of logs. I have an inkling that much of this timber is for gun emplacements and road-making, so I am doing just a little to pave the way to victory in more senses than one. A few days ago I received a letter from Bert. The army routine does not appear to fill him with any excessive rapture.

The newspapers lately make serious reading. Of course we know that the Germans have recently been shortening their line, and we know too, from the experience of our own Battalion, that Fritz is somewhat cowed and willing to throw up the sponge. Did you read the account of a raid carried out not long ago in which we took a great number of prisoners? The Battalion responsible for that splendid affair is a part of our Brigade. But we have not yet liberated [censored] or dealt the death blow to Prussian militarism. The food shortage at home will soon seem a small item when the clash of the great offensive begins to fill the granaries of death.

We are a very happy party of 20 here and could wish to keep on at this work for the duration of the war. My health is excellent, etc.
Laurie.

Dear Mother,

Last Sunday evening I visited the village near our camp and had an unusual luxury over here – some really excellent tea fresh from the pot. The French and Belgians as a rule don't seem to know how to make tea properly. It is quite exceptional to find a villager who drinks it at any time or has any for sale. Coffee, of course, is their great standby.

Yesterday was the 2nd anniversary of the Battalion's departure from old England. Of the 21 in the party of which I am a member only 5 came across on March 17th 1915. So today I commence my third year on the Continent. I fervently hope that it may be the last, under present conditions, that is. Shall I be able to settle down quietly to the life of a Civil Servant? Shall I be long reconciled to journeying backwards and forwards to the same old office every day, after a life of such constant movement? Will Palmers Green be a wide enough sphere for me to feel free in, after living as a sort of citizen of no-man's-land for so long? Try me and see! This is a wild and unsettled life, true, but it is by no means a life without restrictions. I am far more my own master as a Civil Servant than as a Private.

Perhaps to mark off yesterday as something unique we had quite a scare in the evening. Hostile aeroplanes came close over the camp, all lights had to be extinguished and our anti-aircraft guns went "hell for leather" for some time. During the day we witnessed an air accident. A biplane had circled out from the aerodrome and was mounting higher when something went wrong with the machine, which tilted over and fell sideways. I believe both the occupants were killed.

What remarkable news has just come from Russia! It is difficult to get a clear picture of what has happened, but it appears to be a struggle towards greater freedom and democratic government. If the movement will stamp out the hideous police spy system and the forces which barred the way to Russia's enlightenment, then we can feel highly encouraged by the Czar's abdication and the rise of the power of the Duma. *[Laurie greatly changed these views in later years!]*
Laurie

My Dear Connie,

The parcel of the 14th took a fairly long time to reach me. I have been told by our Quartermaster Sergeant that another parcel will be sent up tonight with the rations. You may gather from this that the peaceful days at the Railway Station are ended. All good things must cease, working parties a long way back from the line not excepted.

On Tuesday we received notice that we were to return to the Camp. As a final treat a party of us went to an estaminet where they cooked us some excellent pork chops. This estaminet was an interesting place, being right on the very frontier. By crossing the road you moved from Belgium into France or vice versa. On one side was a French sentry, on the other a Belgian. Moving about impartially in the middle was a British Tommy on road control duties.

I was quite reluctant to leave the place. Rain was falling and we had a long march before us. On the way back we halted and had another little meal – this time eggs and cocoa. We reached the old camp just before six.

The very next day we were off to the trenches which we at present occupy. Part of the journey, which was extremely fatiguing, was done by . . . *[censored]*.

In the line, we (that is the police) are on gas guard. One is in hospital suffering from rheumatism and two others are away on another guard. This leaves us with three policemen, so we do two hours on sentry duty and then have four hours off, day and night. It is not very bad except that we can never get more than three and a half hours sleep at any time. I have now got to go on duty (10pm to midnight) so will continue my letter tomorrow.

Sunday morning.

The weather has been very severe again. On our journey up we had snow and finished up rather wet. Every day we get a stiff frost.

There was soon a little excitement for me. As if to welcome me back to the trenches a small shell burst on Thursday morning about ten yards away, scattering mud about. I was already so muddy that a little more made no difference. The German aeroplanes have been busy and ours even busier still.

Yesterday was full of incidents. A German aeroplane was brought down by our shellfire and fell just between the two front lines. A great cheer was raised as it fell. At one time there were twenty aeroplanes circling over us, mostly British. In the afternoon a furious mutual bombardment commenced. The trenches lay under a tornado of shells, trench mortar bombs, "toffee apples" and "rum jars". These two last are pet names given to special bombs. Things settled down at last and the night was moderately quiet.

Well I must close now. Will keep you posted as to my movements as regularly as I possibly can. Things seem to be going all in our favour now. I believe we shall see the end within the next six months.
My fondest love to you all,
Laurie.

Thursday, 5 April 1917. (Excerpts)

My Dear Mother,
Although I am far too late to catch today's mail, I could not let my birthday pass without sending you my thoughts. Many thanks for your letter and for the good wishes you send me. I shall be very proud of my gold Hunter. What a pity that I cannot come home to wear it! Still all the news is favourable to our cause. The civilised world is behind us as we combat Germany, whose confederates are visibly weakening.

Last Sunday (Palm Sunday) we had a little snow. This was repeated on Monday evening, when the wind rose to a gale. On the 3rd there was a howling blizzard. The snowflakes whirled wildly about and it was difficult to see more than a few dozen yards. In the afternoon the weather improved and some of our officers had some sport. There is a lake nearby and they threw bombs into the water to kill the fish. The explosions were like miniature waterspouts, but only a few small fish were caught.

Good Friday.

I am concluding my letter today. My birthday was a good one. The weather was glorious. Bright sunshine, clean cool air, a touch of Spring in the song of the birds. Hostile aircraft came over once or twice and in the afternoon the German artillery was busy. I started my birthday by going on duty at midnight, so I was awake for the whole 24 hours. Shortly before 9 in the evening, I had to report several signal lights from the line, this, of course, being a part of my duty as a sentry. There was a most violent artillery bombardment on that part of the line and lights went up, not by ones or twos, but by the score. It looked rather a fine spectacle – all these white, red and green lights and the flashes of the exploding shells.

All my love to you,

Yours ever,

Laurie.

War Diary: 7 – 12 April 1917

Front line – Canal sub-sector

Casualties: 15 Killed

                19 Wounded

Saturday, 14 April 1917.

My Dear Connie,

Just a line to assure you that I am still all right and out of the trenches again. It has been a very exciting spell, but I must write about that at my leisure. We have very little time to write or do any mortal thing for ourselves. Still, I will do my best to get a decent letter off tonight or some time tomorrow. Have received your letter of the 10th and Flossie's of the 9th.

Much love to you all,

Yours in haste,

Laurie.

Sunday, 15 April 1917.

Dear Mother,

When I scan the events which have transpired since my last long letter, I feel profoundly grateful that I am still able to write to you. But my stars remained in the ascendant and, who knows, the end of the war may be quicker in arriving than even the sanguine anticipate.

On Saturday evening, the 7th, the British made a big raid upon the German trenches. We had an excellent view of the barrage of fire made by our artillery. As the guns were close behind us the noise became almost intolerable. Hundreds of brilliant signal lights arose above the lines and an aeroplane dropped the most beautiful signals I have ever seen. They burst into a tremendous shower of white stars, umbrella shape, which dropped slowly to the ground. The battalion relieved the raiders the same evening and found everything in a somewhat chaotic condition. Easter Sunday resembled the calm after (and before) a storm. There were naturally numerous casualties among the raiders, and their equipment etc., was stacked up, making a huge pile of smashed rifles, twisted bayonets and tattered pouches.

On the afternoon of Easter Monday, while I was on sentry duty, the German artillery began an intense bombardment, which gradually rose to such a pitch that all the air seemed alive with whizzing, humming, droning fragments. Early in the evening a further bombardment burst on our lines and to our left. The Germans attempted a big revenge for the British raid, but everyone was well on the alert. A great number were cut up by our machine guns and few reached their objective. For a few hours it resembled pandemonium, hell let loose. After things had quietened we went out after our rations, feeling half-stunned still by the din and force of the explosions. The rations were found after a long tramp and then I had to act as guide to a party from one of our Companies. It was 4 in the morning when I turned in for a sleep.

Tuesday *[10th]* was cold and snowy. The line was quiet. Rations were up late and we were not finished until 1 o'clock. From 1 to 3 I was on guard. Wednesday brought us a heavy fall of snow. We went on a fatigue, carrying heavy boxes of ammunition for over a mile through the darkness and the rain. On the evening of the 12th we were relieved and went right back from the line (partly by train) to a camp *[Devonshire Camp, Busseboom]* we have not before occupied.

My health remains excellent. On the whole I have come through this exceptional winter much better than through last year's.
My fondest love to you all,
Laurie.

Monday, 23 April 1917. (Excerpts)

Dear Mother,
You say that the weather has been bad. Ditto for us! We had rain on Sunday and Monday, a very cold wind on Tuesday and slept on Wednesday. Then came a great improvement, for yesterday and today are ideal spring weather.

We left the camp on Saturday evening to go up to the line. The camp had few attractions, being away from the villages and, of course, the rain made any long walk uncomfortable. The journey was a very long and tiring one, but interesting as we were going into a part of the line which was new to us *[Spoil Bank section, Ypres]*. We were over 4 hours on the way and the moment we arrived I had to go back some distance in order to act as a guide for the rations. I got down to sleep at 2.30. We occupy a nice comfortable dugout, well placed on a slope and with quite a picturesque outlook. The air is as exhilarating as champagne. The sky is Cambridge blue, dotted with pillows of cloud. The sunshine brightens up the whole scene.

The aeroplanes have been very active. Ours especially show great daring and fly very low. Shells burst all round them but have no effect. We have a good water supply. Inside the dugout we can show visitors a pretty domestic scene – a cat with four kittens which have just opened their eyes. Two are sandy and two tabbies. They scramble about in a most charming way, but we have to be careful not to tread on them.

While at the camp I got a new uniform. A pity I cannot come home on leave while I look as smart as I can ever hope to look in khaki. We have all been grouped according to occupation and given new numbers. My paybook has also been amended, giving me my first class proficiency pay from the end of August last. So the Army now consider me to be worth one and sixpence a day to them instead of one shilling.

My health remains good, but what a length of time we are separated! Every detail of the old home life seems so attractive viewed across this waste of days.

Goodbye, best love to you all,

Yours affectionately,

Laurie.

Sunday, 29 April 1917.

Dear Connie,

Thanks for your letter of the 21st. Your business did excellently last month and I congratulate you heartily on so fine a turnover. Evidently there is still plenty of money circulating in the old country. One thing somewhat astonishes me, that after a responsible minister has put people on their honour with regard to their consumption of bread they should eat exactly half as much again as they are supposed to. There is little doubt that, if each household bore its fair share of sacrifice, the food problem would be easily solved. Some people seem to give up a son to the fighting forces with less difficulty and reluctance than they will go without a proportion of their food or abstain from the wasteful glass of beer. *[Laurie had been brought up in an entirely teetotal household.]*

On the 23rd and 24th we went out on fatigues, carrying up bombs to the trench stores. On Tuesday the German bombardment was rather lively. Whilst out on a carrying party and on a light railway track which was under German observation we were delayed by some shells coming over and bursting a few hundred yards in front of us. Late the same night we turned out for rations. Thursday saw a big "strafe" by our artillery and a retaliation by the Germans. Small shells exploded all round our Headquarters. One such shell, called by us a "whiz-bang" from the noise it makes, burst on our dugout roof. The nose-cap came through into the dugout, but it had little force left and nobody was hurt.

Late on Friday we left the trenches and marched over eight miles to a camp we had never before used. There were three of us in a little party and we reached our new home in the small hours of the morning. About halfway, we were able to put our packs in a waggon, which was a great help. Yesterday we breakfasted at noon, dinner was at 4 and tea at 7!

My fondest love to you all,

Laurie.

Chapter Eight

The Battle of Messines

*During the winter of 1916 General Sir Herbert Plumer had begun plan-
ning an offensive to take the Messines Ridge, a strategically important
position just south-east of Ypres which the Germans had held since
December 1914. From this point the Germans overlooked our lines and
back areas, and accordingly had proved a considerable nuisance to us for
a very long while.*

*Between January and May 1917 we had dug nearly 9,000 yards of
tunnels under the German lines at Messines. Into these were placed twenty
mines representing 600 tons of explosive which we hoped would remain
hidden until the start of our forthcoming offensive.*

*On 21 May we began a massive bombardment of the German lines,
which became really intense at the start of June. During this bombardment
the two infantry Brigades who were to take part in the attack (which
included Laurie's 15 Battalion), were marched back to Morninghem where
they rehearsed their assaults over taped-out courses. So accurate was the
information supplied by the Air Force's photographs, and so realistic were
the contours of the ground on which they rehearsed, that the attackers later
found the battlefield and enemy trenches virtually identical.*

*As the ensuing letters indicate, Laurie spent the next none too un-
pleasant couple of weeks resting and rehearsing for the attack which was to
follow.*

Saturday, 5 May 1917.

My dear Mother,
Thank you for your letter of the 27th and the parcel of the 26th. Please
do not trouble to send out sardines. We frequently get them in our
rations. I shall not expect such sumptuous parcels now, nor so

101

frequently, in view of the forthcoming rationing of the people at home. The Church always send me a copy of their magazine, so you can leave that out in future as well.

Things have moved smoothly for me since my last letter. Football matches have been the order of the day and have been decidedly interesting. On two evenings I have taken the opportunity to get a pass and visit a small town near by. One evening I entered the Church – not a very old one. The quiet and coolness of the interior were in striking contrast to the bustle in the main street outside. The walls were hung with some very beautiful old pictures and banners which are carried round on Saints' days. The churchyard, like most of those over here, seemed too crowded with big monuments. Very few of these churchyards give the impression of peacefulness and rest, as ours often do.

Nearly every night the artillery get active. The noise is too great for sleep unless you are thoroughly tired. I have to read myself sleepy. On Wednesday evening at about 11 o'clock we received an alarm of a gas attack. For over an hour we had to remain on the alert, with our gas helmets ready to slip on our heads. Fortunately, the "All clear" reached us at midnight.

Some of our winter clothing has been called in and the temperature justifies it. It is more like summer than spring. The young crops are springing up rapidly and every bush and tree is bursting into leaf. Where the constant trampling has worn the ground bare and hard the air quivers with the heat. The sun is working overtime and it is good to be alive.

Our shrapnel helmets have now a device of chain mail, which acts as a visor and protects our eyes. I do not want the war to last another year – by that time we should probably resemble the knights of old. "Every man in his own armoured car" seems to be the ideal.
Much love to you all,
Your affectionate son,
Laurie.

Thursday, 17 May 1917. (Excerpts)

My Dear Mother,
I hope this long gap between the letters – the last one was written on the 5th – has not caused you any anxiety. Three or four service cards should have reached you in the interval. After a short stay in the line, the Battalion has made a series of long marches during which no

letters could be posted. Now that we have settled down again *[at Morninghem]*, I am writing to you and this time far from the line, distant even from the range or sound of shells.

On the evening of the 5th, following an intermittent German bombardment, one of our ammunition dumps burst into flames. We could see the blaze miles away and hear constant explosions. Almost the same thing happened on Monday night (7th) but the blaze was so distant that we believed it to be behind enemy lines. The sunset was perfectly lovely. Great masses of cloud kept shifting and changing, their edges tipped with a rosy pink. The clear spaces of the sky shone green and blue and violet – wonderful, unbelievable colours.

On Tuesday evening we marched up to the line, occupying the old château again. We have heard that just recently it has been violently shelled and great damage done. Both Wednesday and Thursday we had a good many shells over. One pitched a few hundred yards from our cookhouse, wounding a corporal rather severely. The "strafe" on Thursday was mainly over a position held by one of our Companies and resulted in several casualties. *[4 killed; 9 wounded]*

I believe I told you of a small lake near our quarters. The day was very hot. On the lake was a leaky boat. Behold us, your humble and a friend, rowing round, getting aground in shallow places, pushing off again and catching up in the branches of fallen trees. There was one delightful stretch of deep, uninterrupted water on which we made good speed, the boat leaking slowly round our boots all the time. This is just to show you that our life has its lighter passages.

Friday the 11th was hotter than ever. In the evening we were relieved and marched back, along a very dusty road, to a kind of scattered camp not far behind the lines and close to a nearly deserted village *[Dickebusch]*.

My health is good. The marching has made my feet rather sore. Could you send out a small tin of boracic ointment and a little cotton wool for emergencies? I have had a parcel from Annie lately.

My fondest love to you all,
Laurie.

Saturday, 19 May 1917. (Excerpts)

Dear Mother,

Now to continue my last letter. We went to sleep in a small hut at about three in the morning after our night march from the line on the 11th. Soon after five terrific explosions shook us from slumber and the rattling of stones, earth and fragments on our roof caused a speedy exodus from the hut. I am too obstinate to turn out for every German shell, but, after a little while, I slipped on my clothes and looked out. One shell had fallen about twelve yards away, wrecking a small building. This was evidently an isolated shot, for I could see a continuous succession of bursts all along the road near to which some of our batteries were stationed. Reassured that the camp was not the objective, I strolled round, intending to turn in again. Pieces were dropping quite frequently but the hut roof would be strong enough to break most of their force. Then came a little incident which could have furnished a fine subject for a war artist. A shell burst on the roof of an estaminet, one of the few houses still inhabited by civilians. A burst of flame went up and from the house three small fugitive figures – two of them women – came running up the road towards us. A very typical picture.

Most of Saturday, the 12th, we spent lying in the sun on the grass. The weather was glorious and the surrounding country looked green and pleasant. At night we slept under a hedge with the stars twinkling down on us. We rose early and after breakfast set off on a long march to a town about 10 or 11 miles away *[Watou]*. We arrived weary and thirsty and I was very glad to get a bowl of fresh milk at a cottage at which I called. There was a small pond in a field near our barn and most of us went in and had a delicious bath. The sun was so hot that even the water seemed tepid. In the evening I visited the town itself. There were some good shops and I purchased a souvenir ring which I will send to you soon.

We left again soon after 3 on Monday morning in a shower of rain. Our journey was 18 miles this time – a test of endurance. We went through some fine places. Our destination was *[Sercus]* a pretty little village which seemed to be blessed (or otherwise) with a superabundance of young girls! After another short night's sleep, we were off again Tuesday morning. This was to complete our " trek" and we had another march of just over 18 miles to do. To tell you the truth, I was tired before I started. Still, I managed the march all right and finished up *[in Morninghem]* fitter than I anticipated. We went through two splendid old French towns. One was rich in old churches, but the cathedral was in ruins. I believe a bomb was dropped on it at some time or other.

You might send me out an occasional book to read – not very often. My fondest love to you all,
Ever etc,
Laurie.

Saturday, 26 May 1917. (Excerpts)

My dear Connie,

Many thanks for your letter of the 17th and for the parcel of the 22nd. Very sorry indeed to hear of poor Frank being killed out in Egypt.

We have been spending a really pleasant time here. The weather has been all that could be desired. Last Sunday morning our officers had a race on their horses. The doctor came first, the Adjutant second and the second-in-command was third. In the evening we were out having practice tugs of war. The next day we had proper Battalion sports on the transport field. Headquarters Company did very well. All Tuesday and the morning of Wednesday we spent on some rifle ranges. On Wednesday afternoon we all marched off, sweating from every pore, to a special training area, where we practised an advance or so.

Yesterday I at last had the opportunity to visit a large town *[probably St Omer]* which is some two hours walk away. I had two companions. Arrived at the town, our first thought was for a good dinner, which we had in the garden of a very dainty cafe. I had a lemon sole, followed by an omelette and apple fritters. After a leisurely repast, we made our way to the magnificent cathedral. A voluble French verger took us round and pointed out many items. Some of the carvings dated from the 13th century. The organ screen was the finest I have seen in France, with beautiful carved figures mounted on pedestals. The altars were gorgeous beyond description. One was surmounted by a figure believed to have healing powers. Many tablets were let into the walls dedicated to "Our Lady of Miracles" and giving thanks for miraculous cures. The height of the building was immense and it was certainly the most wonderful and impressive church I have seen out here.

You would open your eyes to see the latest additions to the Expeditionary Force – young girls who act as sorting clerks and book-keepers,etc. I had not come across any before, for the simple reason that I am not often so far away from the firing line. They were dressed in a very neat and becoming brown uniform – brown from their hats to their stockings. My companions were of course lovelorn immediately. Quite a red-letter day for me.

My fondest love to you, Mother and Flossie etc.
Laurie.

My dear Connie,

Last Saturday (26th) I walked in the evening to one of our aero-dromes. A concert was to be held in one of the hangers and before it commenced there was time to go all round the place and inspect the score of large biplanes more closely than one is usually enabled to. I was interested in the propeller, the engine and the pilot's seat, with its array of gauges and levers all around it. Each machine was armed with a gun and I could not understand how the propellers escaped injury from the machine-gun bullets, for the gun was mounted just behind them.

On Wednesday I obtained another pass to the cathedral city which I have already described to you. Some of the back streets were near a fairly large canal. There was no proper roadway – just a walk in front of the houses and a waterway where the road runs. This was "Little Holland" and was interesting and picturesque. Most of the houses had small punts tied up at their front doors and many were being used up and down the "street". I went into a Church Army hut and found several Portuguese soldiers there, with whom I exchanged a few compliments in the doggerel French which passes muster out here, like a kind of Esperanto. It seemed strange to see notices up on the walls in English, French and Portuguese. What a war!

The next morning reveille was at 4 and soon after 6 we were all packed up. Off we marched to the station and entrained there *[for Poperinohe]*. At the other end of our journey we heard the old familiar bark of the guns. We are now living "under canvas" *[at Camp Dominion, Busseboom]*. We are not in the ordinary bell tents but in small, low, triangular shelters like those used by gypsies. The ground is absolutely bare and arid. The sun shines with a tropical fury and the wind raises a cloud of thick dust which smothers every-thing in grit. It is the nearest approach to Mesopotamia we have yet experienced.

Yesterday evening I saw one of our observation balloons burst into flames. What fate was suffered by the occupants I don't know. I doubt whether they had time to use their parachutes.

Yours ever,

Laurie.

Laurie returned to the firing line on Sunday, 3 June 1917 in preparation for the scheduled offensive. By 5.00pm on 6 June all the attacking troops had been marched back into their allotted positions in the line. At 2.30am on 7 June every man had had a good hot breakfast and was ready for action. Their spirits had never been better and to a man they were confident of success. They knew they would be given wonderful support by the artillery which was now in full flow and firing extremely accurately. They were further comforted by the knowledge that a section of tanks had been allocated to support their attack. Our own wire entanglements had previously been cut to allow our attacking troops to congregate in no-man's-land, and much good work had been done by our artillery to cut the enemy's wire in front of their lines.

At 3.10am, with the sound of a cock crowing, the earth suddenly quaked. A devastating explosion and an unspeakable noise burst upon the battlefield as the hidden mines were detonated. With an enormous roar great tongues of orange flame leapt out of the ground hurling tons of earth and rubble high into the sky along a 10-mile front. The earth tremors lasted for many seconds and the noise was so great it could be heard in London. Men were knocked flat by the blasts. Massive craters appeared in the ground as if hell itself had opened up under the German trenches, burying enemy defenders and killing an estimated 10,000 soldiers.

Immediately, our artillery commenced another colossal barrage, under cover of which our infantry pushed forward in attack. The artillery fire was superbly accurate and our advancing troops were able to keep within 30 yards of the moving barrage without any danger to themselves. The stunned defenders were initially overwhelmed, but to their great credit the Germans regrouped well and put up a stout defence. Nevertheless, the attack went well and by 14 June the whole of the Messines Ridge was in British hands.

15 Battalion's objective was to take the White Château, the stables and the Damstrasse trench opposed to them. They were detailed to support the initial attack made by 7 and 8 Battalions. 15 Battalion were then to pass through 7 and 8 Battalions to complete the attack and dig themselves in and hold every foot of the ground gained. All of this they achieved. Fighting raged to and fro throughout the next few days until 15 Battalion were eventually relieved and sent back into reserve at Ebblinghem.

140 Brigade, which then consisted of four Battalions, suffered the following casualties in the battle of Messines:

Officers:	*Killed*	7
	Wounded	32
	Missing	1
Other ranks:	*Killed*	157
	Wounded	752
	Missing	47

My Dear Connie,

Many thanks for your letter of the 8th. I am not able to write you a long letter today, time does not permit. You have read the newspapers and I have no doubt drawn a few correct inferences as to why only Field Service cards have come from me recently. As soon as I can, I will write you an account of my experiences. It has been a somewhat nerve-racking time and I am relieved beyond description to be out of the line again, safe and whole. Trust all at home are fit and well.

My fondest love to you all,

Yours etc,

Laurie.

Monday, 18 June 1917.

My Dear Mother,

At last I am able to write you the letter for which you have waited so long. Perhaps the interval will give me a truer perspective of events; it has certainly not yet dimmed the vividness of my recollection of them.

My last letter described our brief stay in the little triangular shelters pitched in an arid patch of land, reminiscent of descriptions of Mesopotamia. It was a constant dust-storm day and night. However, on the evening of Sunday the 3rd – the better the day, the better the deed – the Battalion moved to the line. Our little party were in charge of some stores and ammunition which filled several limbers. We started off later, holding on to the back of the limbers, the better to keep up with the horses, and with the noses of the following pair of horses rubbing up and down our backs. As we neared the line incendiary shells came over. These burst into great flames twelve feet high and lit up the whole surroundings.

Presently my eyes smarted and I guessed we were near some "tear gas". Then my throat began to feel choky and some fellows came tearing past on horse-back. Gas shells were falling on the road in front of us. These fellows were muffled up, some with proper gas-masks, others with scarves bound round their mouths. Several were coughing badly. We all put on our gas-masks and plunged along the very rough track through the gas clouds. It was a mixture of the ordinary lachrymatory gas and poison gas. Out discomfort was acute, as it was very hot and also the goggles got cloudy, making it difficult to see more than a foot or so in front of us.

Presently we got past the danger zone and reached our journey's end. Here, after a spell of duty over a dump of rations, etc., we found our billet – a cellar near an old château.

The next day we received what we fully expected – a heavy bombardment from the Germans. Several shells hit the château fair and square, and brought most of the remaining portion of the roof crashing to the ground. Twice in the day we were compelled to wear our gas helmets. In the evening our artillery started. The German bombardment was fairly heavy – ours beggared description.

Tuesday, the 5th, was a day of much aerial activity. We saw a British aeroplane brought down badly damaged. At one time there were 19 aeroplanes in view – 18 of them being British and Hun a mere speck far aloft in the blue. In the early evening one of our ammunition dumps was hit. You could hear the cartridges exploding like bursts of rapid fire. Two huge dumps were hit at night. One went up with a great roar and a lurid burst of rapid flame like a volcano. The flames were twice the height of the tallest trees nearby.

On Wednesday morning I went out on a water fatigue, which took me past smashed limbers, dead mules and the damaged aeroplane we had seen descend. Across the fields were plainly seen the tracks imprinted by our tanks. In the evening two of the police were put on an easy job in a back trench. A friend and I went up to the front line with our Corporal. In a way I wanted to go up with the Battalion, sooner than take up a "soft" job. We reached the position allotted to Headquarters in the small hours and we had hardly settled down before the great attack commenced.

It started suddenly, as all these affairs do. One minute everything was quiet, and then, with an appalling boom, a huge mine exploded. The whole ground rocked to and fro and the sky turned a brilliant blood-red, more vivid than a sunset even. I have never seen any sight more wonderful or more awe-inspiring. A few seconds later, and while our heads were still reeling, another mine went up and yet another. Then all the British batteries burst into activity, the machine guns started their hellish death rattle, and the first started bravely out to conquer the German first system of trenches.

The German reply to our rain of shells was comparatively slight but a few burst near and so filled our trench with dust and powder that I was compelled to tie my handkerchief over my mouth. After this I got into a large dugout – brick walls and concrete roof – and waited for things to quieten down. Where I stood I could see the Colonel and Adjutant and heard all the messages as they arrived. After a rather anxious wait we had the good news that our Battalion had gained all its objectives with but small loss of life. Batches of prisoners began to arrive, most of them looking white and feeble. They were of poor physique in the main and gave themselves up with ludicrous alacrity.

We now started off from Headquarters carrying two boxes of bombs apiece. We went right over the top and were in the new front line – the sixth German trench – a few hours after it had been captured. Everything was as still as death. The guns were all silent. Only in the trenches men were digging themselves in and stretcher-bearers and carrying parties like our own roamed about in the open. The country had been literally ploughed up by our shells. Our progress was from deep shell-hole to shell-hole. The original trenches were hardly recognisable, so smashed-in were they. We passed a couple of stranded tanks and a huge mass of stones, which was once a fine château. In one place we passed a concrete dugout just peeping out of the ground. No shelling could smash it – the roof and walls were over 4 feet thick. Some of our fellows found a big boiler-full of coffee all steaming hot inside this place. They are no fools, they tried it on a prisoner first (he drank it greedily) to see if it had been doped, and then helped themselves. Our boys were in very high spirits and shouted and waved to us as we went across to the front line.

Little groups of light-blue-coated Germans were wandering about, putting up their hands when they saw a Tommy, and obviously relieved when they were sent off in the care of a slightly wounded man. Many were set to work as stretcher-bearers. I have been over several battlefields now, as you know, and I must say that there were fewer gruesome sights on this one than down on the Somme. From the front line we could look down on some villages still in the hands of the Germans. A commanding ridge had been captured and all our old positions for miles lay stretched beneath us.

In the afternoon we made another journey, this time with ammunition, for a position near the shattered château I have already mentioned. The heat was intense and we suffered greatly from thirst. The Germans were now shelling in a spasmodic manner and one shell burst over our party, killing one man outright. The party scattered, selected a good deep shell-hole, and waited till things were quiet again, when I returned safely to Headquarters.

In the evening we had yet another journey – with two cans of water each. We arrived back at 3 in the morning and this ended my experiences on the first day of the attack.

June 7th.

On Friday we did a gas guard over Headquarters. In the evening there was another attack over towards our left. We heard that it was quite successful. The Battalion's casualties up to Saturday were moderate. The worst loss to our Battalion was our Adjutant (Capt. W.E. Ind, MC), who was killed by a machine-gunner who was making a stand near the château. The runner who was accompanying the Adjutant shot the machine-gunner dead on the spot and afterwards compelled four Germans to carry the body back to Headquarters, threatening them with a revolver. The Adjutant died, however, and we have lost the officer who has been with us since the beginning, a true soldier and the one man who was absolutely typical of, and heart and soul in, the Battalion.

I expect you are tiring of this letter, so I will bring the story up to date in my next letter. Very pleased to hear of the MC awarded to Dennis (Tanner). This is the sixth big battle I have come through, not to mention all the smaller affairs.

All my love to you my dears, Yours ever,
Laurie.

Thursday, 21 June 1917.

My Dear Mother

This is in continuation of the long letter of the 18th, which is, I hope, by this time in your hands. My account took you to the evening of Saturday, the 9th. Sunday was calm and uneventful until early in the evening, when a shell burst very near, wounding two of the fellows who were just bringing along the day's rations. At night Headquarters was moved to the cellars of the château. Although only a huge heap of stones to look at, there were still large cellars, safe and undamaged. The very size of the ruins on top of them helped to save them from destruction. The shells merely served to pile more and yet more debris upon them, and, of course, we always had the feeling that a place which could outlast our bombardment would easily survive anything the Germans could send over.

I went up separately as a guide to a fatigue party carrying water to the château. Somewhere past the original German front line we were forced to take cover. S.O.S. signals were being sent up in front and the guns were getting very busy. When things grew quiet we pushed on and at last were landed safely in the cellars.

Monday was a very busy day. Quite early I went along with the bombs for one of the companies in the firing line, then we were put on digging a communication trench and in the evening I once more acted as a guide. I had to bring up the parties carrying rations and sandbags – two journeys there and back – so you can guess I felt pretty tired at the end of it.

The next morning I was in charge of a small party bound for another part of the front line with sandbags. To our discomfort, we had to go through a trench eight or nine inches deep in liquid mud with sticky clay below that. To get out of the trench would have been to court disaster; there was nothing for it but to push on. Late on Tuesday night we were relieved and marched slowly away from the château to a camp further back than our usual resting places. En route, our travelling cookers met us with some welcome tea.

On Thursday the 14th we did our normal duties in a camp and on Friday we moved away to a town about 12 miles off. Arrived at our billet – a large barn – I was greatly refreshed by a quart of fresh milk, price 5d.

After breakfast the next morning we all turned into a big field and had a bathe in a pond there. The sun was boiling hot and it was delicious to get into the water. In the afternoon we packed up and marched another 12 miles or so, sweating profusely the whole time, to our present village *[Ebblinghem]*. We are doing our ordinary routine here and so far it has been a very pleasant time. The village has a few shops worthy of the name, but there is a plentiful supply of good milk and the people are very well disposed towards us.

This brings me up to date once more. How much longer must I write to you? Leave seems so distant still. How heartily everyone must long for peace. Did you ever dream that I should be away such a time? Still, I suppose we must not grumble. There are so many who will never write home their account of their last battle.

Hope you are all well at home,

God bless you all.

Yours very affectionately,

Laurie.

P.S. I think it is worth mentioning that part of the cellars of the château were used as a dressing station, usually well filled and busy. Our first night there was spent in an atmosphere of blood and bandages and groans. I am glad to be out of it. Certainly I have never lived in so strange a building before.

Chapter Nine

Menin Road and Westhoek Ridge

Laurie was now quartered in proper billets at Ebblinghem where 15 Battalion embarked upon a period of reorganization and training. It was a great relief to be settled in green fields and away from the noise of the guns, turmoil and shell-marked surroundings of the battlefields they had inhabited for the previous nine months. The order to march forward therefore was received with great regret on 27 June 1917, and preparations were immediately made to leave.

Wednesday, 27 June 1917.

Dear Mother,

I was very pleased to receive your letter of the 21st and to hear that my long screed had reached you. Like yourself, I too was awaiting news with some little eagerness, for we had a vague and alarming rumour concerning the air- raid over London, and I could not help wondering how it had affected all of you.

Miss Marshall seems to have had a very unpleasant experience. Altogether, it makes me feel extremely uneasy and dissatisfied. After all, we are out in France for the set purpose of saving England from the misery and destruction which stalks rampant out here. We are to be a living barrier between the ruthlessness of the Hun and the homes of those we love. And yet we find that, despite all our endeavours and sacrifices, homes are being shattered and little children slaughtered behind our backs.

The weather has now become very fickle, sunshine and showers alternating. On Saturday we saw General Lord Plumer, whitehaired but vigorous, and in the evening we had a good concert in one of the fields.

113

On Monday I had another day off duty and visited a large town of which you have already received some views. I spent a very good day and enjoyed some good food. For dinner I had pork chops potatoes and green peas; then liver and bacon with the same vegetables; and, as a sweet, apples and custard. At teatime I had a nice lemon sole, followed by an omelette. We went there by train, on ordinary civilian passenger train, buying our tickets in the normal way, but our return was on Shanks's pony, a distance of just over eight miles.

Two nights recently, as we lay in our barns, we have heard bombs dropped by aeroplanes or Zepps. Fortunately they appear to be aimed at a town several miles away from us.

Your loving son,

Laurie. (New Number 530694)

Thursday, 5 July 1917.

Dear Connie.

There is plenty to tell you, so I will plunge into my account straight away. On the evening of the 27th a rather amusing thing happened. At least it struck me as rather humorous. It was raining hard and an officer asked me to look after his motor-bike and also to guide a number of motor lorries for which he had tired of waiting. When the job was over, some hours later, he flabbergasted me by pushing two francs into my hand "to get a bottle of beer with"! Well, I took his two francs – my first tip as a policeman! – but did not apply it in the way he suggested.

We were up at 4 on Thursday morning and marched off at 6.30 through heavy rain. Our march was on cobbled roads and made our feet very sore. At one point we passed General Plumer. Our new resting place was a lofty barn attached to a farm on the outskirts of a pleasant little village, where we had coffee and eggs for dinner. I afterwards went on alone to look over the church, which, in spite of a most unprepossessing exterior, proved to be full of charm and beauty. I have rarely seen such fine pictures, such gorgeous stained glass, such a profusion of decoration, such images and altars. There was a certain aloofness from the war, from the world in general, about the place. They certainly are the most complete contrast to our Quaker-like little structures.

Again on Friday we had a weary, weary march, finishing up just behind the trenches. My feet were quite blistered and I felt very fatigued. Sleep came on laggard feet. Saturday we had rain, rain, rain.

Our shelter was made by ourselves of old tarpaulins and let in plenty of rain. I was on a water-fetching fatigue through a very smashed-up village. The damage was so great that the very bricks of some houses were pulverized. In the afternoon I helped push a trolley-load of officers' stuff along a light railway. At the end we had a short distance to go over shell-holes and old trenches, barbed wire, etc. to our dugouts.

We had two duties to do in this part of the line – a gas guard and a water guard. We do these on alternate days, dividing ourselves into two groups of three.

The very first day the Battalion suffered some casualties and things got steadily worse until we were relieved. Several guns were only a few yards away from our trench and the noise and concussion when they fired was terrific. We left the line on Tuesday the 3rd and there were quite a large number of casualties while the men were marching out. We had tea on our arrival at the Camp and I felt fairly fit, everything considered.

You wonder that I can save. Well, most of the time I can't spend money even if I wanted to, and then cigarettes never cost me a penny, so my expenses are not very considerable. It is the cigarettes and the drinks that run away with the money out here (and at home too, I fancy!).

Germany does not look like lasting out much longer. We have news that Russia has begun an offensive, and of course the position in Greece is all to our advantage.

I enclose 30 francs for deposit in the Bank.

My fondest love, etc.

Laurie

Wednesday, 18 July 1917.

My dear Connie,

I am going to attempt a letter to you, a feat which is by no means easy under our present regime. The Army, which allows its officers leave every few months, but considers, apparently, that the private in the ranks is well served if he sees England once in a year and a half, is not likely to care much whether he can write home or not. Unless I am greatly mistaken there is going to be plenty of trouble "when the boys come home". What do you expect to see then? A set of lambs? I think you will meet many men with a very bitter grievance, that, having voluntarily and for the love of liberty entered into the war, they have been treated more like convicts. I used to believe that throughout the British Empire slavery had been abolished, but I had no knowledge of the Army then.

On Saturday morning, after a sleepless and uncomfortable night, I found myself in the pangs of neuralgia and with my face nicely swollen. The neuralgia is just leaving me and my face returning to normal (for me) appearance. The Army cure for neuralgia is a daily dose of tabloids – about as effective as a pill to stop an earthquake. However, I have pulled (or pilled!) through, so that's all right. The afternoon was very hot and another fellow and I had the delightful task of pushing a truck along a light railway.

In the evening, racked with a neuralgic headache and loaded with the officers' comforts up to the eyebrows, I set off to our new position behind the front line. Headquarters are in an old German dugout. The walls are more than 4 feet thick and the whole place is immensely strong. We live in a sort of lean-to attached to the wall of the dugout, which is further from the German batteries and we feel quite secure. All the ground about is torn up with shell-holes.

On arrival, I went straight on two hours' gas guard – two hours of standing still after sweating like a bull. Needless to say, I have contracted a slight chill – nothing serious. On Sunday we saw some terrible wreckage while out on a fatigue party of two – myself and a corporal. We turned into a wood to explore a little and found old German gun emplacements with concrete foundations. Blocks of concrete 4 feet thick had been split in two by our big shells. Each evening since we have been here the Germans "strafe" furiously soon after 10. This happens to be the time I go out on duty – 10.30 – 12.30. Gas shells come over in a constant stream; special signals, rockets and Very lights go up by the score; searchlights rake the sky and shrapnel bursts proclaim an aeroplane detected. Yesterday evening our place had a direct hit – its great strength saved us, but all the candles went out. I got slightly "gassed" one night, but a severe headache was the worst result.

We do our own cooking here and I am in my element. They all like my tea or cocoa. I am enclosing a newspaper I found nearby – it might interest you. Trust you are all keeping fit and well.

My fondest love, etc.

Laurie

My Dear Mother,

I have just heard from Bert at Aldeburgh. I hope he will not have to come out to France. By the way, one of our sergeants – Sergt. Begbie – knows Rome Attwell of Thames Ditton intimately. Many thanks for the parcel of the 17th, which reached me in the trenches – such a place! I will tell you about it later. Did you get a letter from me dated 5th? It contained 30 francs and I don't remember you acknowledging it.

My last letter was dated the 18th. That evening was full of incident. After a fierce bombardment, the Germans attempted an attack on our right. Everybody cleared out of our shelter into the concrete dugout. I was just boiling some water for tea, so I and a sniper – a fine, fearless fellow (alliteration) sat together and drank our tea whilst the sky blazed with explosions and the ground quaked. Later on the same evening there was another raid, through which I slept.

Our evenings were all very anxious and our sentry post was no pleasant place. Pieces fell all over the place. One evening a machine gun opened out from somewhere and sent a shower of bullets into the ground not far beyond us. Aeroplanes were always active and dumps were constantly being hit, resulting in huge fires.

Sunday, as usual, seemed more Godforsaken than any other day. In the early evening we sent over one of our indescribable barrages. Later on British troops attacked on our right and returned with a batch of prisoners. On Monday I had a most remarkable escape. We must all be very grateful for these constant deliverances. I was on a fatigue – digging – and a fair number of shells were coming over. Now, it is not my habit to duck at every shell that bursts. I have seen too many for that. Yet for some reason I ducked, and as I did a piece whistled just over my head and buried itself out of sight in the ground in front of me. Had I remained upright I should have caught that piece in the back of my head.

In the evening there was another of our bombardments and another of our raids. The Germans in reply shelled us with shells of every calibre in great profusion. They also sent over so many gas shells that I stood on duty in a fog and half-choked. The effect was only transitory, however. We were relieved on Tuesday night and set off on a long tramp to our present camp. The Germans were shelling the batteries and the roads and we had some anxious moments. The gas sentry who relieved us was killed before he had been on duty half an hour, and our Battalion did not get out without losses. During the whole period we have had constant casualties and I have lost some of the best fellows in the world. What pitiful still bodies! It is heart-breaking. Now I must close until tomorrow. Goodnight, dear ones.

Friday afternoon.

Now I can resume for a little while. Half-way from the trenches we halted for some refreshing tea. It made a curious sight – the weary, dirty soldiers lying in the road drinking tea, while the guns flickered on the horizon and cigarettes glowed in the darkness. We are now living in tents and in a pleasant stretch of country. As I have told you, I found myself very queer on Wednesday. My limbs ached badly, my head throbbed, I shivered and sweated together, and I had a temperature of 101, three degrees above normal. Yesterday I was slightly better and today I am definitely on the mend. If things go peaceably for a few days I expect to be all right again. Any way there is no cause for anxiety.

Connie mentions leave. Well I have high hopes of obtaining my leave – 10 days not 7 this time – before the end of September. That is still two months ahead, but it is something to look forward to with pleasure, isn't it? I long to see you all again and spend some quiet, sweet evenings in our little home in Meadowcroft.

Now don't worry about me any more, there's a good Mother. I am quite all right, only a fit of the hump once a month. Forget that and think of me as most of the time happy and proud to do my share in this great struggle. And I can look any man in the face as to that question.

My fondest love to my two dear sisters and to yourself. Your loving son,
Laurie

The action described above took place south of the Ypres-Comines canal and, after four months holding the line, the Division was relieved and moved back to the Westoutre area, where it remained for only a short time.

Thursday, 16 August 1917. (Excerpts)

My Dear Connie,
My last letter to you was written on the eve of our departure to another billet. It reminds me of a soldier who tried to describe his

whereabouts without upsetting the censor. He wrote as follows (don't attempt to understand it): "I am not where I was, but where I was before I left there to go to the place where I am now!" Let us think of two villages and call them A and B. Very well, we have moved from A to B, stayed at B for a while and are now back in A again.

We marched off on Saturday afternoon with our rainsheets on, but were soon able to take them off. Our route seemed to consist mainly of steep hills, more pleasant to the eye than to the feet. The enjoyment of the soul, in short, was quite the reverse in the case of the sole.

Our billet was a barn, rat-ridden, but otherwise quite good. On Monday and Tuesday, while the Battalion were away from their billets, we had the job of guarding their stuff generally. Things have a knack of disappearing in some of these villages unless there is someone to look after them. On Monday there was an inspection by some General and on Tuesday the Battalion had musketry in the morning and a big inspection in the afternoon.

The Company billets which I had to guard were 25 minutes walk away, in a tiny village with an absolutely unpronounceable name, tucked away in the heart of a clump of trees. There was a dingy old church with nothing of great interest in it. The outlook was superb. Rolling meadows and cornfields, tiny villages nestling amongst trees, a warm sun making everything show up clear and beautiful. The people are all busy in the fields, whenever the fickle weather permits, gathering in the crops. Yesterday afternoon we returned to the village with the fine château which I have already described to you.

Life nowadays seems very largely to consist of getting clean and polishing up brasswork and then going out to get it all smothered with mud. Certainly the men look very smart. Still, there is a war on, I believe! Also, we are all out here not to look like guardsmen, but to get on with the war. There is an Admiral, I fancy it was Sir Percy Scott, who got into great trouble because of a certain signal he caused to be displayed from his ship. He had made arrangements for gunnery practice, but it was decreed by his superior in command that he should get his vessel painted freshly prior to an inspection. So he signalled "Paint seems more important than gunnery." Well done, Sir Percy!

You may receive a visit from a very dear friend of mine who is going on leave in a day or two. His name is Weedon and I am confident that he will be made very welcome for my sake.

My fondest love, Yours ever,
Laurie

My Dear Mother,

I told you in my letter dated 16th to expect a visit from a friend of mine. He left us at 1 o'clock at night and probably was home at teatime on Friday. Has he been along to No. 52 yet?

You know how much the Battalion has to shine up, but I don't think I have ever told you of our ceremonial guard-mounting. I will not confuse you with technicalities, but simply explain that each evening fresh men go on guard over Battalion Headquarters (our billet, ahem!), over each of the four Company Headquarters, and as a fire picket. They are inspected with great precision and then the band have a little musical orgy, finishing up with the regimental march, which smites us all into temporary paralysis – in army phraseology, "standing to attention".

While all this is going on, in the main thoroughfare of the village, all traffic is suspended. This is our function, and we have quite a lot of excited French poured into our largely uncomprehending ears. The French inhabitants hardly see why a public road should be closed to them because a number of Tommies are undergoing an inspection. Neither do I. It is however a delightful illustration of militarism in its disregard for the convenience of the civilian.

Sunday was a very delightful day. While on duty at the village well, (what functions we do discharge, to be sure!) the cable broke, leaving the receptacle 150 feet down the well.

All my love to you, Ever your affectionate son,

Laurie

Monday, 27 August 1917.

My Dear Mother,

I have just read your letter of the 23rd and the one from Arthur. How that wretched asthma does always seem to attack him just when he should be enjoying a rest. Weedon wrote telling me that you had seen him. Don't you think him rather a quaint old bird? I hope he did not buoy you up too much by leading you to expect me home soon. Leave has all been stopped and it seems a little doubtful whether I shall get mine before the end of September after all.

While I was on late duty on the 22nd (9.30 – 10.00) searchlights began flickering to and fro across the sky. Presently the sound of an aeroplane could be plainly distinguished and also the sound of bombs exploding. It seemed to pass over towards the large town two miles off and in the morning I was told by the French postman that several civilians had been killed. There was a vivid display of summer lightning all the evening, the flashes following each other in rapid succession.

On Thursday I witnessed a pathetic little procession marching along through the rain. It was the funeral of a little child. First came the old priest, robed and looking very grave and solemn. Then, on each side of the priest, a little boy in scarlet and black robes carrying a crucifix. Behind followed the coffin, carried on a bier carried by young girls, and then a number of little children, dressed all in black but carrying large bunches of white flowers. Well, it is easy to believe that for the stricken children of this battle-scarred land death is gain. Are there many ministers nowadays with the temerity to quote in their pulpits "God's in His heaven, all's right with the world"?

Friday was a day of delight. The Battalion was on the move, but instead of the usual tramp, tramp, tramp, we went by motorbuses and charabancs. I was in a charabanc. What a ride! We went for over four hours though some of the most beautiful scenery in this part of France. Hill and dale, trees and meadow, clear streams and lowing cattle – I was on my holidays again! Then we crossed the frontier line into Belgium and gradually the scenery changed. Remember Belgium! No need to tell me that. Flatter country, poorer-looking, frail little huts put up for the refugees, and the ever-present khaki. At one railway station we saw a Chinese squad at work. The villages and towns swarmed with troops. No wonder Germany masses her picked troops against us. She needs to!

Our destination was an extensive camp of wooden huts, old and ruinous, by the main road. The boom of the guns is with us now, observation balloons twist slowly up aloft, and at night we look out towards the signal-lights pendant over the trenches. On Sunday afternoon, while I was sitting in a somewhat meditative mood, knowing what lies in front of the Battalion, a small black sheep came up. It was so tame that I had to take my diary out of its too-greedy lips by force. It rained heavily at night and the hut leaked. Heavens, how it leaked! The land is beginning to look rather flooded. I hope the rain will stop soon. Now, in all probability I shall be unable to write to you for a few days. We are going into the line soon and there is an important piece of work we must tackle. You must not worry, but keep a triumphant faith and look forward to what I shall try to make an interesting letter when I return from the line.

My fondest love, Ever your loving son,
Laurie

Laurie was now back at Ypres, a place he had seen much of during the previous winter. The forward positions were extremely unpleasant due to the weather, and derelict tanks were to be found all over the place.

The constant rain was an absolute nightmare. Men sank up to their knees in the mud as soon as they wandered off the duckboards and the deep dugouts were often inches deep in water. It rained every day and 26 August brought an absolute deluge which filled every crevice and shell-hole to the rim.

Trenches were not worthy of the name, so wet, broken down and badly damaged were they, and a series of fortified shell-holes formed the basis of the British defences. Access to the front line was over the open ground, and often under the clear view of the enemy guns, so trips to the front during the day were extremely dangerous. Communications were so bad that pigeons were the main means of sending messages back to headquarters. Laurie spent the first three weeks of September in and out of the line engaged in a series of offensive incidents intended to gain ground slowly from the enemy and to wear down his morale. During the early part of September 15 Battalion advanced our line considerably, until they were relieved on 21 September 1917.

Tuesday, 4 September 1917.

My Dear Connie,

I have waited until I had a special envelope before writing a letter, as the local censorship of letters has become preposterous. Because a few woolly-brained idiots write all manner of details, giving names of places and of regiments, etc., letters are being more rigidly scrutinised than ever. We are not even supposed to say if we are in the line or not. So it's the Base Censor for this child.

A week ago today our Colonel engaged the Divisional entertainers for our Battalion and we enjoyed a show equal, I consider, to many of the London halls. On Wednesday we did special training on ground marked out as an exact copy of a certain part of the German lines. An advance party was actually moving off to the line on Friday when the whole business was cancelled. Strange are the ways of the army. Rumours were rife, of course, and their variety was a tribute to the strength of the imagination and powers of credulity of the average Tommy. I rarely listen to rumours – too blasé, I suppose.

Saturday was somewhat perturbing. In the morning a shell fell in the officers' mess. It was a dud! Miracle of miracles! If it had exploded it would have burst in a small room containing two colonels, a major, an adjutant, a padré and a doctor. Just after an exhilarating Battalion football match in the afternoon, these heavy long-distance shells again began to fall in and near the camp. For a short while we all left for the surrounding fields. Some casualties were reported from a shell which had fallen on a road near the camp.

Yesterday and on Sunday we had air-raids. We were obliged to go to bed in the dark. The German planes were extremely daring and dropped a great many bombs each night. As we are in wooden huts with, at the best, only corrugated iron above us, it was fortunate that nothing came too near.

I enclose a letter which is I think self-explanatory. The certificate is a pleasant surprise to me and I want you to let me know when it arrives, what it looks like – all about it, in fact. I took up this Pelman Course early this year as a pleasant way of keeping my brain from rusting out here. It has, I really believe, saved me from becoming a complete mental bankrupt. There were twelve lessons and they were worked, many of them, in tiny damp dugouts in the line. I can remember doing one exercise by candlelight, while waiting with fixed bayonet ready to move to the front line, where the Germans were attempting a raid, and having the candle blown out by the gust caused by a shell bursting opposite the dugout door.

Trust you and Flossie are all right. Will you please send me out a couple of handkerchiefs?

All my love, etc.,

Laurie.

Thursday, 20 September 1917.

My Dear Mother,

I was very pleased to receive your letter of 14th and to learn that you are now slightly better. A letter from Connie reached me at the same time. As you say, it is indeed splendid the way in which that little business has been developed. *[This refers to the Regent Toilet Co. Ltd, formed in 1916, and of which Miss Constance Attwell was a Director.]* One thing I am quite sure about, and that is that no measure of prosperity, however great, will ever spoil our relations to one another. This kind of life is a sufficient object lesson to me of the relative value of money with regard to the things that really count.

This letter is being written in a loft over a schoolroom which is to be our home, I believe, for one night only.

Saturday, the 15th, was the worst day by a long way that I have spent for many a month. I tell you I draw a sigh of relief now when I think of it. First our heavy artillery fire provoked the German batteries to reprisals upon our devoted heads. Our little German dugout seemed to be the centre of a very maelstrom of flashings and smoke and crashing explosions. Some hours after, hostile aeroplanes hovered over us at so low an altitude that I could see every detail and fully expected a hail of bullets any minute. They appeared to be only reconnoitring, however, and at last returned to their own territory. In the afternoon an attack was launched from our part of the line and a German strong-point was captured with a number of prisoners. Once again it was our corner of the globe which caught the German gunfire. I went on the ration fatigue in the early evening and after, from 7 to 9, was on sentry-duty over the Battalion Headquarters. I have never had so bad a two hours. The whole time shells were landing, first on this side, then on that. The explosions were so frequent that there was one continuous stream of sound. Red-hot fragments, humming wickedly, streaked past at inconceivable speed. The trench became an alleyway of dense smoke and the atmosphere was choky with the powder. I was the only man out in the trench and the whole of my little world seemed to be an inferno of shrapnel, whizz-bangs, woolly-bears, crumps and high explosive. At the very climax, up from the front line soared a great rocket – our "S.O.S." signal. I dashed into the officers' dugout and reported it. Soon afterwards I finished my turn and went into the dugout – glad enough to sit in that comparatively safe retreat. A shell landed full on the roof soon after, but did no damage to us. I think that what saved me in the trench was my experience of shells. As each screamed overhead, I had quickly to decide where it would burst and put a corner of the trench between myself and it.

At midday on Sunday we were relieved – "for which relief, much thanks!" We had a long march out – past the land of continuous shell-holes, past disembowelled horses and sad wrecks of waggons, past the gun batteries, to slightly more tranquil tracks. Here we halted, and I'm blessed if a few shells did not burst in a corner of the road about 100 yards ahead.

In the afternoon we had a cup of tea at an advanced Y.M.C.A. Hats off to the Y.M.C.A., please. We finished our march at a collection of dugouts among the trees, where I slept like a child – 10 hours of glorious rest!

On Tuesday morning we moved by motor-lorries to a pleasant little French town, quite new to me. Yesterday was also spent there, but today we rose at 5.30 and marched to this little place where I am acting, not only as a policeman, but assisting the runners as well. I believe we have another move before us tomorrow and that soon I shall be writing to you from a very different part of France.

Leave approaches – very slowly! My fondest love, etc.,

Laurie

Laurie's letter above refers to action on the Menin Road and Westhoek Ridge. His prophesy of a move to France was fulfilled, and on Friday, 21 September, the Battalion left the Ypres Salient after many weary months of holding the line entrusted to it and moved south towards Arras.

Thursday, 27 September 1917. (Excerpts)

My Dear Connie,

One more letter from a dugout, but nothing so exciting as the last. A postcard has now reached me from Bert, who is now in Rouen. If he could stay there for the duration he would have a really enjoyable time, but if his Battalion is destined for this coming winter to do garrison duty in the line he will make acquaintance with all those discomforts which I have described to you from time to time.

Your last parcel contained a tin of ham. This was already cut into slices and each slice separated by a piece of grease-proof paper. It made excellent sandwiches and was quite the tastiest tin I have had for some time. If this war is to be prolonged into next Spring (I am not at all sure it will last so long) I shall be wanting things like "Campites" and tea tablets, etc. I thought of buying one of those small "Primus" stoves while I am home on leave. Whilst on that subject, I may as well reassure you that leave is going on steadily and that I am once again beginning to entertain high hopes.

Friday (21st) was the second day in our schoolroom billet. Once again I acted as runner. After midnight we packed up and marched a mile and a half to a large station. After two hours' wait in the road, we entrained – 40 men to each cattle-truck – and started our train journey somewhere around 3 a.m. Wonderful to relate, I managed to snatch some sleep, in spite of the cramped positions which our numbers compelled us to take up. On Saturday morning we detrained and after two hours' marching reached a quiet village, situated pleasantly enough, but quite without special interest. Our billet was a large barn which had been converted into a bathhouse for the troops.

Sunday was a perfect day. There was no great amount of work to do and the sun shone fiercely on the chalky roads and white walls of the farm buildings as if we were in Spain instead of France. Towards evening the sky became too wonderful for words. I was on duty near Headquarters and heard the Corporal of the guard giving vent to exclamations of pleasure at the beauties which met his eyes. It was indeed a fine picture. We were standing under an old, high stone archway – the entrance to the farm owned by the Mayor. This tall archway made an ideal frame for the picture of trees and sky beyond.

On Monday morning the wanderlust seized us again – in the shape of Operation Orders from Brigade – and we set off on a long, hot march. At one point we passed an old ruined monastery – a venerable ruin, for once not the work of the Hun. On the road was a truly Oriental sight. A gang of Chinese coolies, I can't call them anything else, with Chinese NCOs, passed us. Some were carrying huge baskets of tools slung on a long pole balanced on the shoulders of two men. It might have been the Celestial City – not Bunyan's – for a few minutes, what with their weird, yellow faces and the glare of the sun on the road. We passed another squad on railway work later on and rested near them, and the Chinese labourers accepted with grins the cigarettes of the British Tommies. This is where you find the true cosmopolitan.

At length we reached a camp – our true destination. Not far off, down the road, lay one of the famous cities of the war, famous in peace as in war, and beautiful in spite of its scars. *[This obviously refers to Arras. Battalion Headquarters were then at Victory Camp, Ecurie.]*

On the very next morning (the 25th) we marched to the trenches. The feature of this place is the extreme length of the communication trenches. When we left the road, just after passing a very shattered village, we entered a communication trench and, from that point, it ran to the front line, a distance, taking into account its windings, of over four miles. Battalion Headquarters are about a mile behind the firing line and our dugout is roughly the same, though in a different trench from the others.

We have a water guard to do. There is a well, cunningly hidden in the ruins of a village captured from the Germans. This is used by the troops for their water supply and we have seen that no crowd accumulates and that nothing is done to invite trouble from Fritz. It is at the very end of a long trench and is half-way to the front line. It is twenty minutes walk from our dugout to our post at the well. The line is very quiet and is likely to remain so.

My health is very good still, except for a little cough, probably

brought on by cooling down after sweating or by a cold bath which I indulged in on the grass in company of many others, at our last camp. All my love to you,
Laurie

Laurie's surviving service records show that on 5 October 1917 his long-awaited leave materialized, which explains the two-week gap in the correspondence until his return to the front in mid-October.

Chapter Ten

The Gavrelle-Oppy Front

By the time of Laurie's return to France, 15 Battalion had moved once more, this time to the Gavrelle – Oppy front. There they enjoyed a few relatively quiet weeks.

WAR DIARY: 18–26 OCTOBER 1917
In the front line.

WAR DIARY: 26 OCTOBER – 4 NOVEMBER 1917
Training and small working parties at Aubrey Camp.

Sunday, 14 October 1917.

My Dear Mother,
If at first you don't succeed —. The authorities have at length managed to transport me to this realm of blood and mud, and I am writing this to you from the transport lines of our Battalion.

Perhaps a few details of my journeyings will be of interest to you. I arrived at Victoria Station at 8.am on Friday morning and found only a small crowd of soldiers waiting. Within ten minutes I was in a corner seat of the train and in less than twenty minutes we were leaving the station behind us.

At Folkestone we went straight onto a mail-boat and had a good passage across the water. It was just a trifle choppy, but not enough to cause any inconvenience. Arrived at Boulogne, we marched up a steep hill to a Rest Camp. I was fortunate enough to espy a friend on the boat and so had a companion for the rest of the journey. We were billeted in a large wooden hut and had a blanket served out to us. At 8.30 I blew out my candle and slept until 6 the next morning. Our

128

food while in the camp was quite good and there was ample for every-body. Connie's sandwiches were very tasty.

We got into the French train on Saturday morning and once again I was fortunate in getting a comfortable seat. The carriage was hardly "de luxe". Two of the windows were missing and the rain flooded half the carriage until a waterproof sheet had been tied up over the missing panes.

On the journey, which was painfully slow, I was responsible for the breakage of yet another window. Giving a man a playful shove, he fell back on the door of the carriage and the window split into dozens of splinters.

We got out of our Pullman carriage at about 6 in the evening and were then marched to a light railway siding. Here we got into – oh, weep for all that scrubbed equipment, – we got into open coal-trucks and trundled along through the darkness like so much inanimate freight. After this, a few minutes brought us to the transport lines, where we reported our return and settled down for the night in a tent. It was rather cold. There was frost on the canvas in the morning.

This is a badly ruined little village with, of course, no civilian popu-lation. The Battalion is somewhere in a quiet part of the line, where we shall join them this evening.

How are you feeling now, my dear? Have you moved to Clovelly Road yet? I am as fit as a fiddle and still very happy in the memories of my days in the dear old home. I will write again in a few days. For awhile we must all live on memories, very precious ones, and on hopes. This war is not going to outlast our affection for each other. I doubt if it will last long into 1918.

Goodbye for a little time, Yours ever,

Laurie

Saturday, 20 October 1917.

My Dear Connie,

Although I have sojourned in this abominable country for eight days now, I have not as yet heard from England. This, however, I know is from no remissness on your part, but from the vagaries of our postal service, and I am rather anticipating receiving something from you by tonight's mail.

I set off on the Sunday afternoon that I wrote to you (14th) to proceed to the trenches. It was a long prowl and brought the reflec-tion home to me very forcibly that I was far indeed from Blighty. The weather fortunately was good and the ground underfoot not more muddy than I expected.

Our position on the map is not far to the left of the place I pointed out to you on that large *Daily Mail* map hung up in Uncle Fred's place. I received a very warm welcome from many of the boys. Accommodation was as usual scanty and, in three nights, I had three different beds in three different dugouts. The line was very quiet indeed and the fatigues we had to do very reasonable. So on the whole, though I returned straight to trenches after twelve happy days in England, I was "let down" fairly lightly.

From our sentry post we had a view over several miles of undulating country dotted with small woods and copses, and here and there revealing a glimpse of a small village. It must have been a good agricultural district at one time and even now looked fairly pleasant with its grass and poppies. The trees are nothing to be compared with our beautiful English woods, even when they have not become scarred by shrapnel and high explosive.

On Wednesday morning the Battalion moved into the front line and Headquarters came up into a trench behind the Companies. My dugout here is really one of the very quaintest I have ever had cramp in. It is so high that I can stand upright in it, but the floor is only four feet square. Two men occupy (!) this little box. I always feel as though I were living in a Punch and Judy box. And yet, believe me, I can manage to sleep in it, though two of the others never seem able to drop off until they are really tired out. If it were on its side it would make a cosy little dugout – unfortunately it is upended.

We work rather harder here, as is only to be expected, but I have no complaints to make. Everybody has treated me well since my return and this naturally eases the sting of being absent from you all a little bit. From our sentry post we have a most interesting view of a large belt of country still in German hands. Behind a dense wood, in which he has concealed several batteries of guns, we can see the smoke of railway engines. In "no-man's-land" is a ruined village and dim on the horizon we can detect through our glasses factory chimneys smoking and a large church spire.

This letter has been rather rushed, but I wanted to get one off today and I know you are willing to make every allowance for me. My very best love to you all.

Yours ever,

Laurie

Thursday, 25 October 1917.

My Dear Mother,

Many thanks for your nice letter of the 19th. I am pleased beyond measure that you are a bit better and also that you are staying with Arthur and Annie. I know quite well that they would do anything to make your visit enjoyable and beneficial.

The torch is a very fine one and is most useful to me in these trenches, for I usually have to go down long flights of dark steps into a deep tunnel to wake people up or get rations, or make some report or other several times a day. Will you tell Connie not to bother sending out big parcels of food while things are so scarce and dear.

I was going to return two of those photos, but on second thoughts I am retaining them. They will make me laugh, anyway, so they are worth carrying. Connie's photo is a real treat. If she could hear some of the ejaculations made by the fellows she would be quite vain.

You have doubtless read of the latest French and British attacks up north. They account for the low, sullen growl of the guns which has been in our ears day and night for nearly a week. The news from Russia seems to get steadily worse. Well, we must win the war in spite of them.

Life has not been very exciting, which is just as well, really, when you come to think about it. One evening I had to conduct a small carrying-party up to the front line. We returned smothered in mud. I was almost a solid cake of mud from the knees downward. We are having excellent food and plenty of it. Our cooks are in the line with us, so we get bacon or porridge for breakfast, hot stew for dinner, tea and a hot supper, when we have porridge, soup or tea and hot rissoles. Not bad, is it?

On Tuesday and Wednesday evenings I had a good view of the distant raids. The Germans sent up the usual brilliant display of rockets – red, green, orange and white. Did you see or hear anything of the Zeppelins? Yesterday afternoon I could just make out the head of a man peering over the side of a German aeroplane. This will show you how low they occasionally fly.

We hope to be out of the line before very long. I shall be glad, for since I left you I have been sleeping fully dressed and in my boots. It will be a relief to be able to undress a little at night.

Give my love to Arthur, Annie and the children, and accept the same for yourself and Flossie. I suppose you see Connie each evening. Give her my love.

Yours affectionately,
Laurie

Thursday, 1 November 1917. (Excerpts)

My Dear Connie,

Today your letter of the 27th has arrived with the photographs. I think them quite good. I suppose I do look something like that at times. My friends out here say the full-length one is like a figure from a stained-glass window, while the other resembles some actor, manager or other.

I have seen quite a number of American soldiers out here. They look like thorough Yankees and their drawl is most amusing. They have very neat uniforms, gaiters and wideawake hats, something like the Australians. One of their Colonels came round our trenches while we were in the line.

Last Thursday we were still in the line. I was on duty late at night, when there was a brisk wind blowing great masses of cloud across the face of the moon. There were several heavy showers of rain, and the brilliant moon shone at the same time, causing a large rainbow, a thing I have never seen before at night-time. Each evening, too, I have seen shooting stars.

On Friday we were fairly "in the soup" as we term it. Soon after midday we were relieved and marched off, heavily laden, through a pitiless driving rain. We had a three hours trudge in the face of a relentless wind and arrived at our camp *[Aubrey Camp]* soaked through to the skin. Things now took a turn for the better. A great brazier flamed inside our hut, so we took our overcoats out of our packs and wore them while we held our tunics and trousers near the blaze to dry. The next day we marched to the large town near us for a bath and a clean change. The water was chilly! On Sunday evening I was able to attend a voluntary service which I greatly enjoyed. Monday evening I went to a cinema a few minutes walk away and saw some good films, including a "Charlie Chaplin".

The camp and the country round about is extremely muddy. There are a succession of ridges and in the valley are small, mined villages. It has a certain picturesqueness and is certainly an improvement on the flat, featureless country found in Belgium. The horses are provided with gas-masks, which are tied on the shafts in an easily accessible position.

I was up at 4 on Tuesday morning and, with a special pass in my pocket, started off for the railway station a couple of miles away. Four men per Company were given these passes. At the station we bought tickets as ordinary passengers and went for a three-hour journey.

Some of the small stations we passed through were terribly wrecked. The line ran through one of last year's famous battle-grounds. In many places the fields and orchards were flooded. Once or twice the permanent way seemed like a bridge across a wide, though shallow, lake.

The cathedral city *[probably Amiens]* which was our destination is one of the famous places on the continent. It has not been touched by the war and is still thronged and to all appearances prosperous. The cathedral is sand-bagged in places for protection against bombs. It is a magnificent structure, smothered with images, ornamentation and gargoyles. But, better than any laboured description of mine could be, I have sent you, direct from the city, a book of views as a souvenir of my visit. The shops were fine, though the prices were ruinous. We left at 7 in the evening after a most enjoyable day.

In the evening we went into the Theatre Royal and heard a splendid concert given by one of Miss Lena Ashwell's parties. It was a red-letter day. We arrived back at camp just before midnight.

The news from the Italian front is very disappointing. There seems to have been some lack of backbone. The Germans will never make a sweep like that on this front.

Ever your affectionate brother,

Laurie

Thursday, 8 November 1917. (Excerpts)

My Dear Mother,

We have been issued with gloves and those woolly hearthrug affairs, which make a soldier look like a prehistoric man or a chauffeur, or Puss-in-Boots at amateur theatricals. Also I have a very smart pair of trousers. For the first time since I joined up I do not feel like Little Willie wearing his papa's cut-downs!

We had plenty of work to do at the Camp, what with duties at the Orderly Room, patrolling the roads and guarding the water-carts – this last, of course, to ensure that only our own Battalion benefited from our supply of water. On Saturday, owing to the wind being in a dangerous quarter, gas sentries were posted at night and we had to do turns at the H.Q.

During the day I had a rather unsatisfactory bath at a village nearby. The bath cost me 3d, by the way, and when I took my trousers off some loose coppers flew out of one pocket and rolled down between the slats of the trench-boards on which we were standing. We were given clean towels at this bath and underclothes as well. My vest is the smallest and most absurd garment I have ever worn since reaching man's estate, but in wartime one cannot pick and choose.

On Monday morning we got up at 5.30, breakfasted at 6, rolled our blankets, (we have two of each, but leave them behind when we go into the trenches) and packed our kit by 7. At 8 we marched off to the very same spot from which I came home on leave. Ah, it does not seem so long ago since those happy days. I occupy the same dugout and we are having the same unexciting time.

We have had some showers of rain and the weather has a touch of rawness in it. Cold feet are easily obtained and not so easily remedied. The Primus works splendidly and is rendering itself quite indispensable to my comfort. This morning a German aeroplane has been brought down, badly crippled by one of our machines. I don't think it can have landed very far from our front line.

My fondest love to you all. Your ever affectionate son,
Laurie.

WAR DIARY: 5 NOVEMBER 1917
Front line immediately south of Gavrelle.

On 9 November 15 Battalion moved back to Brigade Reserve at Roundhay Camp where they stayed until 18 November.

Wednesday, 14 November 1917. (Excerpts)

My Dear Connie,
I wrote to you last on the 8th. The same day we witnessed a daylight raid, which was duly recorded in the official bulletin a few days later. On Friday *[9th]* we left the trenches and marched to our present camp – at least it is called a camp! How can I bring before your eyes an image of our present resting place?

Picture, please, a big sweep of open country, almost entirely tree-less, and minus villages or farms. Long ridges rise everywhere, so that the place looks like a petrified sea. It is an ancient battle-ground, ancient, that is, as this war counts time. When a week can see a nation like Italy changed from a victorious army into a shaken, retreating one, the lapse of months does indeed seem to confer a title to antiquity.

There are belts of rusty and shattered German barbed-wire entanglements, and trenches and saps run web-like all over the place. I walked today through these old German trenches and peered down thirty-foot dugouts and marvelled at the revenge which nature was taking. The sides of the trenches were crumbling and the dugouts were half-filled with debris. Rank vegetation grew over everything. It was difficult to imagine that this place was ever given over to war. The shell-holes were very thick and numerous near to the trench and in among the barbed wire.

Down in one of the little valleys and on the slopes of the land-waves are all kinds of shelters. Some are large and elaborate, others small and very plain. Nearly all have sandbagged walls and a roofing of corrugated iron or proper iron cupolas. They seem to have sprung up like mushrooms. There is no order or system about them. Here we live, and on this ground we move and have our being. When we arrived the average depth of mud was three inches. It is now slightly less. Of course, you can still go up to your waist if you like to fall in a shell-hole, or over the tops of your boots if you go where the limbers have ploughed deep ruts.

Soon after 6 it becomes pitch dark. Last night it was foggy as well. Our camp at evening looks like a gypsy encampment. Dark outlines of shelters loom and little points of light twinkle from braziers and candles. The fog blotted even these out and I stood last night, my outlook limited to a few square yards, feeling almost as though I were the only man left alive in a welter of primordial chaos.

We sleep in a nice little place, dry and cosy, but small for ten men. We have wire netting stretched on wooden frameworks for beds. There are three layers of bunks, one over another. There are two canteens in this place, but we are almost entirely cut off from the comparative civilisation which lingers even around the ruined villages. We had a jolly good bath the other day – a shower, with plenty of warm water, finishing off with cold.

Our present Colonel is away in Blighty. Did I ever tell you that he was the first officer of the British Army to land in France after the declaration of war? He was on the G.H.Q. staff before he came to us.
Fondest love,
Laurie.

Tuesday, 20 November 1917, (Excerpts)

My Dear Mother,
Since writing my last letter to you, I have received a parcel from Aunt
Louey. The contents were weird and wonderfully packed, but I
enjoyed it all right, you guess.

Last Saturday we were to have gone into the line again, but after
full arrangements had been made, the orders were cancelled and we
had to stand by. Rumours grew in wildness as the hours passed. There
is scarcely a battlefield in all this world war that we were not going to
adorn!

On Sunday *[18th]* we left our camp and moved away from the
line. It was a narrow gauge railway with curious little engines pulling
eight or nine open trucks. Thirty-five men got into each truck. I
cannot tell you how it was done. I do know that I sat down on a mass
of equipment and that my legs were buried under still more equipment. It was impossible to move and, before we reached the
journey's end, I had hard work to refrain from shouting at my
agonies of cramp.

Our new camp is near a railhead *[Ecoivres]*. The village is not a
wonderfully interesting place, but it is a pleasing change to see civilians once more and shops, of a sort, but still shops. My health is quite
good, barring a slight cough. I believe we shall soon be on the move
again.
Ever your affectionate son,
Laurie.

Monday, 26 November 1917. (Excerpts)

My Dear Connie,
Your parcel arrived in good condition. It may interest you to know
that I received it on the eve of our departure from camp and so had
to carry it for a distance of 14 miles. I really think I earned the
contents of that parcel! The watch is going well so far. Do you
remember sending me a tube of toothpaste? As I feared, the tube has
squashed all over my shaving brush and soap tin. Enough is left to
last me another fortnight, after which will you please send me out a
small <u>tin</u>?

When I last wrote we were stationed in a certain camp near a railway
station – the station from which I caught the leave train not so very
long ago, though it seems ages. The following morning (21st) we

moved away through some typical French country – long straight roads with a double avenue of trees, great fields without hedges, and small villages hidden amongst clumps of trees. Our new billet was an old barn *[at Hermaville]* which had been fitted up with wire beds. We only stayed there one night and were on the road again at 10 o'clock on Thursday morning.

Thursday's march was memorable by reason of its appalling mud We are accustomed to plenty, but this march took the giddy biscuit. The so-called road was pitted with holes, which were filled to the brim with slime and could not be distinguished from the proper level of the road. We slept in a camp in large wooden huts *[at Wanquetin]*.

Once again we were on the march after breakfast, and once more the mud was the abiding impression, in more senses than one. On reflection, I think the mud on Friday was stickier and more evil-smelling than that of Thursday. We occupied wire beds in an old barn at night. The village *[of Gouy-en-Artois]* was utterly uninteresting.

Saturday's march was a very long one, especially as it was our fourth day on the road. This was the occasion on which I carried a large parcel in addition to all my usual luggage. The route led us over a succession of ridges. The latter part of the march *[to Courcelles-le-Comte where they billeted in huts]* was through ground at one time in German possession. The villages were battered to pieces and at different corners there were German graves, inscriptions and sign-boards.

Yesterday we had yet another move. We passed through some famous places, including one of the great towns of the war – one which for months was looked upon as the ultimate objective of a series of attacks *[Arras]*. It was a woebegone spectacle – not a house intact in all that great place. We were very weary and footsore. The roads were congested with artillery, infantry, columns of motor-lorries and supply wagons. There is not much doubt that we are pressing the Germans very severely in this part of the world.

Both on Saturday and Sunday we passed a great many French colonial troops – strange-looking Algerians and Zouaves. There were numbers of Indian labourers also and Chinese – the latter in the main hatless and with great shocks of hair as rough as a doormat on their heads. We have some weird allies.

The Sunday march was a bitterly cold one. When we finally arrived at our destination *[Beaulencourt]* we had no blankets. Sleep was impossible, so we lit a fire and sat around until 4 o'clock this morning, when we each had a blanket. Even then it was cold. Our packs have

just arrived and I have had a much needed-shave before writing to you.
Ever your affectionate brother,
Laurie

This long succession of marches took them in a lengthy semi-circle around Arras, culminating in their arrival on 28 November at the Hindenburg Line where they were almost immediately to be thrown into some of the fiercest fighting of the Cambrai offensive.

Chapter Eleven

Bourlon Wood

When the Germans retired from the Somme during the Spring of 1917 they devastated the countryside, methodically blowing up every building and cutting down every fruit tree so the land would not be habitable for allied troops following behind. The enemy then retreated into the trenches of their newly constructed Hindenburg Line. This was extremely well constructed, utilizing the high ground effectively, being fortified with sturdy gun emplacements and deep dugouts and guarded by extensive barbed wire entanglements many yards thick.

Nothing much had happened in this area throughout the summer, until suddenly on 20 November the allies launched a massive tank attack on the Hindenburg Line. The tanks surged through the enemy wire and over trenches twelve feet deep, and succeeded in opening up a great salient four miles in depth.

We captured valuable ground in the area of Bourlon Wood and a village west of Cambrai. This allowed us to overlook and enfilade the enemy trenches over a wide area and posed a real threat to their positions. Not surprisingly, the Germans responded by pressing a series of attacks and counter-attacks throughout the following week, resulting in both sides suffering heavy casualties, possession of the village changing hands each day.

A wood is normally best defended by rifle and Lewis-gun posts suitably placed under cover on the forward edge and machine guns positioned with a good field of fire outside the wood. For some reason, despite protests, the strategy adopted on the night of 28 November was to pack the wood with seven battalions of troops. Not surprisingly, the enemy commenced a heavy bombardment with gas shells, leaving the men struggling in the undergrowth half-blinded by gas that clung to every bush.

It was into this arena that 15 Battalion was thrown. On the night of 28 November they were sent with six other battalions to relieve troops holding Bourlon Wood.

WAR DIARY: 28 NOVEMBER 1917
Moved to Hindenburg Line.
Battn. In Bourlon Wood area.

	Casualties:	Killed	4
		Wounded	17
		Missing	2

WAR DIARY: 29 NOVEMBER 1917
In Bourlon Wood   See Narrative of Operations attached

Casualties:	Killed in action	6 Other ranks
	Wounded in action	2 Lieutenant T. Woods
		52 Other ranks
	Missing	2 Other ranks

Narrative of Operations covering period from 28 November to night of 1/2 December 1917

The Battalion took over that portion of the front held by the 2nd Dismounted Cavalry Brigade and the 2/5th West Yorks, on the night of the 28/29th ult. Two Companies were in the front line, B Company under Lt. C.U.Rilner and D Company under Capt. R.Middleton on the right. C Company under Capt. T.H.Sharratt was in support in the Sunken Road. A Company was in reserve in the vicinity of Battalion Headquarters.

The Battalion moved up from the Hindenburg Line leaving there at 9.0pm and proceeded by platoons at 100 yards intervals. When the head of the Battalion reached Relay Station the enemy barraged the ground between this point and Battalion Headquarters with H.E. and gas shells. Gas masks were put on and the Battalion pushed on through the barrage. D and B Companies had no casualties, but C Company lost 18 men and A Company 4 men. The relief was reported complete about 1.30am on the 29th.

Early on the 29th the enemy commenced to bombard the front-line positions, the Wood and Battalion Headquarters. Heavy casualties were suffered during the day. With the exception of gas shelling the night was fairly quiet, and advantage was taken of this to improve the position, and to patrol the Battalion front. Two patrols were sent out from each of the front-line companies towards Bourlon Village. Nothing exceptional was reported.

Our artillery carried out a practice barrage at 5.0am on the 30th, and this drew heavy retaliation for about an hour. All was quiet then until about 8.30am when an intense enemy barrage was put along the whole front. At the same time both the front line companies observed and reported about 600 Cavalry preceded by waves of Infantry and followed by guns and limbers, which were seen to move in rear of Bourlon Village in a south-westerly direction. Our artillery put a barrage in front of these troops through which the Infantry doubled and which caused the Cavalry to retire after suffering casualties.

At about 10.0am the enemy barrage doubled in violence and, the front being obscured by smoke, the S.O.S. was sent up by both front line companies. C Company, which was by this time reduced to two platoons, therefore reinforced the front line as follows:- One platoon going under 2/Lt. W.B.Lacy reinforcing the right of D Company, and the second platoon under 2/Lt C.V.Marchant reinforcing the right of B Company.

No attack however developed until 2.30pm when, after receiving a message to say that the enemy had broken through the Battalion on our left, the enemy was observed to the left rear of the Battalion front. Lewis gun and rifle fire was at once opened by B Company and the left platoon of D Company. OC B Company at once formed a defensive flank of one platoon along the Sunken Road. Lt Col. W.K.E.Segrave then formed up A Company and the whole of Headquarters, including runners, officers' servants and signallers, in two waves and about 4.0pm advanced with the right flank on the Sunken Road in a north-north-westerly direction and dug in. This advance was met by heavy rifle, machine-gun and aeroplane machine-gun fire. At this period our left flank was in the air, and it was not until dusk that touch was established with the 8th Battalion.

Shortly after dusk A Company changed its position to a line being in touch with B Company on the right, and on the left with 8th Battalion. Headquarters had previously been withdrawn.

The next day was uneventful and the Battalion was relieved by the 21st Battalion on the night of 1/2nd December and moved back to tented camp at Femy Wood about Seven Dials.

Harold Marshall, Major
Commanding 1/15th Battn, London Regt
(P.W.O. Civil Service Rifles)
Compiled from reports of officers in
the absence of Col E Segrave, DSO (gassed)

WAR DIARY: 29 NOVEMBER 1917
In Bourlon Wood

Casualties	Killed in action	2 Lieutenant C.V.Marchant, 2 Lieutenant G.E.Tatum 39 Other ranks
	Wounded in action	Captain P.Davenport, MC (Gas), Captain P.Fallon, Captain D.C.McArdle (RAMC)(Gas), Lieutenant & QuarterMaster W.G.Hodge (gas), Lieutenant H.A.Berry, 2 Lieutenant W.E.Hoste, 2 Lieutenant B.A.Fitter (Gas), 2 Lieutenant Rev. Illing (Gas) 122 Other ranks
	Missing	40 Other ranks

Wednesday, 5 December 1917 (Excerpts)

My Dear Mother,

I hope this rather long spell without a letter has not occasioned any uneasiness. As you know my silence has been compulsory. It has been quite impossible to get letters written, or if written, there was no means available of getting them into the post. Even now, I am rather uncertain when you will get this one. I wrote you a long letter on Nov. 26th, and since then have sent Service Cards on two occasions.

By the way, I have sent something home to you – two souvenirs which I found in the trenches during a very critical and exciting time. A great friend of mine is going on leave in a few days and will call on you and deliver the goods. He is a signaller named Holland and is a nice gentlemanly fellow. I think you will agree, now that you have seen some of my comrades in arms, that I am fortunate in belonging to such a Battalion as the C.S.Rs *[Civil Service Rifles]*. Both of the souvenirs are interesting – one is a short German dagger in a metal sheath (carried by N.C.Os), and the other is an Imperial Eagle and Motto from an officer's helmet. These eagles are getting very scarce now, as most of the Germans wear ordinary shrapnel-helmets when in the line.

142

Poor old Uncle Stokes has been killed, you will be sorry to hear. There have been many very sad casualties and I have great cause for thankfulness that I am spared to write you this letter. Three times pieces have hit me on the back and shoulder, but were stopped by the thickness of the clothing I was wearing owing to the intense cold.

Of course, I cannot do any article-writing until we settle down a bit once more, but I intend to keep it up as much as possible. Re Xmas and presents. Please buy little gifts for the kiddies as you did last year and buy and give Flossie a 10/- present. If there is any little thing which would add to your comfort I should like to know that my money had purchased it, and the same applies to Connie. Anyway I give you free hand in the matter.

For myself, I should like a new holdall very much, but it must be small and compact and not very elaborate. I could do with still another pair of socks after all this marching about, and of course I shall want a nice pocket-diary for 1918.

And now to my present wanderings. Please remember it is winter while we are doing these things. That reminds me – certainly send out a candle or two in each parcel. Now that I have a Primus stove, I do odd cooking jobs for myself at every possible opportunity, so you could send out a few things such as coffee-au-lait, tea tablets, soup cubes, an occasional tin of milk, etc. Don't break my back with these things, but please keep up a gentle supply.

To return to my subject. On the 27th Novr. we packed up and left our camp *[at Beaulencourt]* near the great ruined town *[of Arras]* and got into motor-lorries which dumped us down in the dark, the cold and the mud with three miles still to go. We had to carry two blankets apiece besides all our kit and our destination was a field just outside a ruined village *[Doignies]*. The only shelters were tarpaulin bivouacs. We crowded into these – they were only six feet long by four wide – and made ourselves as comfortable as possible for the night.

The next morning we went into the trenches, at a very important point in the line. *[This was the Bourlon Wood sector, north of the Bapaume-Cambrai Road,]* We had no shelter of any kind, but in the evening the Battalion moved into the firing line. We had the job of guarding their packs. So we built the packs up into the shape of a little hut and made ourselves tea and settled down. On Thursday, the 29th, we saw a little air drama enacted. A Fritz airplane darted down with great speed, eluded all attempts to head him off and shot at an observation balloon. In a few seconds the balloon was falling in a mass of flame, leaving a great black trail of smoke, while two white parachutes brought the observers down, I trust without

143

mishap. All day the Germans were keeping up an incessant bombardment of our lines.

Friday morning *[30th]* we ran out of water. We four were feeding ourselves, you see. So I and Weedon went along to a deep lock in a canal *[Canal du Nord just to the east of the Hindenburg main line.]* and drew some. While down there – sixty feet down, I should think – we sniffed gas and for twenty minutes had to wear our respirators. Before we returned to the dump of packs, the bombardment had increased tenfold in its violence. We could see only too well that some mischief was brewing. We got back without mishap and could see from our shelter that the front line was one mass of fire and smoke. Gas shells were coming over by the hundred. Our Battalion and others on our right and left had to face the fierce brunt of a massed counter-attack pressed home by the Germans with the utmost vigour. They were beaten back, but the defenders lost far too heavily. We saw later on long strings of wounded coming down to the dressing stations. On the other hand, the Germans had received as much, and more, than they gave. Their artillery was of course shelling all around our batteries, and this was when I got knocked by the small pieces, but no harm done.

Saturday morning *[1st]* saw all our rations exhausted, so Jimmy Weedon and I set out to find our transport lines – three miles back. On arriving we were told that we would be relieved by another party, in view of the discomforts and so on that we had endured for three days. So we stayed at the transport lines, after guiding our relief party up to the pack dump. I slept the night in an old dugout in Fritz's original support-line.

The next day another policeman and I were put on as runners at Divisional H.Q., which were situated in a rather picturesque wood. I rather enjoyed being temporarily attached to Division, and we heard several interesting pieces of information. It was bitterly cold and we could not turn in until after 10 o'clock when our only shelter was a small bivouac, open at the very end from which the wind blew.

Yesterday the Battalion went into a different part of the line, and we left the transport lines and moved to the rear of the limbers to a Tank park some few miles back. There were any number of tanks but, alas, no shelters. There was a stiff frost and the night before us, so we explored and found a big stack of logs near a light railway. These we built into a fairly comfortable cabin to hold three. Today is bright, clear and cold. Heaven knows where we shall go next or when. I am keeping quite fit and well, and have even lost my cough. I trust you

144

are well. God bless you all. A very happy Xmas to you and may it be the last that sees us separate.

All my love, Yours ever,

Laurie.

As Laurie rightly reported in this last letter, the enemy counter-attacked Bourlon Wood on 30 November in some force. The wood was difficult to defend – the trenches were only 4 feet deep, there was no defensive wire, the men had few tools, trees obscured visibility, and having been treated to an intense bombardment overnight, gas hung everywhere in the thick undergrowth. Gas masks had to be worn for many hours.

Fighting throughout the morning of 30 November was fierce, with many casualties on both sides. Eventually the enemy drove a wedge into 15 Battalion's left flank, and despite counter-attacking by their H.Q. Company, including runners, orderlies and signallers, they were forced to give ground. Nevertheless the wood was held against considerable odds, due largely to the wonderful gallantry of the Lewis gunners, who when an attack was observed ran out with their guns in front of our line, and from positions of advantage in the open, mowed down the advancing German infantry.

On the evening of 2 December 140 Brigade re-took the original line held before the attack on Bourlon Wood on 30 November. Not only did they recapture 300–400 yards of ground but also took fifty-two prisoners and eighteen machine guns.

WAR DIARY: 1 DECEMBER 1917
Out of line. To Havrincourt.

	Casualties:	Killed	4
		Wounded	10

WAR DIARY: 4 DECEMBER 1917
Took up position rt & lt of Graincourt.

Within two days of re-taking this ground, the order was given to withdraw completely from Bourlon Wood. 15 Battalion was one of those chosen to cover the withdrawal to the village of Graincourt back on the Hindenburg Line. By this time the Battalion had been seriously weakened by the previous days' actions and the effects of gas, with the result that they were insufficient to garrison both the village and the high ground to either side of it. By dawn on 5 December they therefore held temporary covering positions on the high ground east and west of Graincourt but did not have control of the village itself.

During the day the enemy had several times attempted to infiltrate the village, and despite being beaten back and shelled, had nevertheless managed to secure a foothold there. Late in the day the Germans managed to envelop the right side of 15 Battalion, thereby cutting off their escape. 2 Lieutenant Lacey gave the order to "make for the sun" and, although pressed hard on all sides at once, the Battalion used the sun to guide them to safety. 2 Lieutenant Chambers and his machine-gun team, who gave such wonderful support, were wounded and captured by the enemy, as were several other officers.

Meanwhile 2 Lieutenant Aylmore had set up a Lewis gun at a forward position to cover the withdrawal of C and D Companies, and was now surrounded by a force of 150 to 200 Germans. After holding out for some while they were compelled to retire under fire from all sides. On the way they surprised a group of Germans who were digging in, and fired on them. The Germans fought back with shovels and wounded one of Aylmore's men in the back. They continued onwards, an officer, three men, a wounded man and a gun, arriving finally at a position of safety. As reported in 47 London Division's official record, "The 15th Battalion suffered heavily, but they could recall no episode in France or Belgium so full of fire and spirit as this refusal of their troops on the outpost line to surrender to an enemy that had already surrounded them."

The following Report of 15 Battalion's Operations during these few days is of particular interest.

War Diary: 5 December 1917

Casualties:	Killed	3
	Wounded	1

Report of 1/15th Battalion's Operations December 4th, 5th and 6th 1917 around Graincourt

On December 4 orders were received for the Battalion to move from Havrincourt in the afternoon and take up a position right and left of Graincourt. This was done after dusk. A and B Coys on the left of the village under Lieut L.C.Morris, MC on the road, and the left was in touch with the 2nd Division. C and D Companies took up a position on the right of the village in some old trenches and gun pits N of the road and connected up with the 59th Division on the right – Capt

L.L.Burtt in command. In this position were also placed 4 guns of the 142 M.G. Coy under Lt Chambers.

The village was not occupied but posts were established in the Sunken Road NE of the village, and withdrawn at dawn. During the night I went over the whole of the dispositions through the front line and in front of the village and arranged with Lieut Chambers for the gun positions covering the front of the village, and with him and an officer of the Sherwood Foresters, for cross-fire at the junction of our right with the 59th. Lewis guns were disposed on the left also for cross-fire and a night gun was put at about E29.C.8.9.

The troops from the old front line passed through us as arranged. The whole front line was patrolled until dawn.

On the morning of the 5th about 10.0am a small number of the enemy were seen advancing cautiously down the slope, and as their numbers increased the artillery were notified and did some excellent shooting – the enemy bolting at once. Later on they appeared and in considerable numbers, forming up in rear of the Sugar Refinery and also lining the Bapaume–Cambrai Road. Some filtered through into Anneux.

Targets were frequently indicated to the Artillery and engaged with good effect. The enemy losses at this period must have been very severe, and some good results were obtained on the right by M.G., L.G. and Rifle fire on many parties of the enemy approaching that portion of our line from Anneux. Fire was also opened on small parties making for the village and in all cases during daylight the enemy was dispersed.

Towards dusk, however, a few of the enemy had penetrated to the cemetery and were engaged by M.G. fire, but nothing could be done to hold the front of the village (other than by crossfire).

During the night our patrols were very active and frequent engagements took place with success to us in every case. We captured one light M.G. and one prisoner, the remainder of that party being killed, except one wounded who got away. Our runners were in several cases involved and did some good fighting, accounting for seven enemy between them.

Owing to the area of the village, and the many means of getting in and out by the enemy, it was impossible to control the situation except to keep patrolling and fighting where he could be found, and in this on the left a platoon of the R.W.F. [Royal Welch Fusiliers], who were consolidating with us, responded to my request and joined in to muck out some enemy who were attempting to get through on the road, and his advance in that direction was stopped. The R.W.F. entered into the spirit of the operations with great zest but had to withdraw at daylight.

It was impossible to stop the filtering through the village on the south and by dawn 40 or 50 enemy had got through and took up a position about the old gun pits. These were engaged by Lewis gun and rifle fire from the strong point and many casualties were inflicted by riflemen as well as L.G. The garrison was R.W.F.

At dusk on the evening of the 5th Major H.F.M.Warne took over command of the right front, and arrangements were made to put a Lewis gun before dawn on the road. He also took confirming orders that on withdrawal the garrison on the right were to occupy the right strong post. He reported that everything was in order and that both companies had already reconnoitred the route.

Rations were sent through from B H.Q. the last party leaving H.Q. about 6.0am 6th inst. (having to make two journeys). This party arrived at the front line safely, but no runners were received from the front line after about that time. Two platoons of the R.W.F. engaged on consolidation work on the right and left about 4.0am.

About 4.30am 6th inst. 2/Lt Aylmore took a Lewis gun and team to the point above-mentioned with instructions from Major Warne to deal with enemy on south side of village as far as possible but not to become too much involved but to withdraw to the post. The Lewis gun was in position about 5.0am and an enemy patrol soon after tried to rush it, but were dispersed with the loss of several wounded and killed and one wounded prisoner was taken by the team.

After daylight two patrols tried to envelop the gun but without success. They were driven off with a number of casualties, but with a loss to our team of one killed and one wounded, who was brought out. As other parties of the enemy were on the move for a further attack, the gun was withdrawn, but before doing so 2/Lt Aylmore sent his runner to Major Warne to acquaint him with the situation. Whilst the gun was in the strong post an enemy attack developed on the right of the strong post and our gun was posted on the Sunken Road away from the post and with the garrison and M.G. and L.G fire the attack was beaten off with very heavy losses.

As to the doings of the right garrison on the 6th please refer to written statements sent to Brigade on 8th inst. from 2/Lt Aylmore, Sgt Cooke and Sergeant Manthorne, no copies of which have been kept.

Orders were sent out for withdrawal at 5.30pm on 6th inst. But it had commenced before the runner could get through. The whole garrison had however a warning order that if after the night of the 5/6th it was impossible to hold on, that they were to withdraw to the post before indicated as might be ordered by the senior officer present.

The garrison of the right sector had apparently a very good time with splendid targets of masses of the enemy crossing diagonally N.W. to S.E. and entered into the defence with good spirit. (Ammunition had been sent to whole line the previous night by the R.W.F. working party.)

The enemy attack developed beyond our right, where apparently not much resistance was offered, and it was discovered that the troops on our left had withdrawn and the enemy was closing round our right rear and at the same time round our left rear from the village. The garrison turned about and the order was given by 2/Lt King and 2/Lt Lacy to cut their way out. A Lewis gun on each flank did splendid work in crumpling up the enveloping troops inflicting such punishment that the riflemens' task was made easier. Both guns got clear, and during the withdrawal again got into action and effectively dealt with bodies of the enemy who tried to bar the way, and on this occasion with only two good men on each gun they were invaluable. Both guns were brought out to the Rest Camp by the same men.

After various bouts of fighting on the way, the post arranged for was reached, the troops being in good heart and much pleased with the day's work.

2/Lt Lacy was brought in wounded. 2/Lt King was last seen in rear of our troops binding up his Sergeant who was unable to walk. As to the other officers, Major Warne, Capt L.L.Burtt, 2/Lt Potts, Lieut Houslop, it is difficult to say what happened, and they were not seen during the withdrawal. I think some or all were probably cut off. As to O.R, the S.Bs and some wounded including Lieut Chambers were in the trench and probably taken prisoners. Probably 12–15.

On the left during the 6th nothing much happened except M.G. fire, and communication was kept up throughout by making a wide detour, and the use of some gallant runners who were tireless and unafraid of M.G. fire. The left garrison withdrew according to orders at 5.30pm.

The Regimental Aid Post was evacuated by the M.O. and staff at 6.0pm, all the wounded having been sent down. Battalion H.Q. arrived at Havrincourt about 11.0pm. 2/Lt Aylmore collected our people in the strong sost and sent them back to camp, also the 1st + 2nd Machine Gunners to their H.Q. He also saw all wounded evacuated. No wounded were left out within 300 to 400 yards of the post, and search was made along the line of withdrawal to that extent.

The operations, coming after heavy fighting and gassing, was trying to the men, added to which the cold was intense, so much so that the water in M.G. sockets in silent guns out in shell holes froze frequently, and the guns had to be changed whilst being thawed out. When, however, the enemy appeared on the 5th, and the patrol fighting started that evening, all ranks responded with a will and showed a magnificent spirit.

Sgd; Harold Marshall
Cdg 1/15 London Regiment

ADDENDA.

On the morning of the 6th Graincourt was occupied by a considerable number of the enemy. On the guns being turned on they bolted out. Two or three hours after they returned and the guns settled down and did some very fine shooting on the village generally and on the position of M.Gs on the West especially.

NOTE. The Battalion Strength:

	On left was 5 Officers,	113 Other ranks.
	On right 6 Officers,	112 Other ranks.
H.Q.:	3 Officers,	25 Other ranks

WAR DIARY: 6 DECEMBER 1917

Casualties	Killed in action	1 Officer
		5 Other ranks
	Wounded in action	63 Other ranks
	Missing =	5 Officers including Major H.F.M. Warne & Captain L.L.Burtt 42 Other ranks

The Battalion had lost ⅗ of its strength in just eight days. When it first arrived in France back in March 1915, the Battalion had initially numbered:

> *30 Officers*
> *1,046 Other ranks*

The battle of Bourlon Wood brought enormous numbers of casualties. 19 Battalion suffered particularly badly. Of the fifteen Officers and 600 men who entered the wood, only one officer and between twenty and thirty men remained a few days later. Ten officers were sent down gassed in the first day or so, five of them dying very soon.

The work of the Royal Army Medical Corps was extraordinarily difficult. The large quantities of gas in Bourlon Wood meant soldiers had to wear their gas masks for long periods. But to avoid the constant stream of shells they had to dig in. They could not dig for long periods without removing their gas masks, so there was a constant stream of gassed soldiers arriving at the regimental aid-posts. One of the most pitiful sights of the war was the long lines of blinded men linking up and being guided back through the wood by R.A.M.C. orderlies.

When they arrived at the aid post, the medical officers found gas still clinging to the soldiers' clothes, so they too had to wear gas masks. But they could not treat the men properly without removing their gas masks, and they also suffered the effects of the gas poisoning.

In the first twenty-four hours of the battle 4,700 casualties entered the dressing stations. The route from the front was heavily shelled, and the R.A.M.C. themselves suffered seventy casualties.

Wednesday, 12 December 1917 (Excerpts)

My Dear Connie,

I wrote to you on the 5th concerning Xmas arrangements and hope you have had that letter by now. Yesterday I sent off several of our Battalion Xmas cards. You will see that we are <u>some</u> Battalion and think no end of ourselves. Still, all joking apart, the fellows did supremely well not long since, and we have had a message of thanks from Sir Douglas Haig and have been told that England and London should be proud of us.

On the 5th the bread ration was one loaf to every fifteen men, so we had recourse to biscuits which the average dog would disdainfully sniff at. For some reason the bread ration remained small – one slice per man per day.

We packed up on Sunday – another march on a Sunday! – and proceeded through a ruined village to our present billet *[in Bertincourt]*. It is an old house, standing at the corner of a village street. I wonder that it still stands, for most of the beams and rafters have disappeared, probably serving as firewood. The roof shows a great many chinks and the floor of the top storey is nearly all gone, so that we have plenty of ventilation. I will not mention the mud. You know all about that now.

For the present, being the senior man, I am in charge of the Police. Our Sergeant got badly gassed and is at present in hospital somewhere. I have just come back from a visit to Clifford *[Tanner – a cousin.]*, who I have at last succeeded in ferreting out. He only came here last night and was very pleased and quite excited when he saw me. He still wears shorts, is covered in mud and looks extremely fit and well. He seems to be very well liked in his Battalion and is as jolly as a sandboy, though, like myself, he longs for the end of all this misery and bloodshed.

So long for the present. I have to go on duty. Much love to you all, Laurie.

Laurie refers above to Sir Douglas Haig's subsequent testimony of the manner in which 47 London Division fought. Commending their efforts at Bourlon Wood, Sir Douglas Haig wrote:

"Though exposed throughout the day to repeated assaults of superior forces, they beat off all attacks with the heaviest losses to the enemy, and by their gallant and steady conduct contributed very largely to the security of the Divisions engaged on the whole front of the attack"

This is especially true of 15 Battalion, who yielded ground only under extreme pressure. Counter-attacks were immediate, determined and successful. Those defenders who suffered from the intense fire and the suffocating gas at Bourlon Wood could look back upon the day with honour and not a little pride in their performance.

Chapter Twelve

Rest and Relaxation

There then followed a period of relative quiet, mostly away from the front, whilst 47 London Division underwent a major reorganization.

Laurie left the front line on Friday, 21 December 1917 for Etricourt. The following day he marched to Marlancourt where he and 15 Battalion spent Christmas.

Sunday, 23 December 1917. (Excerpts)

My Dear Connie,

At last I have the opportunity of writing to you and yet my pencil tarries a little. There is so much to say that I am at a loss to know where to begin. So if my letter should appear to be disjointed and inconsecutive you will realise that it is because I am floating about in a perfect sea of thoughts and can no more follow a single line of thought than a cork can remain stationary on the restless waters.

I hope you will all have a pleasant time at Christmas with Arthur and Annie. When you turn your thoughts to me, I shall also be thinking of you, and believe me, I am not unhappy. Our bad time is behind us, and we are expecting a good Xmas-time and New Year.

The parcel which Mabel supplied was one of the nicest I have ever received. It came, too, when little additional luxuries were very welcome. I have now received your parcel of the 14th and must thank you very much. The holdall is just what I want, also the Diary. Will you give my warmest thanks to Miss Hockley for that fine house-wife, and to Mr Delaloye for his gift of cigarettes. Another parcel to come too! My word, you are looking after me well this Xmas.

You will probably have guessed from the tenor of this letter that the Battalion is at last out of the trenches and has been promised a rest, war conditions permitting, of course, until after New Year's Day. How sorely we need the rest, God knows. I am going to leave the account of my movements until tomorrow, in order to get this letter off by today's post. So look out for another rather lengthy and vivid epistle tomorrow.

I know that Bert's Division had gone to Italy and I sympathise very much with him. In many ways I consider we are fortunate on this front. We get our letters and parcels and are never quite cut off from the homeland.

The weather is most seasonable. I don't think I have ever seen so much snow about in my life before as in the past week. In our present village we look over acre upon acre of dazzling snow. Every tree is a sight to wonder at, every hedge a beauty to bring tears to the eyes, every turn in the road giving a view to thank God for.

There are seven of us in our little upstairs attic. We have a fire and are all boon companions. We shall spend a very happy Yuletide together. May yours be happy too. I am still in charge of the Police – nearly a month now. Hope all is well as I am. God bless you all and bring us together again soon.

All my love, dear,
Laurie.

Christmas Eve, 1917.

My Dear Mother,

Many thanks for your letter of the 16th. I have just received the parcel and feel I shall do very well this Xmas. And now to fill up the long, but unavoidable gap, in the account of my doings.

On the 13th of December we were still in the battered village *[Bertincourt]* in which I met Cliff. He showed me the photo taken by the Press representative after the presentation of Denis's medal at Buckingham Palace. *[Denis Tanner was another cousin.]* On Friday evening I again visited Clifford and we had a jolly supper of fried sausages with his little section.

After dinner on the 15th we packed up and left for the trenches. It proved a weary, weary march. All the suffering and endurance are not confined to the front-line trenches or the moments of actual fighting. Much comes simply as part of the day's routine. At length we emerged from the final desolated village on to a road which was a nightmare. Somehow the road carried an air of misery. Every gaunt tree by the roadside seemed to droop in dejection. On either side waste land

154

stretched away into dimness. A small shrine stood, emptied of its figures and wrecked by a shell. The road led to the very hinterland of the trenches. We had a moment of excitement when some shells pitched over our heads and then we reformed and trudged across to our destination.

Headquarters dugout consisted of two long flights of stairs dug out of the earth and boarded. At the foot were two small rooms. In the first room the Officers lived and in the other was the signal office. One flight of stairs led up to the open. Access to this flight was gained by dropping four feet through a square man-hole. The other flight led up to an eight-foot-deep trench which was completely camouflaged. The trench was boarded over the top and earth piled on the boards, so that it was impossible for an aerial photograph to reveal its existence.

We slept on the stairs – three steps to each man. Our steps led up to the open and therefore the entrance could only be used when it was dark or misty. The Colonel would not permit any traffic through his room, and so, once we were out early in the morning, we had to wait in the trench till dark before we could return. The weather was far and away the coldest we had known this winter and snow soon covered the ground. We had a very limited water supply and it was 3 days before we could have a wash and shave. I only got it then by collecting a large amount of snow and boiling it down. We had two warm drinks a day from the cook, who used a tank-trap as his cookhouse.

Now, what is a tank-trap? I had never come across one before. They are very large and deep pits with almost perpendicular sides, big enough to hold our house and one or two more besides. Netting is thrown across the top and brushwood covered with a thin layer of earth. So the crew of the tank imagine there is solid ground in front and go plunging helplessly into the pit. So does the wily German endeavour to beat the tank menace. Though there were many stranded tanks about, I did not see any in the pits, but I did notice that the side of one pit was crushed down a lot. Perhaps the tank had been hauled out.

We had a fair amount of work to do, in addition to our gas guard. At night we had a double post, so we had little sleep. I doubt whether I averaged more than four hours a day during our stay there. We were relieved on the 21st and marched out over the snow *[to Etricourt]*. The road of gloom was altered now. Every tree was a thing of beauty. Snow lay everywhere. Our route led us over a plank road winding through a large wood. What a fairyland that wood was! The planks were as slippery as glass and few men kept their feet for the whole journey.

We were bound for the same village we had left earlier and were billeted in a small but comfortable hut. Up again the next morning and away through two villages to a point on the railway. Hurrah! We are leaving the trenches behind and here are villages with civilians and civilisation. I saw bonny little French boys and girls – the first children I had seen for nearly a month. How happy the men were. Men who had been gassed, who had been shelled, who had fired into dense waves of German infantry, and who at length, cut off on all sides, fought their way out to safety. Thirty or forty of us in one small truck – sang and joked the whole journey through. When we disentrained *[at Marlancourt]* the snow was six to eight inches deep. Where the road ran between high banks huge snowdrifts had collected and often went up to our knees. The whole countryside lay wrapped in a fleecy mantle and looked like a scene in Canada.

The village is partly deserted. Many of the houses and farms are tenantless, but there were several shops of sorts and it is not at all a bad place. We are to have special meals and junketings tomorrow and on Boxing Day. I will tell you about them in my next letter. As far as we know, we shall stay here at least until the New Year.

We do police duties and close the estaminets at the proper hours. I have decorated our little attic with the Xmas cards and we are going to have "A Merry Xmas" in cotton-wool on one of the walls. We have a small French stove, so can keep nice and warm.

Now my dear ones, you see that my Xmas is going to be a happy one. This letter is, I suppose, going to reach you by the end of the year. Let me tell you my New Year resolution – to try to be worthy of such a Father and Mother as I have had. God bless all of you, and keep you happy and content.

All my love, dear. Yours ever,
Laurie.

Monday, 31 December 1917. (Excerpts)

My Dear Mother,
I hope you have received the letter written on Christmas Day, *[This was either not received or has not survived.]* and also the parcel sent off on Boxing Day. My postbag has been very interesting recently.

I have already told you of our Xmas dinner of roast pork, apple sauce, onions and potatoes, followed by Xmas pudding and custard. We had a nice tea in our little room, toasting bread at the little French stove. In the evening we played cards and did not get to bed until eleven.

On Boxing Day morning I was up quite early, for I was lucky enough to get a special pass to that splendid city of which you have a book of views *[probably Amiens]*. With two companions I trudged through the snow to a little station about three miles away. While waiting for our train we had coffee at a little estaminet. It was served in tins and cost threepence – about ½d a spoonful. We followed a pleasant journey through the wintry country – streams all frozen over and the sheet of snow dazzlingly white.

Arrived at the city, we had a good breakfast of ham and eggs and coffee, and then thoroughly examined the grand cathedral. It was snowing hard, so the cathedral was a welcome refuge. As I was the only one who had been twice, I acted as showman. I found one new thing this time, or rather it was a very old thing. Set right in the middle of a very elaborate mounting was a small box with a glass lid. In the box was a relic – part of a bone of John the Baptist. I offer no opinion, but merely tell you what I saw. In another part I came across a lovely old book, evidently the work of monks. It was a series of Latin chants with musical scores, and each page was decorated with scroll-work, or dragons, or scenes from Scripture. Every bit had been done by hand, so the volume must have been very valuable. The high altar was quite the finest I have ever seen.

The cathedral visited, we had a splendid dinner and went to a French cinema for British and American troops and we greatly enjoyed the films. One showed French troops marching through various Italian cities and being greeted rapturously by the inhabitants.

We changed to another billet *[at Méricourt]* on Saturday. This was a very draughty barn. With a temperature well below freezing point, this was not at all tempting, but a friendly Frenchman gave us several large bundles of straw. The next morning we moved into a much better place, from which I am now writing. It has a tiled floor, there is a fine stove in the centre and on the whole it is a good billet. The village is almost large enough to be called a town, boasting a railway station and a fair number of shops.

Today I have been doing duty at a village about 1½ kilos away, where three of our companies are billeted. The snow, after a fortnight, is gradually melting away, but the roads are wicked to walk on. The poor horses slide all over the place.

How are you all? I do trust you, Connie and Flossie will have a New Year of ever-increasing happiness and that before long I may have the supreme desire of my life – to be with you again for good.
Ever your affectionate son,
Laurie.

My Dear Connie,

I was overjoyed to hear from all sides that your Xmas was so happy and especially that dear old Mother was able to share in the games and pleasure. I am also glad that your selection of gifts on my behalf was appreciated. Many thanks for your trouble in the matter.

While in the trenches some time ago, and in rather depressing circumstances, I was chaffed for reading a book called *The Retreat from Mons* by an eyewitness. Nevertheless it was a fine book and one I could hope to find on my bookshelves when I return, were I not ashamed to keep on asking for things. Please remember that the battery for my torch is due in a week or two.

There is not much to say about these opening days of the New Year. They have all been spent in the one French town with its snow-covered roofs and slippery streets [*Méricourt*]. It is surprising how long the snow lingers. Our band turned out just before midnight on New Year's Eve and played the Regimental March and the National Anthem. German prisoners have been used to help clear away the snowdrifts all round our district.

The shortage of sugar is now very obvious in France. Coffee is frequently unsweetened or else honey is used in place of sugar. Eggs have increased in price, also biscuits. It is a terrible misfortune that we have been unable to cope with the U-boats. Still, nobody is starving, as yet, I fancy.

I hope you are all well and that business is satisfactory. My cough is better and this year I have not lost my voice as I did in 1917.
My fondest love to you all, Your affectionate brother,
Laurie.

Friday, 11 January 1918.

My Dear Mother,

It is a raw, cold morning and the rain is coming down steadily. I have just come in from a spell of duty and my fingers are somewhat numbed. Our hut is quite comfortable, but dark. Candles feebly illuminate the gloom. Outside the scenery is undoubtedly depressing – ruined houses, and a large factory, now a mass of broken machinery, fallen girders, old fly-wheels, etc. So I turn to my writing pad, and in thinking of you all in the dear old place, lose any sense of desolation that might have depressed me.

Since I last wrote to you there has been a thaw, then a further heavy fall of snow, followed by a steady thaw which reaches its climax in today's downpour. The snow is at last vanquished and those roads which have been so treacherously slippery are, even if slushy, more easy to march along.

On the 9th I paid another visit to "a certain city" *[Albert]* you know something of already. I enjoyed this visit as much as I did the two previous ones. For one thing, I had a very fine bath for two francs. There was an unlimited supply of hot and cold water, and each customer was given a couple of clean towels and a piece of scented soap.

Then at teatime I went into a large Canteen and, after my meal, saw a really good selection of cinématograph pictures. One lengthy film was the *Prisoner of Zenda* – very interesting, as I have both read the book and seen the play.

I have almost missed telling you of my most interesting experience. Knowing the centre of the town so well, I decided to walk to the outskirts. It was a little after ten when I passed a modest-looking café with the usual board announcing that "Coffee-milk, biscuits, beurre, eggs" were to be had. You will observe that French and English are mixed in a most impartial manner. I went in for an egg breakfast and was greeted by a fine-looking old French dame. With her I had a most interesting conversation, though of course I found it easier to follow her than to enter into any very lengthy sentences myself.

During the conversation she spoke of her ruined home in Contalmaison. I told her I had probably seen it and she stooped and brought out from under her feet a brick. "From my little home in Contalmaison," she said, with tears in her fine eyes. She also told me that her son was about my height and age and had been buried about a month earlier. I asked her if she was staying in the city after the war was over. Her eyes flashed. "No, monsieur, I shall go back to my own home in Contalmaison. My husband lies there." We drank to an early victory and a durable peace. She said that the Germans (les Boches) must be driven back – out of France and out of Belgium and right away from Contalmaison. She must have been over sixty years of age, and I could not disguise my admiration for her fire and spirit. Here was France at its best. Home and dear son gone, but unfaltering yet. I went straight from her into the cathedral – somehow it seemed fitting. I met a very different type there – a young United States soldier, thoughtful and a delightful talker, though nasal, like all of them.

Yesterday we moved to this place *[Bertincourt]* by rail. We have been here before. It is the town in which I met Clifford before Xmas and, strangely enough, I have just met him again. Arrived at our destination, I proved unlucky, being one of a large party detailed to unload the train. This meant letting down the travelling cookers and all the limbers (fully loaded) from the trucks down a ramp to the ground. We finished at 10 at night, working in the rain by the light of lamps held by the Officers.

I am keeping quite fit and hope you are well. My fondest love to you all, Ever your affectionate son,
Laurie.

Saturday, 19 January 1918.

My Dear Mother,
I want to make plain to you our movements since the letter of the 11th. We were then in a town in the "back area" of our Front *[Bertincourt]*. When you read of back areas being shelled it means that these different towns and villages a few miles behind the trenches which are used as rest billets have been bombarded. I saw Clifford in this town, not long before he was due to go up the line with his water-cart. The cart is emptied and he returns late the same night. I saw him to some purpose too, for I got some petrol from him for my Primus stove.

After an early tea on the 12th, we left for a village *[Ribécourt]* which is but a stone's-throw from our trenches. We entrained in open trucks and were jolted slowly along a light narrow-gauge railway. The wind was very cold and we were glad to reach our journey's end. After an uphill march of just over three miles, we arrived at our new resting place.

It is a veritable French Pompeii – a city of the dead. Few of the houses have their walls intact and none have a sound roof. But this ruin was no worse than of the town we had just left. What was so impressive was the daylight life of the village. Although it had had so many khaki-clad inhabitants, the streets were deserted. Very occasionally a man, bound on some errand, slides cautiously along, hugging the wall as much as possible. At night things are different – there are groups of men working and quite a bustle of movement.

From our observation box we can solve this mystery. Away to our right rises a dim-looking ridge with woods and towers crowning its summit. From that ridge the Germans have direct observation of the streets of our village. So we become like the early Christians in the catacombs – we live in our cellars all day and creep forth into the open after dusk.

Our cellar was quite a comfortable abode. We are able to use an upstair room as a living-room. The door and windows are hung with blankets, to prevent our fire or candle-light showing outside. One day a shell knocked a great hole in a wall about two houses away. The rubbish blocked the roadway and we had to clear it before the food limbers could pass.

The village was spasmodically shelled day and night. The shells were very scattered, too, so that it was impossible to guess when or where the next would burst. On Tuesday, the 15th, we had a great gale. The wind was accompanied by torrential rain, which left the roads like miniature trout streams. Several walls and roofs collapsed, and tiles were falling all day long.

The following day the Battalion moved into the trenches. This did not necessitate a long march for H.Q. Coy., who are billeted on the very outskirts of the village.

We do our gas-guard at a deep dugout up a trench which commences literally at our back door. The trench has an average depth of water of four inches, so we are pretty muddy. Each day adds its fresh deposit and we have mud splashes from head to foot.

We are on duty two at a time for eight hours, and then we go back to the village for eight hours' rest. Part of our eight hours' duty is done in the signal office at the bottom of the dugout. It is interesting to watch the operator at work. The dugout is very damp and drips in a score of places. Pumping goes on almost continuously or the bottom would be flooded out. We are getting good food and sleep well – when we can.

I had a parcel from Arthur the other day and a nice letter. My best love to you all.

Your affectionate son,
Laurie.

Saturday, 26 January 1918. (Excerpts)

My Dear Connie,
Last Sunday we had a good deal of artillery and aeroplane activity. It was a very clear day and we could see the towers and spires of a big city behind the German lines. In the afternoon we moved out of our dugout Headquarters back to the brasserie in the village. This move was very convenient for us, as we had been sleeping in the brasserie

161

(brewery) and doing our duty at H.Q. The move was a precautionary measure. It was believed that Fritz had an idea that H.Q. occupied that particular dugout.

On Monday four guns were mounted to deal with the German aeroplanes – Lewis machine guns. The weather through the day and on the following day was wet and dull. Tuesday *[22nd]*, in spite of the rather poor conditions for observation, the village was heavily shelled and the brasserie suffered some direct hits. The cellars were all right. While this was on, I was shifting bombs and ammunition in the trench.

We left Ribécourt on Thursday evening and marched a few miles to another village where our cooker waited with hot cocoa. We then clambered onto open trucks and trundled along the light railway to our present resting place *[Bertincourt]*. I sat with my legs dangling over the side and found it an icy cold journey.

We reached our billet – a nice enough little shanty holding four – at two in the morning. Yesterday the weather was truly delightful. At night the moon was bright and we had a proper air raid. The bombs shook our frail little hut several times, but I believe only one horse was injured in the whole town.

The shortage of candles is phenomenal. Please make it your practice, if possible, to send some with each parcel. The old Primus has been a great boon this winter. I am enclosing a few razor blades for resharpening. There is no hurry for them at all. I hope you are all in the best of health. Weedon and Sims frequently ask after Mother. My fondest love, etc.
Laurie.

WAR DIARY: 1 FEBRUARY 1918
Battalion fighting strength = 22 Officers + 536 Other Ranks
B Company:
>Two platoons + four Lewis guns front line
>Two platoons, gunpits

WAR DIARY: 2 FEBRUARY 1918
Front line – Flesquières

Sunday, 3 February 1918.

My Dear Connie,
Whilst most probably you are at the morning service, I am writing to you with my writing pad balanced on my knee at the bottom of a very

large and deep dugout. The dugout, which is of German construction, and therefore well and strongly made, is in a trench running through the wooded grounds of a much-battered château. Beyond is a village [Flesquières], an unspeakable wreck, still unsafe in daylight and frequently the target for the enemy's shells. One more name to add to the already lengthy list of places I have dwelt in, in this much-suffering part of France.

I have seen a newspaper account of the big raid on London and notice that Paris did not go unscathed. I hope your sleep was not entirely destroyed.

Last Sunday [27th] we had a much-needed bath and change of underlinen. I also had a new tunic and pair of trousers. It was the anniversary of my being wounded and during the evening I was wounded again – by the Medical Officer, who re-inoculated me. After this I did not expect to feel very well on Monday. I was not disappointed.

On Tuesday evening, the 29th, we had another air raid and again on the 30th. The weather turned extraordinarily cold. The trees had half an inch of rime on every leaf and twig. I have never before seen trees so thickly frosted. In the early morning sunshine they shone like Xmas trees – it was a really beautiful sight.

Yesterday we left our billet in the ruined town and went in motor lorries to another place much nearer the line. It was not safe to move further in daylight so we halted until the sun had set. Then we went right across country, across sunken roads, along ravines, and in mud literally a foot thick. Progress was so tiring that we were all thoroughly exhausted. I tell you, I never came within miles of such fatigue in civilian life. As a civilian, one simply cannot appreciate the strain which one can be called upon to endure. I am sure of this, that many and many a time a man would welcome a machine-gun bullet as a happy release.

But even this journey came to an end and we found ourselves entering a ruined village – our halting place. We were put, temporarily, in charge of a drying-room – a room in which a coke fire is kept burning day and night beneath racks from which thigh-boots are hung to dry.

This morning we are back on our usual trench work – the gas guard over the Officers' and Headquarters Staff of the Battalion.

My health is quite good. I hope Mother's back will get better and that you and Flossie are quite well. My fondest love to you all,
Your affectionate brother,
Laurie.

War Diary: 16–21 February 1918
Relieved – to Bertincourt.
War Diary: 21 February 1918
Marched to Manancourt.
In reserve – training.

Saturday, 23 February 1918. (Excerpts)

My Dear Connie,
The position as regards candles is rather comical. Ever since I appealed so desperately for candles, I have received little else. Now after Arthur's gift of eight, Miss Marshall has sent me a dozen, and you drop hints of more from you. I scarcely know whether I am a Roman Catholic altar or a common soldier, I have so many. My present stock will last about ten days, so please send out no more until after the 10th March. After that, I shall probably want, not an avalanche, but a steady reasonable supply.

There is no real news to tell you. I will write again soon, My best love to you all.
Yours affectionately,
Laurie.

Wednesday, 27 February 1918.

My Dear Mother,
Many thanks for your letter of the 21st and for the parcel of the 20th. You will be glad to hear that we have had a quiet time since I last wrote to you.

Last Wednesday, the 20th, we shifted billets, moving into a cupola dugout. The inside had been coated with Stockholm Tar by some ingenious maniac with a sense of humour. When I stood upright I found my hair sticking to the roof! Our caps all caught it!

The next morning, we marched through three dishevelled-looking villages to our present home *[Manancourt]*. We have a brass band now (some Battalion!) and marching to a band is, of course, twice as easy as marching without. We have large huts with wire beds. They are very comfortable, though the roof leaks a bit.

The village is a total wreck and has few points of interest. It is prettily situated and is well supplied with trees, whilst our huts on the outskirts are on a broad open expanse, reminiscent of the downs at

Brighton. This part of the country is well peppered with bomb craters intended for a well-concealed aerodrome not far away.

I had a look at what remains of the church. A stone archway has the date 1720. The altar is badly smashed. It must have been rather an imposing one. In the small churchyard are some graves of German soldiers and some crosses erected by the Germans over English soldiers.

The weather has been extremely changeable. We have had stiff frosts, pouring rain, boisterous winds and mild muggy days all on top of each other. I have been fortunate enough to find a youngster, a nice bright boy, who plays chess a bit. I think I shall give him a pawn and a move to make the games harder.

Will you please send out some razor blades as early as possible. Fondest love to you all, Your affectionate son,
Laurie

At this point there is a break in the correspondence, no letters being available until the end of March. From the subsequent April letters, and the fact that the great German offensive involving the retreat from Cambrai took place at this time, lack of letters is understandable.

Chapter Thirteen

The Retreat from Cambrai

The big German attack was expected in March, but exactly when, nobody knew.

WAR DIARY: 17 MARCH 1918
Third anniversary of Battalion's arrival in France.

WAR DIARY: 19 MARCH 1918
By train to Etricourt.
Relieved 1st Berkshire Regiment.

Then at 4.15am on Friday, 21 March, while Laurie was in the front line, the bombardment began. Trench mortars pounded the front-line troops and heavy concentrations of gas shells targeted our lines. Long-range guns sent high-bursting shrapnel shells over our Headquarters and support lines miles behind the forward positions.

140 Brigade was sent to hold the right front which was adjacent to the 9 Scottish Division. By 9.00am the bombardment was particularly intense and we had suffered many casualties, especially from the gas-shells. The men of 15 Battalion had to wear gas masks for long periods whilst continuously repelling the enemy's fighting patrols.

WAR DIARY: 21 MARCH 1918
Heavy hostile bombardment.
   Casualties: 2 – killed
         38 – wounded or gassed

During the night 17 and 18 London Regiments fell back leaving 15 Battalion trenches as front line.

During the night, the position on the right flank deteriorated and the Battalion withdrew in accordance with a pre-arranged plan to a line of trenches some 2000 yards behind. The Germans made repeated endeavours to reach our new positions, but our machine guns, Lewis guns and snipers had been well placed, and all day the enemy was prevented from gaining further ground.

But on the right flank things were going badly, and as early as 7.30am it was clear the withdrawal of 9 Division meant 140 Brigade was now dangerously exposed and was forced once again to withdraw, but not without considerable pressure. The new trenches were only half-dug and there was little wire. The artillery were moving to new positions, and a protective barrage during the night was out of the question. No sooner had preparations been made to defend this line than 9 Division retired once more, again leaving the right flank open. Should the enemy succeed in turning this flank, the disaster would be incalculable.

15 Battalion was on the extreme right flank. It had an anxious and heavy task to perform, and the fact that no Germans filtered through throws great credit on the way the patrols and machine gunners did their work that night.

The situation changed in the morning. From that point on, the fighting was more open. Up to then we had been prepared to defend for a long period every new position taken up as we retired. But the operation was far more extensive than we knew, the enemy's success more penetrating than we could have imagined, and from now on the Battalion's task was not to hold definite positions to grim death, but to keep the enemy's advance in check and at all costs to prevent him striking in behind us, thereby cutting off our troops and rolling up the flank of the entire Army.

15 Battalion once more gave ground when a gap on the right allowed the German machine guns to enfilade our flank. The enemy realized the situation and made desperate efforts to get through the gap and behind 140 Brigade, and it was due to the prowess of 15 and 18 Battalions and R.E. Companies that he was prevented from doing so. Heavy fighting took place. The enemy advanced, supported by trench-mortar, machine-gun and artillery fire; close fighting ensued, in which one Company of 15 Battalion was surrounded and, unfortunately, never extricated.

There is no doubt that the frustration of the enemy's plan of rolling up our line from the position to which he had penetrated on our right rear on this occasion saved the Division and the right of the Third Army from disastrous results.

WAR DIARY: 22 MARCH 1918
Orders received to withdraw to Desert Ridge Switch

23 March was a hard day. The enemy continued to attack in strength. Our men were tired from the strenuous fighting of the previous few days and continued to fall back. The gap on our exposed right flank was for ever widening. All day the artillery was in action covering the infantry's withdrawal. Batteries "leap-frogged" back to new positions.

For three days the troops had been fighting and marching, digging and manoeuvring without ceasing. From now on the operations were of an even more open nature. The men adapted themselves well to the new conditions, and Lewis gun and rifle fire were very effectively maintained throughout. The men were still unshaken, but tired. There had been no sleep; food had been eaten when and how it could. Casualties had been heavy, and men had become separated from their units. The consolidation of a definite line of defence was a practical impossibility.

WAR DIARY: 23 MARCH 1918

During the day a concerted German attack was launched resulting in D Company being surrounded by the enemy and the Battalion became seriously fragmented.

Casualties:	Killed	2	
	Wounded	6 Officers,	71 Other ranks
	Missing-	6 Officers	210 Other ranks

5.30pm	Orders received to withdraw to Martinpuich Battalion strength now 230.

On the morning of 24 March, massed attacks were made against our positions round Mesnil village. Fighting was severe, with hand-to-hand encounters. Attack after attack was repulsed with a vigour which must have surprised the enemy, and it was not till 2.00pm that most of our men finally left the village. The afternoon saw more hard fighting and yet more ground was given to the enemy.

Feet were sore with marching over rough country; stomachs were yearning for nourishment; mouths parched; bodies tired with a heavy, numbing fatigue; these things produced a desolate feeling akin to the quiet sorrow of the desolation of the Somme countryside. It was a sharp, cold night. German aeroplanes had been flying low all the afternoon, firing machine guns at our retreating infantry, and bombing the transport and areas where men assembled.

The rumble of wheels was the only sound to be heard. Occasional Very lights reminded the men the enemy was very near; where, exactly, no one knew – nor did one worry, for what was uppermost in the mind then was food and sleep. Food there was – for the convoy got through safely – but very little sleep.

During the morning of the 25th a determined attack by the enemy was repulsed with rifle, Lewis-gun and machine-gun fire. After this we were able to inflict many casualties and 140 Brigade was able to consolidate its position. Then, for a while, the left flank became exposed. (At this point, as Laurie makes clear in his letter of 3 April, he and two friends were positioned on the extreme left flank and found themselves in a highly perilous position.) Then, late in the day, fresh reinforcements arrived, but at 6.00pm the enemy entered Pozières on the left. 37 Brigade then set the ammunition dumps on fire, and during the evening the ammunition exploded all over the area where the village had once been, and a great fire lit up the surrounding countryside.

Then came the order to retire, and finally, – for the first time since 21 March – there was no need to fear a big outflanking movement on the sides. This gave everyone a feeling of enormous relief since for several days there was a very real fear of attack coming from all sides.

15 Battalion, along with the rest of 47 Division, were relieved during the night of 25–26 March. This was no ordinary relief. It embraced much more than the mere handing over of the battle-front to another division. It meant that the anxiety of having to protect the flank of the great Third Army was over. It meant rest, food, shelter and – sleep.

War Diary: 25 March 1918

10.0am	Battalion withdrew to a position along Contalmaison Ridge. This position was held by rifle fire and bayonet fighting until withdrawal.	
Casualties:	Killed	4
	Wounded	5
	Missing	4

The troops were now exhausted. Everywhere men slept – in stables, barns, beds, wagons, and even by the roadside. Wherever a man could find a quiet place he slept, not caring where the other man was, or what was happening. There was, for the moment, no longer need to care. Many had not slept for six days. After the day's hard fight was over there had been no rest. Night after night the troops had to march back to the new position assigned to them for the morrow's fighting. A more strenuous six days had never been endured

169

by the Division. The casualty list was a heavy one. The total losses of the Division had been:

	Officers	Other ranks
Killed	16	166
Wounded	75	985
Missing	70	1,079
Total	161	2,230

WAR DIARY: 26 MARCH 1918
3.00am   Battalion marched cross country to Aveluy + Bouzincourt.
4.00pm   Battalion marched to Louvencourt.

WAR DIARY: 27 MARCH 1918
9.00am   Battalion marched to Clairfaye Farm.
4.30pm   Battalion marched to Toutencourt.

WAR DIARY: 28 MARCH 1918
12 noon   Battalion marched to Warloy.

Easter Sunday, 1918 (31 March)

My Dear Connie,

I hope you have received the P.P.C. sent off yesterday and the Field Cards of various dates *[These have not survived]*.

My long silence needs no excuse. Your daily papers are a sufficient explanation. In the course of a few days I am hoping to get off a long letter to you. Meanwhile, will you please come to my aid as quickly as possible. As I told you yesterday all my personal belongings have "gone west". During the past days of difficulty and exposure I have been without overcoat, waterproof sheet, clean socks, towel, soap, razor, etc. Most of the things lost will, of course, be replaced by the Army as soon as possible.

Will you send out as soon as you can some safety razor blades (or safety razor complete), some notepaper and envelopes, two pairs of socks, a stick of shaving soap and a spoon? These are my most urgent needs. Fritz has got some fine things of mine, including half a dozen little books in art bindings, bought as souvenirs in various large French towns and cities. Still, I am out of his clutches and I guess that is what you are keenest about.

By the way, leave is now naturally washed out. Don't expect me now until my knock comes at the door. The cold in the head is no worse, although yesterday again I got very wet. We have recently been acting as runners. Food has, of course, been plainer and more scanty. It is a long time now since I tasted bread. Another thing which I greatly regret losing is my diary for 1917. Still, if you have kept the long descriptive letters, I shall probably be able to remember most of the places with the aid of a good map.

I hope Mother will keep her spirits up. I believe the worst is over now and that the tide is slowly turning. Trust you and Flossie are alright.

All my love to you, Yours ever,
Laurie.

Another letter dated Easter Sunday, 1918

My Dear Connie,

The time has at length arrived when I can attempt some description of my small part in these last momentous days. I have been sorely buffeted by Fate and indeed have often felt more like a feather in a whirlpool than a free agent in an orderly universe. If I can succeed in making you appreciate the suddenness with which events moved and the extreme gravity of our peril, you will readily join with me in a prayer of gratitude for my deliverance and preservation.

As is so common, there was a calm before the storm. We were spending a not unenjoyable time in the camp on the fringe of the ruined village. On the 13th an American bishop spoke to us as we lay on the grass under a genial sun on America's participation in the war and the genuineness of their efforts. I remember also hearing a new word for the first time – "Tankodrome" – it is self-explanatory.

The Battalion went out up the line on working parties and we Police were on a kind of guard over the camp each evening. So we were the right men to notice the gradually increasing intensity of the artillery fire during the small hours. Enemy aircraft were pretty active, but did no damage locally.

On the 18th March we had the official celebration of the Battalion's arrival in France. It was a wonderful day. The sun did its best. Early in the morning we had a short commemorative service. Special food was provided – eggs with our breakfast bacon, very rich stew at dinner-time with cabbages, onions and carrots, and stewed fruit with milk at teatime. During the afternoon there was a good concert, the Band played at intervals, and there were some amusing sports. There were no parades all day! And so to bed, as Pepys would say.

Tuesday the 19th was a very different sort of day. It marks, too, the commencement of that long series of misadventures which has left me in so bedraggled a condition and which bade fair more than once to give me my quietus altogether. It poured with rain from very early in the morning and we received orders to proceed to the trenches. Part of the way we travelled by light railway [to Etricourt]. We took over a section of the front line which we had never before visited, though it was near enough to several well-known villages. The accommodation was poor and the trenches were very muddy. I shared a little cubby-hole with another fellow. It poured all night, so each turn of sentry-duty made us wetter than before.

The weather improved greatly the following day. The wind and sun dried our clothes but made such a sticky paste of the mud that walking became an exertion. I went down to our Brigade H.Q. on a bomb-carrying fatigue.

In the early hours of the morning of Thursday, the 21st, the storm broke upon us. At 4.45 the Germans commenced a furious bombardment. Predominant among the crashing clangour rose the curious whining whistle of the gas-shell. The trenches were soon foggy with gas, helmets had hurriedly to be donned and we prepared ourselves for the worst that might follow. For seven hours we sweated and suffered inside our gas masks. An occasional peep out to test the strength of the gas showed the sun shining as through a cloud. At length the air cleared. The bombardment, and our reply to it, continued, however, with unabated vigour. Towards evening a welcome lull came and we crept back to our shelters to snatch a few hours sleep.

Friday was a much more tranquil day for us, although conflicting reports kept reaching us concerning a great German attack. In the evening we moved for a few hours into a very large and deep dugout, formerly used as a Brigade H.Q. Then we marched out thinking we were bound for billets and a rest. Fond illusion! Try to imagine what it means to the infantryman, weary, half-gassed and coated in mud, to be on the way to some barn or cellar in a much-shattered village. It is home to him. There he has comforts unknown in the line. He sleeps in a blanket, and with his boots off. Some kind of social enjoyment is usually possible. This however was not for us.

As we marched along, great fires were blazing in different quarters, some with reverberations and explosions like the outpourings of a miniature volcano. We emerged from a cross-country track onto

172

a high road, along which we marched merrily, all unsuspicious of the menace which stalked ahead. Presently the head of the column halted. A short consultation of officers was held, and then quickly we were ordered to dig ourselves in. The Germans were not far off up the road! The remainder of the night and the morning hours were spent in making our position as safe as possible. Meanwhile, other Battalions were gradually being withdrawn from the encircling movements of great masses of German troops. They came trooping across through our positions, pursued by machine-gun fire. The Battalion held on to facilitate their retirement. At length our companies were being hard pressed and in places badly bombed. So H.Q. Company, including, of course, myself, were sent out to cover their withdrawal. We lay down in a thin line across a bare open field, loaded our rifles, fixed our bayonets and waited for the enemy.

He was not long in coming! A German aeroplane heralded his approach and fired some unavailing shots at us. The young runner with whom I had spent so many delightful hours over the chess-board lay next to me. A bullet came from somewhere and he crawled back – a hole clean through the centre of his hand. At this moment I remembered my letters, received that morning, one from home, one from Arthur and one from Miss Marshall. Flat on my stomach, in the field with Fritz gradually tightening his net around us, I read them and drew courage from their affectionate messages.

Not long after, the Battalion retired and after a few shots at a sudden swarm of active blue-grey figures on both our flanks, we followed. All the way up a long exposed hillside under a hot sun, we were pursued by a hail of machine-gun bullets. Hardly any experience in warfare is so painful as to retire under intense fire like this. Still, it was done, and, on the crest of the hill, we reformed and once more faced our foe. It was now certain that only great good fortune and clever leadership could extricate us from the trap which Fritz had laid for us. On each flank he had made such progress that only one small avenue of escape was left, like the neck of a bottle.

Twice we retired and twice reformed, to delay the enemy's progress. The time thus gained enabled guns, transport and other troops to get through the neck of the bottle. Our duty was to fight rearguard actions and get out as best we could afterwards. Towards evening, weary beyond measure, but not beaten, we ourselves stood in the last trench across the avenue to safety. Again enemy aeroplanes located us, dropped signal lights and got their artillery to work. We served our purpose. He stayed his advance a bit in order to batter our trench with his guns. Soon after, we retired once more, this time through a hell of cross-fire. It was as though he knew we were eluding him. How we got through that belt of death I hardly know. After that he followed us with heavy shells, but we were contemptuous of these.

We reached our appointed resting place and had two hours' rest on the grass. Then, to our dismay, we were told to occupy a defensive line once again. We could hardly drag one leg after the other, yet, such was the personal magnetism of the Colonel who now commanded our very mixed ranks, that we followed him without hesitation. As we topped a little ridge we were observed and immediately shelled so heavily that for three hours there was nothing to do but lie flat in shell-holes. One shell fell in water and splashed me with evil-smelling mud, and another made me deaf on one side for the rest of the day.

After this episode the scattered remnants of our party were gathered together and marched several miles to a little village, where our transport lines were. We had some hot tea (how we needed it!) and some bread and cheese and then turned in. It was half an hour after midnight and we had been continuously in action for nearly twenty-four hours. My bed was a shell-hole. Frost had made the grass stiff and white, and I had no scarf, no overcoat, no ground-sheet, no gloves. Yet I slept!

This is as much as I will tell you this time. In a day or two I will try to send you some account of my further experiences. They are, I can assure, not less exciting than these. I have just received your parcel of the 16th. Oh, many, many thanks. Those biscuits were a Godsend. We have had no bread, nothing but Army biscuits since the 23rd. *[That is eight days since.]*

My health is still alright, barring the cold. I have found a scarf now. Hope all are well.

My fondest love. Yours ever,

Laurie

Wednesday, 3 April 1918

My Dear Connie,

I hope you have duly received the long letter sent off on Easter Monday. Will you please let Arthur see it. I am too tired to write a separate account to him, and indeed my little stock of paper will not allow it. Where you find that I have only succeeded in bewildering you, he will probably be able to explain things. It is difficult to maintain coherency in any description of these last chaotic days.

Before continuing to the point where my last letter ended, let me make a few general remarks. The great German push commenced with artillery fire of overwhelming intensity, but each day this factor became of less and less importance. Soon the enemy was using only a few field pieces which he had managed to push forward behind his waves of infantry. As for our artillery, it simply was not there. It was all retreating post haste. The same applies largely to the air service. Instead of our relying on their aid, we ourselves had to form a flesh and blood barrier against their capture.

At length trench warfare was over. Both armies worked in the open. In spite of his losses, Fritz had massed such numbers of men against us that for days his pressure remained constant. Each stand of ours dwindled our numbers and soon units were isolated. There was no connection on the right or left. Both flanks were usually "in the air". The German plan of advance seemed always to avoid a direct frontal attack. This was lucky for them, for we have a good proportion of fine shots and were also never short of machine guns. A frontal attack could have been staged, but instead the enemy would feel cautiously till the gaps were found and then creep through these gaps, concealed from view by the numerous ridges which are the conspicuous natural feature of this part of France. With our flanks exposed to lateral fire we were helpless, and a further withdrawal would follow.

Motor machine guns were much employed on either side. Ours are mounted on motorcycles with sidecars. They were of course limited to the roads.

You left me asleep in a shell-hole in the transport field. Two or three times I had to get up and stamp about to induce a little warmth. At 6.30 I decided I had slept long enough, and lo! where was the transport? They had moved hurriedly and I was stranded. So for this day my fortunes were not shared with the Battalion. They were away in a fresh position where we will join them later. I made what enquiries I could of traffic control police, who were themselves preparing for instant flight. Then off I trudged to find the transport lines.

A mile up the road I came upon lines of troops awaiting an attack. Fritz was still advancing and further progress along the road was barred. So I left the main road and pushed off through a large wood, passing the most completely ruined villages I have ever seen. You could always pick out the church, however. The church bell on top of a huge mound of bricks revealed it. For several hours I was thus walking on the fringe of an engagement, with the rattle of musketry and machine guns in my ears. At length I came out onto one of the great main roads. What a spectacle! As far as the eye could see – and the road was dead straight – spread one great, long snake of traffic, all in one direction. An Army was in retirement, our trench system had been perforated, and here were all the guns, ammunition limbers, motor lorries, ambulances, staff cars, G.S. waggons and travelling cookers.

It was past midday and I had not eaten since the night before. On the side of the road were derelict camps, deserted hutments and lines of tents. In places great stacks, including officers' valises, had been abandoned. I found a loaf in one hut. Half I gave to two other hungry stragglers and half I kept for myself. Later I found some bully beef and a delicious bottle of pickles. I feasted royally on the roadside, while the stream of traffic poured on and on. An hour or so later I had definite information as to where to go, and also met a few of our own fellows, stranded like myself. We fried some bacon for tea and had some bread fried in the fat. I have had no bread since then, nothing but biscuits.

At one point we passed a Chinese labour squad, carrying huge loads hung on the ends of bamboo rods, which they balanced on their shoulders.

At length we reached our new transport lines and, after a short rest, paraded and formed part of a group which was to rejoin the rest of the Battalion. That night we lay out along an embankment as an outpost guarding a string of transport. In the small hours of the 25th (Monday) we were taken off and rejoined the Battalion. They were occupying a position not unfamiliar to the old men. This was the very battlefield where so many of our comrades fell in 1916. Then we were attacking, now we were being forced back over the very ground we had torn from the clutch of the enemy. *[They were once again on the Albert – Bapaume road.]*

Soon after daybreak news was brought to Headquarters – a ditch – that the Germans were massing in great numbers behind a certain wood *[High Wood.]*. I was standing as a sentry with a whistle ready. As soon as an observer in front gave a signal, I should blow alternate long and short blasts as an alarm. Meanwhile the padré held a very short service. A solemn prayer, with Fritz massing for an advance not many hundreds of yards away and no artillery to stay his passage. The wood, however, frightened him. He feared a trap and commenced pushing round the edges, so that our lines held him up for several hours.

We were then marched to a very high ridge *[Contalmaison Ridge]*, overlooking an important town, where we began to prepare an emergency firing-line. A friend and I managed to make a small fire and enjoyed a drink of cocoa, made with rainwater from a shell-hole. A curious little incident occurred here. We heard a sudden buzzing behind us and turned to find a German aeroplane swooping down upon us. He was only a couple of hundred feet up when he was met with a volley of rifle bullets from our fellows, which evidently "put the wind up him", for he quickly mounted and flew away.

Soon after, we had a long cross-country march to a fresh part of the line. Once more we were front-line troops. In front was a village *[Pozières]*. It was not known whether Fritz was there or not. Two roads led towards us from this village and we commanded these roads. I was on the extreme left of our Battalion with two friends. On our left was a gap and a ridge which hid the further country from view. No one knew where the Battalion, supposed to be on our left, actually was, but we had to hold on till morning. Evening came and dark, and with the darkness two famous Battalions passed through us to push the Germans out of the village, if it were found to be occupied. They found it empty, but, before leaving, set fire to a great dump of shells and s.a.a. (small arms ammunition). The flames rose to a great height, with a loud continuous roar. There were frequent explosions, and at times, although it was night, the light was too fierce to be looked at steadily. The dump burned for a good twenty hours.

Early in the morning of the 26th we found that the Germans were forming up along the ridge I have already mentioned. We were accordingly withdrawn and wasted no time over the manoeuvre. We marched so far that we had high hopes that we were being taken back for a rest, and heaven knows we needed it. But not for us yet. Once more we were formed up in a line and told to dig ourselves in. We understood that it was an emergency position and that we were to get it ready for fresh troops to occupy.

Each man dug himself a little pit from which he could comfortably fire, with plenty of head and shoulder cover. They looked horribly like vacant graves when they were done. By this time German shells were falling on the little village *[Aveluy]* which lay in front. This task completed, we marched a further three miles to another village *[Bouzincourt]* and had a few hours' rest. I had the first shave (with a borrowed razor) since the imbroglio started and changed my socks. Our band was playing bright marches in the village square. It struck me as somewhat incongruous, but quite British, for the band to play ragtime in one part of the village, while shells burst on the other, and the great tide of German invasion swept irresistibly on.

Our orders to move soon arrived and we marched out, band still playing merrily, to a village five or six miles away *[Louvencourt]*. Here we billeted in a barn and I managed to get five hours' sleep.

We rose early the next morning (the 27th) and marched beyond a certain village *[Clairfaye]* and aerodrome. Here we composed an outpost. All we knew was that certain troops had to arrive at some unknown destination and that, if they could get there, Fritz would probably receive a definite check. We had to see that they arrived before Fritz did and therefore must hold on, whatever happened, until our troops had arrived. The Padré held another service in which he prayed that our reinforcements might arrive in time – a prayer which was answered. You can guess perhaps a little of the responsibility and solemnity of these days. But how inexpressibly weary we were. But not beaten. Never accuse us of that.

Early in the evening the danger was over. We marched to yet another village *[Toutencourt]* and slept in an empty house. Before dinner on the 28th we were off again to a larger village *[Warloy]*. Here the Police were told off to act as Battalion runners. It was very showery and, as I had no overcoat, I was soon wet through. I was doing runs for the Battalion until half past twelve at night.

This, I think, is a fitting point at which to close. I trust this very lengthy epistle has not wearied you, but the newspaper accounts of the affair are all written from the Staff point of view, so that of the infantryman in the line may be fresh. My next letter will, I hope, bring my account right up to date.

My own health is fairly good. I cannot get rid of my cough and cold, but don't worry. It will go sooner or later.

Fondest love and best wishes,

Laurie.

The respite was a brief one. The following day Laurie's Battalion was on the move again – and back to the front at Martinsart.

WAR DIARY: 29 MARCH 1918
6.00pm Battn marched to Front line – Martinsart

WAR DIARY: 30–31 MARCH 1918
Quiet day

It was at this point Laurie learnt that at last the withdrawal was to cease. Each unit received a copy of Sir Douglas Haig's stark order, which read:

"Every position must be held to the last man: There must be no retirement. With our backs to the wall and believing in the justice of our cause, each one of us must fight on to the end."

The Battalions were very much reduced in strength and the men were weary. A composite battalion formed from the remnants of 19 and 20 Battalions relieved 15 Battalion on 1 April. They moved back to Senlis for a few day's rest before again returning to the line on 4 April.

WAR DIARY: 1 APRIL 1918
Battalion relieved by 20 London Regiment to proceed to Brigade Reserve. Billets at Senlis

	Killed	4
Casualties:	Wounded	4

WAR DIARY: 2–3 APRIL 1918
Reorganization and bathing.

WAR DIARY: 4 APRIL 1918
Battalion relieved 21 London Regiment in front line. B & D Companys in reserve.

Sunday, 7 April 1918.

My Dear Mother,
I have received Connie's letter of the 26th and yours and Flossie's of Easter Day. I am very pleased and proud to find you all keeping so resolute and cheerful during these days of waiting. Surely by now you have received one of my cards or letters. Field cards went off on 20th, 21st, 26th, 27th and 29th. Then on the 30th I despatched a picture card and wrote a letter on the 31st. So you see it is the fault of the postal authorities if you have been without any news of me.

My letter of the 3rd took events down to the Thursday *[28th March.]* before Easter. On Good Friday we found, in a cellar of a deserted house, a jar of honey and some potatoes. These later we cut into pieces and fried in fat. The Battalion went into the line in the evening. The Police were left at the Stores and Transport lines to act as runners. We take messages from the Battalion Orderly Room to Brigade and Division 1 H.Q., to Transport, the Stores, and so on. It keeps us on our feet a good bit, but it is interesting and heaps better than in the line just now!

There was heavy rain on the 30th and the streets were awash. In the afternoon we loaded up Lewis-gun magazines for despatch to the line. It rained again on Easter Day. In the evening I saw the regimental band of a very famous regiment play what is known as the "retreat". They were a wonderful sight in that filthy, nearly-deserted French village. Not a spot of mud on them, brass glittering, drumstrings and belts pipeclayed – good enough for Hyde Park or Buckingham Palace! Hopelessly useless here, though, I thought. The most unkempt, ragged, out-at-elbows boy in the Battalion has without a doubt done more to hold back the German peril than all that "posh" band put together.

On Easter Monday *[31st]* I met Cliff (Tanner). He is quite all right and was very pleased to see me again. The Battalion moved out of the line to a little village *[Senlis]* not far behind and the Police were sent for to make a Battalion gas-guard. We were roused from our beds in a loft and marched off to the village, reaching it at 3 in the morning. For three days we did this day and night gas guard. There was a great deal of rain and a great deal of shelling, but we spent a fairly jolly time there.

In the evening of the 4th the Battalion went into the line again and the Police became runners at the other village as before. My birthday was quite a happy day. We had our first bread for a fortnight – a fifth of a loaf each. In a farmhouse where the people still remained, I had a plate of fried potatoes and some lukewarm coffee. After waiting an hour and a quarter in a queue outside a Canteen I got a tin of sardines for tea. One house was demolished and a lorry was blown to atoms, a bridge damaged, and the hospital had a shell through the roof. The casualties were not very numerous fortunately.

We are still in this village and carrying on as runners. My cold is slightly better. Fondest love to you all, etc.
Laurie

WAR DIARY: 5TH APRIL 1918

7.00am	Enemy opened heavy bombardment with high explosive and gas shells on our front line & support trenches & on Bouzincourt. Except for these short intervals of about half an hour each, this bombardment continued until 4.30pm. From 1.30pm to 4.30pm the bombardment of Bouzincourt was particularly

	intense. Enemy's machine guns were very active all day on our front line & support trenches with both direct and indirect fire. Before 7.00am enemy were seen on the crest in twos and threes (total about 150) some carrying timber. Our rifle fire caused these parties to keep down & dispersed them.
10.00am	Enemy in twos and threes dribbled over crest & made use of cover afforded by huts and sheds to get to the trees & broken ground (total about 300, with light machine guns). Rifle and Lewis gun fire was opened on these targets as they appeared. Enemy's machine guns (two) & minenwerfer (two) enfiladed our trenches all day. The enemy in the broken ground pushed forward & in some places were within 100 yards of our front line. These parties showed up several times as if about to rush our trenches, but never succeeded in leaving the broken ground. Our rifle and Lewis gun fire was opened on them whenever they appeared.
11.00am	Enemy seen digging-in along the crest as if consolidating a position.
1.00pm	No further signs of enemy advancing. Our artillery was sweeping the ground and the crest with great effect. Between 7.00am and 9.00am parties of enemy were seen advancing in a north-westerly direction towards the south-west edge of Aveluy Wood. Lewis gun & rifle fire was opened on them from our front line at range of about 1,800 yards.

Casualties:	Killed in action -	2 Lieutenant S.G.Clarke & 5 Other ranks
	Wounded	2 Lieutenant E.S.Shepherd, 2 Lieutenant L.A.Nutbrown & 37 Other ranks

	Lieutenant. Colonel W.H.E.Segrave, DSO slightly affected by gas and ordered by G.O.C. Division to proceed to Transport lines for a rest.
9.00pm	D Company relieved No.2 Company 21 London (on left point) who proceeded into support.

WAR DIARY: 6 APRIL 1918

7.00am	Enemy in twos and threes were walking about open ground under cover of the mist. Our snipers got many

targets and one of above enemy was captured after being wounded.

There was shelling by the enemy throughout the day. Enemy machine gun was very active. Our artillery was put on to it and obtained several direct hits on target, which silenced the machine gun.

8.00am	Enemy opened heavy bombardment to our right which spread to our front & continued till 10.00pm gradually dying down. No infantry movement was seen. The remainder of the night was quiet
11.00pm	B Company relieved C Company (centre front) who proceeded to support.

Casualties:	Killed	3 Other ranks
	Wounded	3 Other ranks

WAR DIARY: 7 APRIL 1918
Battalion relieved. To Billets in Senlis

Casualties:	Killed	1
	Wounded	4
	Missing-	3

WAR DIARY: 8 APRIL 1918
Marched to Hédauville

WAR DIARY: 9 APRIL 1918
Draft of 590 Other Ranks joined the Battalion.

WAR DIARY: 11 APRIL 1918
Marched to Domart.

WAR DIARY: 12 APRIL 1918
Marched to Cachy.

WAR DIARY: 13 APRIL 1918
Re-organisation – Cleaning up.

The Spring German offensive in France involved three million of their men in a bid to smash the allies before US troops arrived at the front. Their forty-mile advance resulted in 80,000 allied prisoners being taken.

The success of the German offensive at the end of March shocked the

Government and the nation at home into seeing the urgency of the need for more men, and large reinforcements were hastily sent across the Channel. During the first week in April over 3,000 new troops, mostly boys of eighteen, joined 47 Division and had a very uncomfortable first taste of active service. They were absorbed into the Battalions on 9 April.

Saturday, 13 April 1918.

My Dear Connie,

It is a great relief to know that communication between us has been restored and that you are gradually receiving my letters. By now you have probably had those of the 3rd and 7th – sequels to that commenced on Easter Sunday.

There are many things which I, on my part, must acknowledge. First, I want you to thank Mother and Flossie for their nice birthday cards and wishes. Words fail me when I think of the two parcels – that of the 28th March and that of the 5th April. All my wants supplied, supplied lavishly and with extreme speed. My smallest expressed wish complied with, many of my desires anticipated. What other man can boast so good a Mother and sisters?

Now for the latest news. My last letter took us as far as the 7th. On Monday one of our Policemen put his foot between the beams which composed the floor of our loft, fell, and sprained his ankle badly. He was in pain all night and on Tuesday morning was wheeled into hospital in a wheelbarrow – our first casualty in the force during this "do". The rest of us left the village soon after. Our route lay through several villages lying in a pretty belt of country. A few miles took us clean beyond the ever-increasing belt of battle-scarred country into unspoiled France. We had a lift in a lorry for some 7 miles.

We halted near one of the largest aerodromes I have ever seen and watched the machines ascending and descending with as much precision as your train pulls up or starts again at Palmers Green station. At a large town we stayed for a meal. We were only able to get chocolate, biscuits, cake and a large tin of pears. After some hours the remainder of our Battalion, which had been in a different village nearer the line, came along in motor-buses. We joined them and were taken to our destination.

Our billet here *[in Hédauville]* was a poor one – a dilapidated barn with a damp earth floor. We were very tired and sleepy. It was

2.30 a.m. and we had travelled 16 or 17 miles. A very large draft had joined the Battalion. All our losses in men were made good and we were as strong numerically as we have ever been in France. Quite a number of the new recruits were nineteen or under. To see them makes me feel profoundly sad. I have seen many similar drafts before, and seen, too, what havoc War, that greatest of iconoclasts, plays among the ranks of these fair, young images of their Maker.

We remained in this village throughout Wednesday and I at last got a soft cap to wear in place of the heavy steel helmet which had been my only headgear for so long. After dinner on Thursday we marched for 12½ miles through some of the most lovely hill and vale scenery imaginable. At night we slept in a coachhouse *[in Domart]*. Jimmy Weedon and I slept under the coach itself. We were off again next morning for a tramp of 14 miles, so you can see we give our legs something to do. Our journey ended in a large straggling town *[Cachy]* and in a barn more draughty than most, even in France. Our pioneers have hung up sacks over the large holes, so it is a little more habitable now. The church has a quaint old stone figure over the porch, showing Christ seated, crowned with thorns and with hands tied.

This morning I attended the Nonconformist Church Parade. My cold is a bit better and, as we are expecting a period of rest, I shall soon be fit again. Events move so quickly nowadays that we cannot forecast where we shall be a week hence, but as far as we know we are to spend at least a week here.

I hope Mother is in good health, and yourself and Flossie. How long, how long have I to bear this agony of separation and loneliness? We sang this morning:

> "Holy Father, in Thy mercy,
> Hear our humble prayer.
> Keep our loved ones, now far absent,
> 'Neath Thy care."

I nearly forgot that I was a man. Ah me, a sad world when the humble ones sit and eat their hearts out for the lack of a word and a smile from those dearer far than life; when men must degrade themselves below the beasts, become more murderous than the tiger and steel themselves to look coolly at sights which must horrify the angels of God; when the military caste, devils incarnate, grow in power and force tortured humanity to work their wicked will. Yes, an evil world, yet we do not despair.

> "Oh, Joy that seekest me through pain,
>   I do not ask to turn from Thee,
> I trace the rainbow through the rain
>   And feel the promise is not in vain."

All my love, dear ones, Ever yours,
Laurie

Sunday, 21 April 1918.

My Dear Connie,

Before me lies quite a budget of letters. If I continue to receive such delightfully bulky posts I shall expect to read that the paper shortage is assuming alarming proportions. You know by now that all the parcels have been safely received. The Army, moving more tardily, supplied me with a ground-sheet and an overcoat two days ago. The overcoat is a good one, warm and yet very light to carry. As a matter of fact, one of my friends in the tailoring staff put it on one side specially for me.

Many thanks for your remarks concerning the letters. I am glad and sufficiently rewarded to know they are appreciated, but really you seem to be trying to turn my head a little by your flatteries. Should time permit I want to start another little effort in the course of the next few days. Has the Welsh paper published that other thing yet? As for after-the-war questions, I will deal with them as and when they arise, but it certainly is not my intention to throw up my Civil Service employment on the strength of the little (though cherished) successes I have had while out here.

In my letter of last Sunday I told you something about the peaceful little place we are now in *[Cachy]*. In spite of cold weather and some rain, the days are passing very pleasantly here. On Tuesday we were inspected by our Brigadier, and on Thursday by our Divisional Commander, who, in quite a good speech, after thanking us for services rendered in the recent operations, compared this present crisis with the Battle of Waterloo. In that battle the British, greatly outnumbered, withstood numerous attacks by Napoleon's picked regiments, waiting for the arrival of the reinforcements which turned the tide of fortune for the day. They held on stubbornly until at length the great leader gave the historic order "Let the whole line advance" – and Victory followed.

So, said the General, we believe and trust it will be in this great offensive. Hold on yet a little longer and victory will again be ours.

In the afternoon of the 18th I obtained a pass permitting me to visit a city some seven miles distant *[Amiens]*. We gave the grand old church a thorough inspection and then had a very nice meal in a French restaurant. It was a quaint, interesting place and I greatly enjoyed the visit.

Yesterday morning I did some firing at the ranges and was fairly successful. We only fired ten shots and I got ten hits! In the rapid they made a 6-inch group, in the deliberate a 3-inch. Rather nasty for the Hun, five bullets in a 3-inch ring.

Today there were some sports, but I was on duty some distance away from the field, directing officers, etc., and also competitors in the cross-country race.

I must make special mention of the great encouragement I draw from the letters sent to me. They are so brimful of helpfulness and love. Arthur wrote me a wonderful letter and Miss Sharp has also written very nicely. Miss Marshall is a faithful correspondent and the letters from home never fail. All my thanks.

My fondest love to you three, Ever your affectionate brother,
Laurie

Sunday, 28 April 1918.

My Dear Mother,

Thank you for your letter of last Sunday's date. I am sorry to hear you have not been quite so well lately and hope that your health will soon improve.

We are still where we were last Sunday *[Cachy]*, but there are sure signs of an imminent move. The week has passed very pleasantly and we have all benefited greatly by our rest. The mornings have generally been spent on the range, either firing or acting as a Range Warden, i.e. superintending the posting of sentries with red flags, the pasting over of the targets and so on.

The Battalion have played several football matches and yesterday a match was to have been followed by a concert given by our Divisional Follies. Unfortunately it came on to rain just as they commenced and, as the stage was erected in the middle of an open field, first the spectators and then the performers took a hasty departure.

It is good news that Bert is at the Base. These are weeks when the ordinary risks of the line are doubled or trebled. I hope he will be allowed to stay there.

The news is still serious reading. The affair at Zeebrugge was glorious, but the Germans have not yet made their final throw. Not yet are their reserves dissipated, not yet is the crisis for the Allies past. By the time you receive this letter the Battalion may be under very different conditions from those under which I write. Still, I beg you to remain calm and confident. "So long Thy power hath blessed me, sure it still will lead me on."

My cold is certainly better. I hope Connie and Flossie are both well. All my love to you, Your affectionate son,
Laurie.

Chapter Fourteen

Summer 1918,
and the Hundred Days

May, June and July were very quiet months, but there were many alarms. At first it was confidently expected that the Germans would make another attempt to capture Amiens and to force their way down the Somme. However, apart from a number of incidents, no serious operations erupted.

The summer months of 1918 were remarkable for two arrivals. The first was an epidemic of influenza, which during the following winter spread with alarming results to the United Kingdom. The fever itself was not particularly severe, but it had the effect, particularly on the younger men, of making them unfit for hard work for some weeks after the attack. The effective strength of the Division was thus seriously impaired.

The second arrival was the American Army. The appearance of these new troops, with their fine physique and frank inexperience, had a valuable effect on all the men and gave them a wholesome sense of being old soldiers.

47 Division then had a valuable spell of rest and training in Corps Reserve towards the end of June.

Postcard dated Sunday, 7 July 1918.

My Dear Flossie,
I hope you are getting out a good deal for walks, etc., while this splendid weather lasts. H.Q. Coy had their photos taken yesterday. I will send you a copy as soon as possible. The latest craze here is the game of baseball. Our American doctor is, naturally enough, the best exponent. My health is A1 again now. Hope all at home are well,
Fondest love,
Laurie.

My Dear Connie,

Thank you for your letter of the 3rd and for that very nice parcel. I am glad to hear that you have escaped the all-prevalent influenza so far and hope your good fortune will persist. Probably a general change in the weather will sweep it all away. There seems little doubt that it has been a contributory factor in delaying the German offensive this summer. And as time is supposed to be on our side, we must regard the influenza as an ally.

It is quite foolish to allow speculation as to when I shall get my next leave to interfere with any convenient plans for a seaside holiday. But, anyway, mind you get as much open air as possible. I fancy you will find a great change in me in this respect aprés la guerre. I shall feel cramped within the four walls of a room. So here is something to look for in our new house. It should have a good open aspect and a garden large enough for one to read and write in without feeling the presence of neighbours almost at one's shoulders. There should be an abundance of unbuilt-on land within easy reach and plenty of trees.

On Tuesday the 2nd I heard our Divisional Follies and on Monday, the 8th, there was an excellent Battalion Concert. Both these events took place in the beautiful grounds of a fine château here. The surrounding woods are very fine. In their abundance of fern, they remind me of Winchmore Hill. I have had a few wild strawberries from these woods.

I have had some good walks, visiting woods and villages not far distant. On Monday last I had to go to a large place about seven miles away as a witness at a district Court Martial. After the trial was over we spent an hour looking at the shops, etc. before marching back. Halfway home we halted at a farm and purchased some milk from a French refugee who had come from beyond Villers Bretonneux.

This is a poor village but I have enjoyed my sojourn here. There are not wanting signs that we shall be off in a few days time – where, I don't quite know.

Fondest love to you all, Your affectionate brother,

Laurie.

Saturday, 13 July 1918. (Excerpts)

My Dear Mother,

I am enclosing two copies of the H.Q. Company photograph which I told you about in my last letter. The Colonel is right in the centre with the Adjutant on his left and the R.S.M. on his right. As for myself, well, it would save you a violent shock if you could not find me, but look for a very cadaverous individual on the extreme right. When you have recovered from your fright will you please lock up one copy for me après la guerre and give the other away (or burn it!). *[This photograph still survives and is reproduced in this book.]*

Our clothing looks very rumpled. That is because our khaki has all been baked in a "Foden" fumigator. This operation caused some fun and excitement. In reading out the orders various names were substituted. One sergeant called it an incubator and another an incinerator (which is where we burn all our rubbish). I fear these errors were not quite as unintentional as they should have been.

The amusement was great when we paraded with our stuff ready for the fumigation. Shirts, pants, vests, trousers and tunics had to be made into bundles and carried to the boilers. This left us with only our overcoats to wear, and some of the fellows were frantically borrowing safety-pins and putting on buttons before venturing into the village streets.

Fondest love and best wishes to you, Connie and Flossie,

From your loving son,

Laurie.

Sunday, 21 July 1918. (Excerpts)

My Dear Mother,

My last long letter was written on the 10th. The following day the Battalion sports took place and were extremely interesting *[B Company won the 15 Battalion's three-legged race!]*. After the sports an open-air concert was held near the château. One of the West Indians (we have a batch of fellows who came all the way across the Atlantic to join up) is very clever at card tricks and he gave a most amusing exhibition of his skill.

On Friday morning *[12th]* we rose at 4.15 and breakfasted at 5. After a short uphill march we got into a long string of motor-charabancs and proceeded linewards. After a glorious ride we

190

dismounted at a place at which we spent some time early in April. It was not greatly altered, just a few more buildings bombed or broken down by shellfire.

On Saturday we had a bath and a change of clothes. The Colonel and Brigadier came round on a tour of inspection and included the baths. That is a feature of a soldier's life which I am not yet used to, even after three (nearly four) years in the Army, – there is no privacy. There is no moment in the whole 24 hours that you can spend free from intrusion.

Last Sunday I was on duty at Church Parade, held in the girls' school by permission of the French priest. On Monday afternoon we had a final treat before proceeding up the line. Our Divisional Follies gave a splendid entertainment to our Battalion only. I was doorkeeper and saw that only our men got in.

Our position that night was on the side of the road protected by a high bank. In the morning I went with a small party to a battered village a mile and a half away to draw water. Would you like your water to mean a three-mile walk for you? In the evening we went to a nearer village, as this time we should not be under observation, it being nearly dark.

We had a wonderful thunderstorm on Wednesday. The lightning lit up the ground with a queer radiance and the thunder was like a great barrage of guns. It was rather cold, too, for we do not take over-coats to the line now and of course have no blankets.

On Thursday evening we moved to another position, again behind a bank. The hot weather has been glorious for us. While in this position we did working parties, building dugouts, in addition to our normal police duties of gas guard, S.O.S. sentry, water and ration guard, traffic control, etc.

We are now in yet another position, having moved here with morning. I am in very good health and hope you, Connie and Flossie are the same.

All my love, etc., Your affectionate son,
Laurie.

Marshall Foch's great offensive in the Champagne began on 19 July and from that time on it became clear a move was imminent. On 2 August there were indications the Germans were withdrawing – explosions were heard in Albert and they began to shell their own line.

Then on 8 August, the British offensive began, and the Fourth Army's "Battle of 100 Days" started. More than 400 tanks spearheaded the allied assaults, backed up by aeroplanes strafing the enemy infantry and day and night bombing raids on their rear positions.

The Germans were pushed back to the position they held at the start of the spring offensive – the old Hindenburg Line. As the advance progressed small pockets of German infantry began to surrender. They were found hiding in shell-holes and ruined buildings, and offered no resistance. But many others still offered stiff resistance.

By 13 August Laurie's Battalion had been successively in and out of the line just east of Tailles Wood, and they maintained this uncomfortable position until the next advance on 22 August.

WAR DIARY: 22 AUGUST 1918
At 6.10am the Battalion marched forward by Companies at intervals of 100 yards, from the trenches near Marett Wood where they had rested for the night. By 7.50am the Battalion was in position at the rendezvous – the vicinity of the sunken road where we found a squadron of Cavalry – about eighty strong – waiting its turn to go forward. At 7.55am this squadron advanced to the attack, accompanied by Tanks, but both came dribbling back, about an hour later, having met with serious opposition.

WAR DIARY: 23 AUGUST 1918
At 4.30am the Battalion stood-to till daylight.

During the day the position occupied by the Battalion was subjected to considerable shelling from the enemy, mostly ineffective.

Orders were received for an attack to be made during the night on the Green Line and Happy Valley, in which 15 Battalion were detailed to act as "moppers up".

WAR DIARY: 24 AUGUST 1918
At 12.55am the Battalion assembled in the Chalk Quarry.

Soon after 1.00am (the zero hour), each Company having previously been allotted an area for the mopping up of which it was to be responsible, the Battalion moved forward under Major G.G.Bates, MC, and by 2.00am parties of prisoners began to reach H.Q. The operation had been entirely successful, the Battalion having captured some 300 prisoners in Happy Valley, as well as a considerable number of machine guns and some trench mortars.

At 4.45am I went forward to the Bray–Méaulte road where Major Bates had established his H.Q. The Division on our left had apparently been held up and a dangerous gap existed between their right and the left of 21 Battalion. For some hours the position at this point was precarious and, several times, enemy counter-attacks were threatened: in fact, as I crossed the open to reach my Companies an S.O.S. Rocket signal was fired from our outpost line. The enemy shell-fire was considerable at the time, and the ground was freely swept by his machine gun fire. The S.O.S. was repeated at 8.15am, but my Adjutant, Captain Paul Davenport, MC, whom I had sent forward to rearrange the Companies with a view to assisting the 21 Battalion to secure their exposed left flank, shortly returned to my H.Q. and reported the situation as well in hand.

WAR DIARY: 25 AUGUST 1918

The Battalion advanced to the attack behind a creeping barrage at 2.30am and reached the neighbourhood of the objective, some 2,500 yards in front of the starting line, practically without opposition. The casualties incurred, some thirty-five in number, were caused almost, if not entirely, by our own barrage.

A thick fog had settled down, and considerable difficulty was experienced in finding even so prominent a landmark as Bronfay Farm. However, in due course the objective was reached.

During the day walking round Happy Valley, we counted twenty-one enemy machine guns, which had covered this small valley; and there were probably more. There were also several Minenwerfers. The German dead, at a moderate estimate, must have exceeded 100. There was also a considerable number of German wounded, who, after their wounds had been dressed, we evacuated.

At 5.00pm an order was received to withdraw the Battalion to the Green Line for the night, and the following day it marched back to the trenches near Marett Wood taking with it one captured Minenwerfer, four heavy and ten light enemy machine guns.

WAR DIARY: 28 AUGUST 1918

At 11.45am Brigadier General H.B.Kennedy, C.M.G., D.S.O., inspected and addressed the Battalion, congratulating all ranks on the part played by the Battalion in the recent fighting.

WAR DIARY: 29 AUGUST 1918

At 2.00pm the Battalion marched. The Companies took up a line in front of the Briqueterie.

WAR DIARY: 30 AUGUST 1918

At 7.00am the Battalion marched to Maurepas Ravine where the day was spent. Considerable shelling from the enemy's heavy artillery was experienced during the day.

At 3.15pm the Adjutant (Captain Paul Davenport, MC.) was wounded by a shell which fell about 1,000 yards away from him. This point is of interest as evidence of the great spread caused by the instantaneous fuse, now almost universally employed by the enemy.

A draft of 100 men joined the Battalion this day.

WAR DIARY: 31 AUGUST 1918

The Battalion rested the day at Maurepas Ravine.

At 3.00pm orders were received for an attack to be made on the following morning.

Casualties 22–31 August 1918:

Officers:	Killed	–
	Died of wounds	1
	Wounded	2
	Missing	–
Other ranks:	Killed	7
	Died of wounds	1
	Wounded	48
	Missing	1

**M Fielding, Lt. Col.
Comdg. 1/Civil Service Rifles
(1/15 London Reg)**

It is apparent from the following letter that events were too hectic to allow frequent letter-writing and it is quite possible that some mail was lost in the rapid advance.

Wednesday, 11 September 1918.

My Dear Connie,

I know that in attempting to bridge the gap which exists between this letter and the last written to you I have taken up a heavy task. In fact, any adequate description of the storm of events which has swept us along during these days would require far greater powers than I possess. So please deal kindly with the writer grappling with a subject far too big for him and give your imagination a free rein to fill in and colour the vague outline which he offers.

In the letter of the 25th *[Missing]* I spoke of the cloud of an impending move hanging over us. The cloud burst that very after-noon, for I came back from the sunny hillside where I had been writing

194

and feeding a goat with biscuits to find everyone in the throes of packing up. We marched off across hilly and sparsely-populated country towards the line. Soon there were no civilians to be seen working in the fields and gradually we entered the zone of deserted villages, ruined houses, shell-holes, old gun positions, the hinterland of the actual war zone. I carried one of your hefty parcels on this little trek and earned its contents by the sweat of my brow.

The village at which our journey ended was crammed with troops and every available barn and shelter was crowded, the more so as a heavy thunderstorm came on, driving those indoors who would otherwise have slept in the open. The church here was not badly damaged, though every window was shattered by concussion. The following evening we moved again and slept, in the intervals of our gas guard, on little shelves cut out of the side of a trench.

On Tuesday morning *[27th]* we hunted out two nice little dugouts and occupied them (I am speaking now, of course, of the Police). Our Brigadier addressed the Battalion on Wednesday morning in a thunderstorm and gave us an inkling of what lay before us. That same evening our Divisional Follies were brought right up to the trenches and gave an open-air performance in a pretty little village. It would have made a good picture – the entertainers in their Pierrot costumes, the crowd of laughing boys, so many of whom were spending their last days on this troubled earth, the gathering shadows in the valley and, beyond, the flicker of the guns. After one very merry piece I chanced to look across the valley and there, in the last rays of the sun, lay half a dozen little white crosses – graves of the infantry. Such a wave of feeling swept over me then that for a time my own petty life and circumstances were lost. I was one with them, that glorious company of men who had fought and suffered for an ideal of righteousness, and who now gazed on the struggles of Time from the vantage ground of Eternity. But, alas, I cannot put my feelings into words. When I try I merely babble like a child. But, here we were, enjoying life to the full, all our cares forgotten. Yonder lay men who, in a quite true sense had died for us, and soon we must be prepared to make our own little sacrifice for the common weal.

"Rank graves of spendthrift infantry, who did not count the
     price,
"Nor asked the unborn world to mark their splendid sacrifice.
"You found the things of use and waste, all that you take or
     give,
"Upon the bayonets of men who died that you might live.

"Again you draw your wealth, your peace, again the world is
   free,
"Because of certain nameless graves that held the infantry."

On Thursday *[29th]* then, we set off once more, each man carrying a
pick and shovel, following up the retiring Germans. That night we
slept near an old German encampment, cleared of the enemy the day
before. His devilish ingenuity was still a menace, however. We were
in the area of hidden mines and traps. Special orders were issued and
great precautions taken. Nevertheless we suffered casualties. Three
innocent-looking stick bombs lay wired together. When picked up
they immediately exploded. In the roads at certain places lay buried
charges. A heavy lorry passing over would be blown up. Old dugouts
were filled with poison gas. On the steps were glass tubes filled with
gas, only requiring a slip of the foot to be released.

   We had a very early breakfast on Friday, the 30th, and moved off
on a long march immediately after. We are now *[at Maurepas Ravine]*
just in the rear of our attacking troops and we police were sent forward
to intercept straggling prisoners and to direct escorts where to conduct
their parties. We lay in a shattered wood under somewhat heavy shell-
fire and could watch the attack proceeding. It was very successful and
after midday we saw the guns moving forward and fresh troops
pressing on. Later in the day we returned to the main body of the
Battalion.

   On Saturday *[1st]* no water turned up and no rations for some long
time, so our breakfast was very late. We had to move from one trench
to another on account of the shelling. The evening was very cold and
we knew that Sunday morning would see the Battalion right in the
thick of it.

   Here I think I will stop for a while, but I want you to try to picture
the country as well as you can. Remember that all these woods and
villages have changed hands in this war, some as often as six or seven
times. The woods are mere collections of splintered stumps with,
however, a fairly strong undergrowth. The villages can only be identi-
fied by the notice-plates. Not a house stands and the heaps of ruins are
so overgrown with grass and weeds as to be indistinguishable from the
surrounding country. On most of the roads and tracks lie dead horses,
polluting the air, and in the fields and along the slopes run old broken-
down trench systems and rusted lines of barbed wire. It is a dreary,
desolate region, the greatest battlefield, I suppose, in the world.
Fondest love, etc.,
Laurie

War Diary: 1 September 1918

At 2.45am the Battalion moved up to its assembly positions.

Battalion H.Q. was established in a shell-hole near the assembly positions. A certain amount of shelling was encountered on the way up, and one shell which burst in the mouth of the new Battalion H.Q. unfortunately killed three, including Sergeant Moore the Signalling Sergeant, and wounding others.

Zero was fixed for 5.30am. After a five minutes "crash", the Battalion moved forward behind a creeping barrage. The attack was completely successful, prisoners beginning to come down within five to ten minutes of Zero.

Lieutenant E.R.Laselles, commanding C. Company, and 2 Lieutenant R.L.Kirk, whose first day in action in France it was, were killed early in the advance, but otherwise losses were slight, and by 7.30am all objectives had been reached, and were being consolidated.

Large numbers of prisoners and machine guns were captured – the Battalion's share amounting to about 150 – 200 men and some 10 machine guns.

During the process of consolidation, B and D Companys were subjected to heavy shelling from a German field gun battery which remained in action in the open, firing over open sights from about 1,000 yards range.

An attempt by the enemy at infiltration through a gap on our right was prevented from developing by Lewis gun fire.

At 6.05pm a warning order was received that 1/15 Battalion would be relieved during the night, and would take part in an operation the following morning. At about 11.30pm the Battalion was relieved by the London Irish and marched to a position just S.W. of Bouchavesnes.

War Diary: 2 September 1918

The plan was for 74 Division to conduct the main attack, and capture and "mop up" the village of Moislans, their final objective being Nurlu. 140 Infantry Brigade was to follow them closely in support, wheel left past Moislans and form a defensive flank on the high ground.

Zero hour was 5.30am. The Battalion was in position at the place of assembly at about 3.00am, A and B Companys leading.

From the outset the Battalion came under heavy shell and M.G. fire, and, as it moved down the slopes to the S.W. of Moislans, under still heavier M.G. fire directed from the village and from both flanks.

The enemy were found to be occupying both Moislans Trench to our left, and Quarry Trench to our left rear, while they could clearly be seen moving in Moislans, and assembling in the village and in the huts immediately to the S. of it.

Simultaneous counter-attacks were developed on our left rear and our right front, while the enemy at the same time attempted to bomb up the trench on our left. Both the parados and parapet were manned and the attacks across the open were beaten off, but the bombing attacks continued all day, and owing to scarcity of bombs, were with difficulty held up.

It was at once obvious there were no British troops to our front, though elements of 74 Division could be seen in the distance on the right, on a level with Moislans Trench. In the face of the very heavy flank and frontal M.G. fire, of the heavy casualties incurred, and of one flank at least being in the air, it was impractical to attempt, without a barrage, to capture the village which was still firmly held by the enemy.

A small local attack by about two Companies was actually delivered by 74 Division on our right, but though it made some little progress, it hardly did more than establish our right flank. With this exception, there was no indication of any attack having been delivered by 74 Division in the vicinity of Moislans.

A German field gun battery was in action for some four hours in the open immediately S. of the village, and less than 1,000 yards E. of the canal and firing over open sights on our trench. A very careful examination of the battlefield afterwards confirmed no British dead either in Moislans or to the E. of Moislans Trench. The only dead in rear of Moislans Trench were those of 140 Infantry Brigade and of Germans killed in the counter-attack on our left rear. In this area twenty-five men of this Battalion alone were found and buried in an hour, and many others of the Brigade still lay there.

The only dead of 74 Division whom I personally saw in the section of ground with which my Battalion was concerned, were lying about 300 yards from our starting point. Since these dead were not there when we originally advanced, I can only come to the conclusion, which is shared by all who were with me on the battlefield during the action and after, that 140 Brigade, instead of being in support, found itself with its flanks unsecured, and with the barrage so far ahead as to be useless, carrying out the main attack on a strong enemy position, and that 74 Division, so far from being in front of us, was behind us.

Orders were received to withdraw the Battalion at 10.30pm and to rest the men in the trenches.

M Fielding, Lt. Col.
Comdg. 1/Civil Service Rifles
(1/15 London Reg)

As can be seen from the War Diary above, it was with the greatest difficulty that 140 Brigade established itself in the Moislans Trench west of the village. This was indeed some of the hardest fighting during the whole advance, and it was all the more difficult owing to the fact that the Brigade was officially not fighting, but following up what should have been a successful attack over ground outside their Divisional boundary.

In the centre Laurie's 15 Battalion lost half its strength in casualties, and was at one time being attacked from the left rear and right front, and by a bombing party in Moislans Trench itself. But they still managed to consolidate the line of the trench and protect their exposed flank with a battery of machine guns.

WAR DIARY: 3 SEPTEMBER 1918
The Battalion rested.

WAR DIARY: 4 SEPTEMBER 1918
The Battalion rested. Owing to its heavy losses, the Battalion was re-organized on a two Company basis, each of two Platoons.

Early on 5 September the line advanced towards Nurlu Ridge, but met with a number of obstacles. It was decided to attack again under barrage in the evening, and at 7.00pm in a violent thunderstorm 140 Brigade pushed on to the top of the ridge without difficulty.

WAR DIARY: 6 SEPTEMBER 1918
At 8.00am the 18 London and 1/15 Civil Service Rifles, who had formed up behind the new front line, moved forward, their objective being a N. and S. line on the right of Lieramont.

The Battalion reached its objective about noon. The 18 London on the left had not yet arrived and heavy enemy M.G. fire was raking our men from that direction, as well as rapid fire from his Field Artillery, as they appeared over the crest.

The men behaved with the utmost steadiness, falling back slowly to the reverse slope, where they immediately turned and dug in.

During the night the Battalion was relieved and moved to the Valley which they reached about 3.00am in the morning of 7 September and where they bivouaced.

The casualties sustained by this Battalion during the fighting, was as follows:

22–30 August

	Officers	N.C.O's & Men
Killed in action	–	7
Died of wounds	1	1
Wounded	2	48
Missing	–	1

31 August – 6 September

	Officers	N.C.O's & Men
Killed in action	4	35
Died of wounds	–	4
Wounded	6	241
Missing	1	38

Total: 389

WAR DIARY: 7 SEPTEMBER 1918

In the morning, the bodies of those killed on 2 September, near Moislans, were buried.

I have already forwarded the names of those officers and men whom I wish to bring to the Brigadier-General's notice for special gallantry.

M Fielding, Lt. Col.
Comdg. 1/Civil Service Rifles
(1/15 London Reg)

Thursday, 19 September 1918

My Dear Mother,

I hope my three lengthy letters have reached you safely. *[Sadly, only one was received or survives.]* They were an endeavour to furnish, without dwelling on the simply nauseating aspects of the battle zone, a straightforward account of my own little experiences. Many a time it was necessary to tighten up the nerves in the face of some sight ghastly beyond the normal. One scene lingers strangely in the memory. I was sent to where a bit of trench emerged on to a road strewn with wreckage, in order to intercept the runners with messages. In the trench lay a German with a wonderfully boyish face, by his name probably a Pole, and in the roadway a dead horse lay stretched out just in front of me.

Nothing very remarkable in this till I looked more closely. Then I saw a hand still clutching at the reins and a few inches of sleeve, a dark stain on the road, and nothing else!

But now I have done with horrors for a while and this letter is written from a civilised and hospitable town. On the morning of the 12th we marched over rather flat country to our present quarters. Soon we came to small mining villages and presently could see the towering slag-heaps rising above the huddled roofs like pyramids. The town we are in has two of these mining suburbs. It is interesting to watch the little trucks of slag on their journey from the shaft to the heap. They cross the streets hanging from an overhead cableway and on reaching the foot of the slag-heap are emptied into larger trucks which run up a miniature mountain railway to the top of the heap where they automatically discharge their contents.

The streets are almost always lively, especially when the shifts change at the mines. A great number of lads and girls are employed. In the evenings most of the estaminets provide some form of music – either a mechanical piano, a gramophone or, in a few more pretentious places, a small orchestra. Then all the tables are pushed closer to the walls and the miners choose partners and waltz round at an amazing rate. Some are really clever at solo and eccentric dancing, and the scene is always merry.

On the outskirts of the town is a camp occupied by a Chinese labour Company. Queer looking allies, these, but affable. A few can speak French and one or two, who have lived in the U.S.A., know English. It is a strange experience to have a wierdly dressed Chinaman wish you "Bon jour". One evening as I passed their camp they were all togged up in bright coloured wraps and were amusing themselves by walking about on stilts.

Apart from these, there are a great many French soldiers and a sprinkling of Belgians and Portuguese, so the crowd is fairly cosmopolitan. The church is well worth a visit and dates from 1637. Our Regimental Band plays in the square in the afternoon and is a great centre of attraction. Our billet is in a cinéma and is somewhat out of repair. One night we had a particularly fierce thunderstorm and the rain found out every weak spot in the roof. I have been for walks to two other towns, but ours is the finest in the neighbourhood.

Last Sunday we had a very special Church Parade at an aerodrome, at which we were on duty. A very well-known General attended and made a speech to us all. Prices are very inflated and many things are almost unobtainable.

On the evening of Saturday (the 14th) the order was issued that I was appointed an unpaid Lance-Corporal. This is a promotion which is almost without significance. There is no pay attached to it and, in practice, if not in theory, I have been in charge of the Police for a long time, as the Sergeant of Police is also Quartermaster Sergeant, and has always left me to arrange the duties, etc. Still, it gives me a little more authority and is an acknowledgement of past work. When writing, just put "530694 L/Cpl. L.W.Attwell" and the rest of the address as before.

I am nothing more nor less than a dandy just now, having secured a well-fitting new tunic, trousers and puttees. I only hope I shall be able to get home before all the shine is taken out of them. My health is good.

It is necessary to warn you that this may be the last letter I shall be able to write to you, perhaps for as long as a week. You know how restless this Division has always been, and how it has shifted from North to South and back again, how we have seen almost every sector in France and Belgium in which British troops have held the line. And now another big move seems inevitable. It may end, who knows, in your two soldier sons shaking hands. But whether in Belgium, France or elsewhere I have to spend my days, my heart will always rest in that dear little home with the best of mothers and fondest of sisters.

With all the intensity of my being I send you my love. Every good wish my dear ones.
Yours ever,
Laurie.

It was soon known that Laurie was due to move to Italy by the end of September, and a small advance party set off to make arrangements for the 47 Division's arrival there. The 140 Brigade were supplied by an enterprising Brigade Headquarters with maps and a list of useful phrases in Italian, and rations had actually been loaded onto the train when the orders were changed.

The great success of the Allies in France culminating in the capture of the Hindenburg Line by the Fourth Army, Major T.E.Lawrence's triumphant entry into Damascus in the East, and the capitulation of Bulgaria, showed the end of the war was near. It was a race against time to settle the issue on the Western Front before the winter set in, and neither the time nor the rolling stock could be spared for the move to Italy.

Orders came on 1 October to move to Lestrem west of Lille, where the Germans were retreating fast.

Saturday, 5 October 1918. (Excerpts)

My Dear Connie,

Very many thanks for your letters of the 24th and 29th September. You have my sincere sympathy for the bitter disappointment you are feeling, just after your hopes had been raised so high. But personally, I simply feel that my leave has been postponed – not that all prospects of it are destroyed.

I see by the amounts of the August and September warrants that there are no 'big' months now. Each month they send exactly one-twelfth of my annual salary less the 1/- per day and the other small deductions. The Bank account is certainly growing quite fat.

My silence during the first few days of this month must have set you wondering whether the big move had at length commenced. It has not and is still in abeyance. There still seems little room for doubt that it will eventuate in due course. The military news seems almost incredibly good however. It is something to know one has played a part, however small, in securing this dramatic swing of the pendulum, and that on some of the most famous battlefields of the war. It is like a game of chess. The players have reached that part of the whole game known as "the end game". We have the advantage in pieces and in position, and a referee would award the game to us. Germany may choose to play on, in which case the game may last for a long time, but only a stupid blunder could rob us of the final checkmate.

On Friday the 27th we breakfasted at 6 and then set off on a 21 kilometre march. The country we passed through gradually became more and more lovely and we finished in a little village situated about five miles from a great railway centre *[in the neighbourhood of St Pol]*. Our billet was a lofty barn, one of the outbuildings of a big château. We had heavy rain the following morning, but in a clear interval I got into the fields and picked about a pound of blackberries, which I consumed with the rice at dinner. On Sunday we had no church parades but went for baths instead. Cleanliness next to godliness again! A reading and writing room was opened – under the care of the Police, who also had to partol two villages in which the Battalion was billeted, close the estaminets at 1.30 and 9, and send a man to the big

203

city daily to inspect passes and be responsible for the orderly behaviour of the men. As the Lance-Jack, I had to fix up all these duties, and to act occasionally (don't laugh) as Orderly Sergeant for H.Q. Company. This means that you take the sick men down to the Medical Room, draw rations, go in charge of any fatigue parties, collect the letters, read out the orders to the various billets, superintend the grub, give out passes, and do any other little job that turns up. For the Companies, a Sergeant is appointed, with a Corporal to help him. For H.Q. Company a Corporal alone is considered sufficient.

The 1st of October was our last day in the village. We are far away from that peaceful spot now, being in fact in territory which was in German possession only two days ago. However all this I will leave for my next letter. So far I can assure you the danger has been negligible, so do not commence worrying. My health is excellent.

Fondest love to you all, Ever your affectionate brother,

Laurie

Saturday, 12 October 1918. (Excerpts)

Dear Connie,

Your letter of the 8th reached France very quickly and proved most interesting reading. The way in which, from small beginnings and in spite of manifold difficulties and discouragements, you have built up your business interests is quite romantic. The bank balance is a magnificent endorsement of your abilities. That is what I most appreciate – that the home can be kept cosy, with no wolf threatening at the threshold; that as far as possible Mother can enjoy the comforts which were denied her whilst we were younger; and that Flossie's future is no longer a source of anxiety. I am very proud of my sister and very glad to have this opportunity of telling her so. When I am next on leave – unless the war ends first – we must have a good talk about the business.

And now to steer your thoughts to a very different sphere – to where the greatest historical events of this age are being enacted. I am not sure whether I mentioned our railway journey in my last letter. We entrained in the rain at a certain station and travelled in trucks through the night towards a sector of the line never before visited by us. When we got out a very different station loomed in front of us. The buildings were riddled with shell-holes and the outlines of the houses against the sky resembled the outlying crags one sees off the Cornish coast. A very weary march in the early hours of the 3rd took us to our halting place. Here we slept under a tarpaulin fixed up as a triangular tent and fastened with our bayonets.

The following afternoon there was a general move forward, for the Germans had commenced a retirement and it is our policy at such times to harass them as much as possible. However fast they retire, they cannot shake off our pursuit, and so guns and prisoners are captured. The country through which we passed was flatness itself. The land was wonderfully green. Every road has two deep ditches full of water. The water squelches under your boots. Dykes and ditches run everywhere – all filled to overflowing. If you dig a 3-ft hole at 2 o'clock it will be three parts full of water in less than an hour. Innumerable little willows grow by the roadsides and round the fields. The villages in this country have been very badly shelled. We slept that night in a small hut in a German "lager".

The next morning early the pursuit was continued. We soon passed through a fairly large town *[Radinghem.]* and from this point onwards, being well beyond the original German front line, we had many evidences of his occupation. Houses had been shattered by our shells, but inside the broken walls wonderful shelters had been constructed of solid concrete – obtained, I suppose, from us through Holland in those early days when we let neutral nations have everything they asked. These had been blown up by German mines as they retreated, so that we should not benefit by them, and presented a marvellous spectacle of gigantic masses of concrete piled up one on another. Without exception, every crossroad had been blown up to hamper our progress. R.E's were busy cutting wires which were suspected of being attached to unexploded mines. Some of the concrete shelters were intact, but marked "Dangerous". No trick is too vile for the Germans. They are very bad losers.

In the more open country 'pill-boxes' were a very common sight. They were of concrete three or four feet thick, cunningly camouflaged, and cleverly loopholed for machine-guns. At length we reached our destination – an old farmhouse. Here in a wooden shanty formerly used by Fritz we had our billet while the companies were in reserve, support and front line positions.

We had a fairly quiet time here. You commented on the variety of our jobs. Well, here I was in charge of the aeroplane guard by day and the gas guard by night. Also I was made "sock king" – collecting socks from the men to go to the laundries and giving out the clean pairs received in exchange. This seems a job that will stick with me whenever we are in the line.

On the evening of the 9th we moved back a short way to an old

German camp which is surrounded by barbed wire ten feet high. Think of all these defences given up by Fritz. He makes his peace overtures to the U.S.A. but I am hopeful that John Bull will have <u>the</u> say in the matter. England has been the backbone of this war for a long time. The U.S.A. is still second fiddle. They have definitely turned the scales in our favour, but the months when almost all the burden rested on Britain's shoulders must never be forgotten.

Like yourself, I am in the seventh heaven of delight at the news. Bulgaria out, Turkey going out, Austria waiting her opportunity – I expect to be no longer on "active service" on my next birthday. At the same time, there is still a lot to do. Nobody must relax now. Everyone must press home the advantage we have won. He retires one mile – Good! Let us drive him back another. As for discussing peace terms – why should we? Germany must accept what we dictate. For four years she has wilfully plunged the world into Hell and now we are the appointed instruments of her punishment. Not in vindictiveness, not in revenge, but to vindicate the principle of justice and the binding nature of a nation's word. Germany must be made to suffer. She must foot the bill, and if she rejects the militarist party which has been her undoing, then, <u>after she has paid the bill</u>, she may be admitted into the fellowship of civilised nations again.

Yours, etc.

Laurie

Saturday, 19 October 1918

My Dear Mother,

Very many thanks for your letter of the 14th. In my last letter I attempted a description of our surroundings in the old German camp. At our back was a low-lying rather swampy field. On Saturday afternoon (the 12th), with a sublime indifference to the war and the nearness of the enemy's outposts, the Battalion played football in this field against a team of artillerymen. The evening was wet and dark, and Fritz sent over so many gas-shells in our vicinity that we had to sit with our masks on for quite a long time.

Very much the same thing happened on Sunday evening, only this time there were fewer gas-shells and more containing high explosives. We were also shelled in the small hours of the morning to the detriment of our sleep, for our huts were very frail.

On Monday we were relieved and marched out through the gathering darkness to a large town behind the lines. Here four of us had a very comfortable little hut as a billet. It was originally Portuguese. Weedon was a bit queer as a result of the rather long march, but is recovered now.

The next morning we had a long march to do. The town we were in was now revealed to us as a mere husk – the pitiful remnants of a once splendid place. Few sights have roused my indignation more. Whole acres of buildings were levelled to the ground. Many of the streets were untouched by gunfire, but these had been reduced by fire. Just the walls were left. Most of these were large houses of three, four and five storeys. A few French people were walking round, having just arrived in farm waggons and carts. At the door of one ruined cottage on the outskirts of the town a woman sat crying into her apron to find her home wrecked. Much of this damage must have been wanton. No military advantage was gained by it and surely those in authority will see to it that restitution to all those thousands of ruined households is made one of the first conditions of peace. And this was one town only. The total destruction caused by the Germans has no parallel in history. You can march for hour after hour through country once rich and happy and look in vain for one habitable house.

Our journey ended in an old French town where we were billeted in a deserted convent. The buildings were very substantial, and though much damaged by shell-fire, still capable of sheltering several hundred men. A tablet on the outer wall dated the place in the 1700's.

On Wednesday, the 16th, we drew leather jerkins, winter gloves, thicker pants and vests. In the evening I took a walk along the banks of a certain river of which mention is frequently made in the communiqués. The next morning we were marching again – still away from the line. This time we got clear of the devastated areas and into unspoilt country. It is very flat everywhere, with long straight roads running between avenues of trees. We slept in a barn.

The French people are extremely well disposed towards us. Yesterday evening Weedon and I were invited to use a little room, containing a bed. I can assure you I slept very cosily. There was a tame magpie with clipped wings here. He is a good thief. If you throw a half-franc down he will snatch it up, hop away with it and bury it under some rubbish or poke it into some crevice. He eats out of our hands and is a most entertaining little rascal.

This morning a long and ornate funeral procession wound its way to the church. Choirboys wore lace vestments, the priest was wonderfully attired and the hearse was covered in black plumes.

The war news goes from one climax to another. The very highest hopes seem now to be justified. Who knows? Before Christmas maybe the spectre of War will no longer stalk the world and the message of Christmas may come this year to a world that is making a new start. For surely all this agony and sacrifice have not been in vain. Surely the nations have learnt on these stricken fields "that men should brothers be, and form one family the world o'er". The clash of ambitions may give place to the spirit of co-operation and mutual service. If this be so, then I for one am content.

"Nor any prize we ask, Lord,
When this our work is done,
But to have shared the travail
That makes Thy Kingdom come."

I hope you, Connie and Flossie are in good health, as I am. I may be with you sooner than you think.
Every good wish, Your loving son,
Laurie.

P.S. Have just received a form which entitles me to vote in France should there be an election!

By 16 October, the Germans had retreated as far as Lille, and the following day the city was liberated by the allies. The 47 Division's official procession into Lille started at 10.00am on Monday, 28 October.

It was "roses, roses all the way". The tricolour was flying everywhere, with a sprinkling of extemporised (and rather inaccurate) versions of the Union Jack, and American and Belgian flags. Several hundred small flags adorned the rifles and equipment, and there were flowers on the guns. Brass bands played, and great crowds along the road and at every window cheered and sang as the troops marched by. An enterprising printer had produced posters in red, white and blue with the inscription "Honneur et gloire à la 47me Division, nos Liberateurs", and others with the same message in English.

The Army Commander presented his fanion (the small red flag with a black cross which is carried behind an army commander in the field) to the Mayor of Lille, and received a flag from the city. Then a large gathering of officers and civilians – among them the Secretary of State for War, Mr Winston Churchill – watched as the 47 Division marched past.

However, as you will see, Laurie missed all this.

Wednesday, 23 October 1918.

My Dear Connie,

Your letter of the 20th received this afternoon. Many thanks. I shall not attempt a long reply, for this reason. I am to entrain on the afternoon of the 25th and shall probably cross over to England on the morning of the 26th. So unless something most unfortunate and highly improbably intervenes, you can expect me at No. 52 quite early on Saturday morning – perhaps before ten o'clock.

Fondest love from,

Yours, in wild excitement,

Laurie.

Thus Laurie's long awaited home leave materialised. He arrived home on Saturday, 26 October, and after two glorious weeks with his family, once more left Victoria Station for France on Saturday, 9 November 1918.

Two days later, at the eleventh hour of the eleventh day of the eleventh month, the guns fell silent over the battlefields of Europe. Germany had capitulated and an armistice had been signed. So ended The Great War, with a human cost of ten million dead.

Postcard dated Monday, 11 November 1918.

My Dear Mother,

Have not yet nearly reached the Battalion, but am steadily tracking them down. French railways and travelling generally are still hardly up to the English standard. Have been through some interesting places and will have a long letter to write to you when I do reach my destination.

Yours, etc.,

Laurie.

In fact, on 11 November 1918 Laurie's Battalion was still in pursuit of the fast retreating German army.

There was nothing dramatic about the end of the war for them. News of the Armistice reached the troops on their march westwards towards Tournai. It hardly raised a cheer.

My Dear Connie,

As you know our train had quite a good send-off at Victoria on Saturday morning. The ride to Dover and the Channel passage were quite enjoyable. We arrived at the Rest Camp at 3.30p.m. and spent the night there, sleeping ten men in each tent and two blankets per man. During the evening there was a concert of sorts in a Y.M.C.A. hut. Sunday was very far from being a day of rest, for reveille was at 3.30 and breakfast at 3.45 a.m. An hour later we marched out of the Rest camp to the station, where we entrained, after receiving some salmon sandwiches and plain scones as rations for the journey.

The train, which was not overcrowded, did not start until 7 o'clock. The compartments were unadapted luggage-wagons. Seats ran along the sides and down the centre, and there were large hooks on which to hang equipment. I had no knowledge of the whereabouts of the Battalion and therefore no idea where to detrain. There was only one thing to do – to rely on the station police. This proved a safe policy. I detrained at a certain station and waited from 11 o'clock to 4 for another train. This was to take me to the city which I just missed visiting through going home on leave. *[This obviously refers to Lille.]* It was a most interesting journey as the line ran through some notable battlefields. Several towns and villages were passed, all in a ruined condition. The country was very flat and wet, with great pools of water standing in the fields. Soon after 8 o'clock we reached the great city and in failing light our party had their triumphal entry. It was a beautiful city, with lofty public buildings, large squares and wide boulevards. We marched right through from one end to the other and, after an hour and a half, reached our destination – the Divisional Reception Camp. Here I am still. When I shall rejoin the Battalion I don't know. You might let me know when you have received this letter and address your reply to: "L/Cpl. Attwell 530694. 1/15th Battn., London Regiment, (C.S. Rifles), 47th Divisional Reception Camp, B.E.F., France". Don't send a parcel along until I ask for it, please.

Wednesday, 13 November 1918

I was unable to finish my letter yesterday, so will resume this morning. Well, as I told you, I shall not have any more fighting to do. The armistice terms, which I have just read, are splendid. One can hardly conceive of a greater humiliation for the German war-party. Our great objective has been attained. The military domination of Prussia has been finally and wholly destroyed. It is very good to be alive to see this day.

On Sunday night I slept in a large barn-like room with no glass in the windows. The following morning I changed into a large linen factory. The looms are still standing and some are still usable. There are hundreds of heavy machines all driven by means of shafting and pulleys. I had not been here long before I was asked to do some clerking for the Brigade Sergeant Major. At present I am the sole clerk of a sort of orderly room for the men of the Brigade who are down here. Up to now I have not had too much to do.

The French people are still in a very excited state at their new liberty and, now that the Armistice is signed, they are hoping to see their relatives – soldiers and civilians – who have been in German hands. They hold the Germans in utter detestation and have many tales to tell of the reign of terror when they dominated the district. I am billeted with one other fellow, a permanent Orderly Corporal, in a private house. We have full use of a little kitchen and sleep in a bed in a nice clean bedroom, so that's all right. There is not much grub going. All the shops are empty. The city is only slowly recovering from the depredations of the Boche. All brass fittings, copper, etc. was stolen. The French people buried stuff beneath their floor-boards and up chimneys. Nothing is hidden now. They have the completest confidence of the British troops.

I will keep you informed of any interesting movements in the inter-regnum of the armistice. Have you heard from Bert recently?
Fondest love to you all, Yours, etc.,
Laurie.

Postcard dated Saturday, 16 November 1918.

My Dear Mother,
Hope you have received my letter and cards. I have good reason to believe that before long I shall be with the Battalion again. A small parcel would not come amiss – but it should be small in case it goes astray. I could do with some shaving soap, writing paper, a couple of handkerchiefs and some Neloids for a bit of a cough. My billet is absolutely grand. Home from home! These first days of the Armistice are full of interest. The more we know, the harder Germany is seen to be hit. Her defeat is crushing beyond precedent. What I could tell

you would not incline any of you to mercy. Let us be sure to feed all our allies before we feed these reptiles.
Fond love to all,
Laurie.

Thursday, 21 November 1918.

My Dear Flossie,

In spite of all my instructions, your misguided sister sent off a parcel before I had written home to say that I had definitely settled down. As a result it reached the Battalion just as they were about to go on a twelve-mile march. The shaving soap was saved for me. All the rest went – quickly! I understand that Weedon and the others enjoyed the cake and chocolate very much.

I am back in the Battalion now and anything sent to me will reach me alright. Connie enquires as to how the fellows received the news of the Armistice. Well, the Battalion were in the line a long way in front of Tournai somewhere. They had been having a curious time, for the front line ran through a village, part of which was still held by the Germans. There was hardly any shell-fire and the different platoons were in houses in which the civilians still went on with their work. It was quite customary for civilians to go walking through streets which were theoretically, no-man's land. The houses were properly furnished and the civilians made coffee for the troops – in the front line! The news was of course anticipated and brought merely a deep sense of relief and personal satisfaction. The men feel that their lives are spared. Other than this, the Army carries on. There are the same fatigues, the same duties to perform, the same discipline. The Armistice brings very little outward change to the life of the troops except it is as if they are always away from the front line, since there is no gun-fire or danger.

I had quite a good time at the Divisional Rest Camp. My work in the Orderly Room was not such as to overtax my brain or make excessive demands on my time. In the evenings I used to sit in the kitchen with Madame Canis, Yvonne, Marie-Louise, Madeleine and young Raymond, and to the best of my poor ability, maintain a lively conversation. Madame used to declaim against the Germans. She had many stories of their brutal treatment of the people of Lille and the surrounding villages. They hid some of their brass and copper articles up the chimney and others beneath the floor-boards. The German soldiers would sometimes taunt them when they wanted food and tell them to eat the rats and mice. Many young boys were forcibly deported. The mothers were always in deadly fear as to their daughters' honour. She declared that she would never, never forget the four years of misery during which the Prussian brute lorded it over Northern France.

One evening we had a sing-song and the three girls sang some patriotic French songs very prettily. On Sunday afternoon they took a gramophone out of some hiding-place in the loft and gave us a number of Pathé records. On Friday evening the Sergt. Major down here got some tickets for the Cinéma. He wanted to take two of the girls and asked me to come to help him out with the French. We had a very merry evening.

On Tuesday afternoon we left to rejoin our Battalions. It was a march of about six miles over rough cobbles. We passed a great number of returning French people, some pushing barrowloads of stuff and others carrying huge bundles. Many were very footsore and inexpressibly weary. There was a pathetic look about them – pinched, white faces, with a big hope dawning in their sunken eyes. We also saw several hundred German prisoners – gaunt and animal-like.

A heavy mist rose and we finished our journey by groping through a wall of darkness. Our billet was a clean, bare loft – bitterly cold. I made a bed in some straw and with two blankets was quite comfortable. The village is called Willems and is not far from the borderline with Belgium. There is not much of interest.

My health is quite good. The cough is no worse. I hope Mother is quite well.
My fondest love to you all, Your affectionate brother,
Laurie.

A fortnight after the Armistice, on 25 November, Laurie moved back by road through the devastated country behind Lille to billets in the familiar area behind Béthune. He was to finish the war in the same area in which he first entered it.

Postcard dated Wednesday, 4 December 1918.

My Dear Connie,
Thanks for your letter of the 30th. Can't imagine what made you think that we were marching to form part of the army of occupation. Anyway, if you have received my letter of the 4th *[either missing or not*

retained.] you will know exactly where I am. I share all your misgivings about the Coalition, without having, as yet, fallen in love with the Labour leaders. There are too many of the old style place-hunters and professional politicians among the Coalition candidates and too many of these confounded lawyers, who make the laws purposely obscure. If Locker-Lampson has an opponent with any force of individuality about him, that opponent will get my vote. I did not receive the Cooker which you mention. My cough is better.

Fondest love to all, Yours ever,

Laurie.

Throughout Christmas the talk was all about demobilisation, and when the men would get home. Laurie was fortunate, for his active service records show he was transferred back to the UK on board the S.S. Lydia on New Year's Eve, and "disembodied on demobilisation" on Wednesday, 29 January 1919.

Afterword

Laurence Wesley Attwell served his country with the British Expeditionary Force in France for 4 years 152 days, earning himself the 1914–15 Star, the British War Medal and the Victory Medal, as well as a lifetime of experiences he assuredly would rather not have endured. He fought many times on the great battlefields of France, and in some of the most famous actions – Festubert, the Battle of Loos, Vimy Ridge, the Battle of the Somme, Ypres, the Battle of Messines, Menin Road, Bourlon Wood, Cambrai, and the final advance on Lille.

That he was fortunate to survive the war goes without saying. Although he was once wounded and suffered the effects of gas, he remained fit and well for many years after the war. As one of a very small force of military policemen attached to HQ Company, his duties were more varied than those of the ordinary infantryman, and allowed him a certain freedom of movement. This probably made his life in the line a little more palatable, but certainly no less dangerous. Besides his long spells in the trenches, he also spent lengthy periods on patrols and guard duties out in the open, enduring often intense barrages of high explosive and gas shells. As time went on, Laurie clearly gained in experience, after a while knowing how best to react to the sound of an approaching shell, which undoubtedly on several occasions saved his life. As it was, he tells of many very close shaves with death, yet only once, in all that time was he wounded.

It is a great tribute to his passive nature that throughout the whole of his active service Laurie managed to maintain a wonderfully objective, moderate and equable tone in his correspondence. Only very rarely can the reader detect the slightest sense of discontent or irritation in his writing, when in truth, he must have been under the greatest provocation to "sound off" about the high command's appalling mistakes, and the manner in which so many lives were so shamefully sacrificed.

It is noticeable how in Laurie's letters he spares his mother and sisters too much detail of the horrors of the war, yet he still conveys to them all the intensity, drama and danger of his experiences in this quite remarkable series of letters.

W.A.Attwell

Index

Canadians, 19
Canal du Nord, 144
Cauchy à la Tour, 3, 9
Chocques, 11, 12, 39
Churchill, Winston, 208
Civil Service Rifles, viii, xi, 1, 34, 39, 40, 41, 141, 142, 194, 199, 200
Clairfaye, 178
Clairfaye Farm, 170
Comines, 118
Contalmaison Ridge, 169, 176
Courcelles le Comte, 137

Dickebusch, 103
Doignes, 143
Domart, 182, 184
Drucat, 81

Eaucourt l'Abbaye, 85, 86
Ebblinghem, 107, 112, 113
Ecurie, 126
Essars, 14, 39
Etretat, 72
Etricourt, 153, 155, 166, 172

Farquhar, Captain H. B., 73, 74
Festubert, 14, 15, 16, 19, 20, 24, 39, 45, 215
Flesquières, 162, 163
Foch, Marshal, 191
Folkstone, 128
Franvillers, 81
French, General, 24

Gavrelle, 128, 134
Givenchy, 10, 11
Gorre, 14, 20, 21, 39
Gosnay, 43
Gouy-en-Artois, 137
Graincourt, 145, 146, 150
Grenay, 29, 39, 44, 45, 50, 58

Haig, Sir Douglas, 151, 152, 178
Haillicourt, 58